DAVE McNALLY

THE MONTANAN WHO REVOLUTIONIZED BASEBALL

Dennis Gaub

Mechanicsburg, PA USA

Published by Sunbury Press, Inc.
Mechanicsburg, PA USA

www.sunburypress.com

Copyright © 2025 by Dennis Gaub.
Cover Copyright © 2025 by Sunbury Press, Inc.

Sunbury Press supports copyright. Copyright fuels creativity, encourages diverse voices, promotes free speech, and creates a vibrant culture. Thank you for buying an authorized edition of this book and for complying with copyright laws. Except for the quotation of short passages for the purpose of criticism and review, no part of this publication may be reproduced, scanned, or distributed in any form without permission. You are supporting writers and allowing Sunbury Press to continue to publish books for every reader. For information contact Sunbury Press, Inc., Subsidiary Rights Dept., PO Box 548, Boiling Springs, PA 17007 USA or legal@sunburypress.com.

For information about special discounts for bulk purchases, please contact Sunbury Press Orders Dept. at (855) 338-8359 or orders@sunburypress.com.

To request one of our authors for speaking engagements or book signings, please contact Sunbury Press Publicity Dept. at publicity@sunburypress.com.

FIRST SUNBURY PRESS EDITION: October 2025

Set in Adobe Garamond | Interior design by Crystal Devine | Cover by Hina Zubi | Edited by Andrew Smith.

Publisher's Cataloging-in-Publication Data
Names: Gaub, Dennis, author.
Title: Dave McNally : the Montanan who revolutionized baseball / Dennis Gaub.
Description: First trade paperback edition. | Mechanicsburg, PA : Sunbury Press, 2025.
Summary : A biography of star pitcher Dave McNally, who won 184 major-league games for the Baltimore Orioles and the Montreal Expos. When he retired, McNally, a Billings, Montana, native and Montana's greatest athlete of the Twentieth Century, took the lead role in a groundbreaking arbitration ruling fifty years ago. That ruling gave baseball players and other professional athletes workplace rights they had never had before.
Identifiers: ISBN : 979-8-88819-328-0 (softcover).
Subjects: BIOGRAPHY & AUTOBIOGRAPHY / Sports | SPORTS & RECREATION / Baseball / History | HISTORY / United States / State & Local / West (AK, CA, CO, HI, ID, MT, NV, UT, WY).

Designed in the USA
0 1 1 2 3 5 8 13 21 34 55

For the Love of Books!

To the hundreds of Billings youngsters who have played American baseball over the decades and dreamed of making the major leagues. Several have gone on to the Big Show, and they've helped make Billings one of the best baseball towns in the country. Dave McNally was your North Star.

CONTENTS

Acknowledgments — vii
Introduction — 1

CHAPTERS

One	Billings Beginnings	7
Two	Foundation for Fame	21
Three	Prelude to Glory and a Lifetime Match	36
Four	Best in the Land	44
Five	Learning in the Bushes	60
Six	Serving Notice	65
Seven	Building Towards Greatness	70
Eight	Nearing the Promised Land	81
Nine	Best in the American League	88
Ten	Shaky Series Start	96
Eleven	Champs of the World	99
Twelve	A President Takes Notice	107
Thirteen	Post-World Series Funk	109
Fourteen	Return to Glory	128
Fifteen	The Streak	134
Sixteen	Another Series	140
Seventeen	The Grand Slam	146
Eighteen	Lutherville Days	157
Nineteen	Greatest Pitching Rotation Ever	161
Twenty	Winding Down	171
Twenty-One	Life with Weaver	180

Twenty-Two	The End . . . and History	184
Twenty-Three	Back Home	194
Twenty-Four	Montana's Greatest Athlete	201
Twenty-Five	The Last Battle	204
Twenty-Six	McNally's Legacy	210

PostScript		218
Endnotes		220
Index		227
Afterword		236
About the Author		237

ACKNOWLEDGMENTS

I wish to acknowledge contributions to this work from Dave's widow, Jean; their oldest son, Jeff; Dave's sister, Dee Nobles (only surviving sibling); other friends from his Legion baseball days, Bob Fry, Pete Cochran, Ed Bayne, Jr., and Woody Hahn; two former Baltimore Orioles teammates who offered insight, Hall of Fame pitcher Jim Palmer and slugger Boog Powell; Bill Stika of the Birds' front office; and former Baltimore Sun writer John Eisenberg, whose 2001 book on the Orioles, *From 33rd Street to Camden Yards: An Oral History of the Baltimore Orioles*, helped me understand team dynamics.

Also, thanks to my former *Billings Gazette* colleague, now retired sportswriter Bill Bighaus, for your wonderful, evocative reporting on McNally during his final years of life. And to Joe McIntosh for sharing memories of that fateful day in June 1975 when you were a pitcher for the San Diego Padres and you defeated fellow Billings guy Dave McNally, then wearing a Montreal Expos uniform, during his final big-league game. A priceless story!

And thanks to one of my best friends from my RightNow Technologies days, Steve Zillis, a lawyer and sports agent in Los Angeles before he pivoted to the tech world. Steve convinced me to forget my initial urge to try boosting McNally into the Hall of Fame and instead concentrate on his biggest achievement: helping pro athletes gain basic worker rights. Thanks, buddy!

Also, thanks to the two fine editors who polished my words: Sunbury Press' Andrew Smith and Jim Thomsen, who took a crack at the manuscript before Sunbury accepted my proposal.

Finally, I thank my wife, Cathie, for her understanding and support as I researched this book and then worked through multiple iterations of it.

INTRODUCTION

"They owned you, lock, stock, and barrel."
—Dave McNally's description of how owners
of major-league baseball teams dominated
relationships with players until the 1975 Seitz
ruling evened the playing field.

Long before he was an adult and expressed those sentiments, Dave experienced the first of his several life-changing moments while growing up in Billings, Montana. There, chatter among baseball fans on October 11, 1951, centered on the World Series that had finished the day before. What a thriller it had been! Casey Stengel's New York Yankees had won Game 6 of the Series, nipping their cross-town rivals, Leo Durocher's New York Giants.

Let's suppose that those digesting the news included a fourth-grade Billings boy eating his breakfast that Thursday morning before another day of school. He picked up the copy of his hometown newspaper, the *Billings Gazette*, delivered to his home, and flipped through it to the sports section. On page 18, he found what he wanted, a story headlined, "Yanks Nip Giants, 4–3, to Win Third Straight World Championship." A photo below the headline showed Stengel with his arms draped around the game hero, Hank Bauer, who hammered a sixth-inning, bases-loaded triple off the Giants' Dave Koslo. Bauer's hit gave the Yankees the cushion they needed, but they had to hold off the Giants in the ninth inning to clinch the title as more than 61,000 chilled spectators at Yankee Stadium shivered in their seats before they boarded the subway for a happy trip back to their Bronx homes.

Dave may have daydreamed as he read the account for a minute or two. He could have imagined himself playing in the major leagues and pitching in the World Series someday (though his imagination was unlikely to have included the notion that he would play in a World Series under the management of Hank Bauer, which he did fifteen years later). It was time for a schoolboy to face reality; he continued preparing the day ahead at Fratt School, part of Billings' Catholic school system.

Dave, who celebrated his ninth birthday on October 31, 1951, had plenty of baseball-related material to fuel his imagination. In June of that year, he discovered Little League, the country's premiere baseball program tailored to the abilities of youngsters like him. Three years earlier, in 1948, Jack Skinner, an infielder for Billings' minor league Mustangs, an affiliate of the Brooklyn Dodgers, married the former Dorothy Yokem; the wedding reception took place at the home on Elm Street where his widowed mother, Beth McNally, was raising Dave and her three older children. Dave's older brother and future business partner, Jim, served as a batboy for the Mustangs during their inaugural 1948 season in the Pioneer League.

Millions of American boys have played Little League and sandlot baseball over the decades, and some of them have dreamed of and achieved careers as major-league players. Dave was one of those whose dreams came true—but he did that in a way unique to members of his and future generations. Fresh out of high school, he signed with Baltimore, starting a thirteen-year career with the Orioles, during which he became the winningest left-handed pitcher in team history.

McNally certainly found stardom as a pitcher for the Baltimore Orioles. He won 181 games during his Orioles career, from 1962 through 1974. He won three more games for the now-defunct Montreal Expos in 1975, giving him a career total of 184 wins. He won twenty or more games for four straight years and, in 1971, was part of the greatest four-pitcher rotation in modern major league history. Also, he remains the only pitcher who has hit a grand-slam home run in World Series play, that coming in the 1970 Series against the Cincinnati Reds.

Billings people, schools, and places laid the foundation for Dave's greatness, beginning as a star pitcher for some of the best American Legion baseball teams in the country in the late 1950s.

Beyond that, however, Dave made a contribution to baseball and professional sports that endures to the present. His 1975 accomplishment left an effect that is still felt today in professional sports. When a reader has finished this book, they will have become familiar with an unassuming man from Billings who developed into a star major-league pitcher and then became a champion of workplace fairness for professional athletes. What he did in 1975 proved to be a thunderclap that reverberated in professional sports then, and it continues to resonate today.

His life serves as a lasting lesson that someone with a sense of purpose and the discipline to focus on a goal—playing big-league baseball—can not only achieve that goal but do more. They may change the world in a seemingly modest but meaningful way.

Dave McNally took a stand opposing the power of major league baseball's establishment: wealthy team owners; sportswriters with little or no empathy with the athletes they wrote about; many, if not most, of that era's fans; and others on the wrong side of history. Dave's efforts culminated in a landmark victory in 1975, which created a legacy that is the foundation of this true account of his life.

Statistics and accolades aside, Dave earned his place in history by taking part in the baseball arbitration case that resulted in the so-called Seitz decision. When the ruling, named for arbitrator Peter Seitz, was announced, Dave and former Los Angeles Dodgers pitcher Andy Messersmith found their names inscribed in professional sports history.

The ruling overturned baseball's reserve clause, which had been in place since the start of the twentieth century, and ushered in the modern era of free agency. The reserve clause essentially tied baseball players to the team that signed them to a contract, allowing them to seek a place on other teams' rosters only if their original team consented. As some labor observers said, baseball players before 1975 were chattel, the legal property of the team that held their contract. Almost slaves.

But with the reserve clause outlawed and free agency in effect, baseball players were free—with some restrictions—to do what most other Americans could do to improve their lot. Players could now announce their availability to other teams and, often with the help of an agent, negotiate deals worth millions of dollars. Katy bar the doors! The era of handsomely paid athletes, even those with average skills, began in the years after Dave and Messersmith allowed their names to be affixed to the Seitz case.

Now it's time to give Dave his due. That's why I've written this book. I've lived in Billings for most of my adult life, except for time spent out of state going to college and later when my twenty-five-year career as a newspaper reporter and editor took me away from the Treasure State. I spent most of my career as a working journalist employed by the *Billings Gazette*; my twenty years on the *Gazette*'s staff included more than a decade as a sportswriter before I took on other reporting assignments.

That experience included my interview with McNally in 1978, three years after he retired from baseball and came home. Dave emphatically stated that while baseball had been an enormously satisfying part of his life since his Little League days, he was through with going out to the pitching mound.

Instead, McNally wanted to become a better businessman, fully engaged in his new career as a co-owner with his brother Jim of a major car dealership in Billings. He wanted to raise his growing family, which then included the four children he had with his wife, Jean, and which grew to five children. He wanted to play golf to relax, and he also wanted to give back to the community and the state that lifted him to fame, evident in ways that included being named one of the first members of the Orioles Hall of Fame.

Dave, sadly, died of lung cancer in 2002 at age sixty. I have had conversations with several of his immediate family members, including his sister, Dee, his widow, Jean, and Jean and Dave's oldest child, Jeff, who shared stories about a man they all called kind and, occasionally, funny. And, as Jeff said when he eulogized his father, he was someone who could be stubborn and, in Jeff's words, "bull-headed" when he felt his sense of right being challenged.

I've also spoken with several of Dave's old teammates from their American Legion baseball days, and I've interviewed two of his Orioles teammates, Jim Palmer and Boog Powell. That material, plus abundant newspaper clips available through digital archives, gave me a rich vein of material to construct stories about someone whose life was well-lived, although too short.

Join me as we go back to those days in Billings, in the early 1950s, when a youthful Dave McNally first got a taste of the sport he loved, a sport that made him a household name first in Montana and then in Baltimore.

Before we proceed, though, allow me to provide a quick description of the structure of the book. While I have extensive material about Dave's baseball career, as well as his growing-up days, gaps exist in the material available to me. These could be experiences Dave may have had as a typical Billings youngster navigating the 1950s, or they could be a story about a true event where some details, including everyone who took part, are not available to me.

As a journalist, I firmly believe in staying true to facts. There are no such things as "alternative facts." Yet, my goal is to make this an enjoyable work of narrative nonfiction, complete with stories that include scenes, settings, and dialogue. Thus, at times I've had to imagine what likely happened almost seven decades ago, based on my interviews and research, and write based on that. I've clued you, my readers, into content such as that. Also, I've derived everything between quotation marks from verifiable sources: newspaper accounts, interviews, other published books, etc.

With fair notice to you of my method, I hope I've given you the true story of one of Billings' and Montana's more memorable people—and insight into his contribution to basic professional athlete rights throughout the United States.

A letter to the editor published in the *Baltimore Sun* on December 6, 2002, put Dave's career and his impact on baseball in perspective. The letter writer, Gary Rostkowski, said other Orioles pitching greats–Mike Cuellar, Mike Flanagan, Mike Mussina, and Jim Palmer–surpassed McNally in various ways, especially their statistics. Rostkowski then summarized the love that Orioles fans in Baltimore and back home in Montana felt for Dave when he played and, in the decades, afterward.

"But if I could have one Orioles pitcher to pitch one game for all the marbles, it would be No. 19, Dave McNally, who died last week at the age of sixty. Mentally and physically tough, McNally never gave an inch to anyone or anything. He was quietly but fiercely competitive and pitched every game with the same approach–work quickly to keep the defense sharp, keep consistency at the front of your game and keep throwing."

Rostkowski said "blisters and injuries never interfered with this man's job. Though he hailed from Billings, he was all-Baltimore every fourth game."

With Mr. Rostkowski's words in mind, let's begin McNally's odyssey.

CHAPTER ONE

BILLINGS BEGINNINGS

One morning in mid-June 1951, Dave McNally said goodbye to his mother, Beth, as she got in her car, headed to her job as a social worker with the Yellowstone County Welfare Department in Billings, Montana.

What are you going to do on this fine day? Mrs. McNally might have said to the youngest of her four children she was raising by herself, her husband, Alfred "Jimmy" McNally having been killed in combat at Okinawa as World War II wound down.

Dave told his mother about what he had read in the *Billings Gazette*: a new baseball program designed for kids like him had started at Lissa Field. He asked her if he could go there and see what the program was about.

Knowing about her son's love of baseball—he threw balls all the time at the walls of their garage so he could practice fielding them—his mother assented.

Beth, her motherly instincts kicking in, told Dave to be on his best behavior. And she probably told him to come home for lunch and to let his sister, Dee, then 15, and the only girl and oldest of her children, know where he would be and what he would be doing. Dave said he would.

He had finished the school year, the third grade in Fratt School, part of the Billings Catholic school system, and June 18, 1951, was a glorious spring day for the start of Little League play in his hometown. A few puffy clouds blended with the big, blue Montana sky that swept the horizon. The forecast called for a high temperature of 72 with the possibility of afternoon thunderstorms. Dave and other Billings youngsters couldn't have asked for a better day to play baseball.

He left his house on Elm Street and walked up Virginia Lane, accompanied by his black dog, a stray he had rescued in the neighborhood. Their destination was Lissa Field, where two games were scheduled that morning. In the first, at 9 o'clock in the morning, the White Sox took on the Hotrods. A coaching period followed and then came a game pairing the Blackhawks and Dodgers. Another coaching period concluded the day's action.

The youngster reached the field and soon spotted a man who seemed in charge. It was Cecil "Cec" Musburger, whose sons, Brent and Todd, were already playing youth baseball in Billings.

Brent Musburger, who became a famed TV broadcaster, returned to Billings in 2016 for the naming of a Little League field in honor of his father, who started one of the first if not the first Little League programs in Montana. On that occasion, Brent recalled a conversation between his father and Dave more than six decades earlier; it went perhaps like this:

Mr. Musburger, could I rake the infield for you? Dave said.

Cec Musburger assented.

"Brent says he's allergic to manual labor," Cec said, according to his son's recollection.

Cec's belief in the potential of Billings youths may have led him to say something more, perhaps like this:

So, Dave, get that field smooth. These boys need a good park. Who knows? Maybe one of you will turn into a major-leaguer.

Neither McNally nor his mentor, Musburger, could foretell the future. They couldn't have predicted that *Sports Illustrated* magazine would name McNally the greatest athlete of the 20th Century in Montana—and that he would be ranked as No. 14 among all-time greats for the Baltimore Orioles. Then, after retiring and moving back to Billings, McNally joined fellow big-league pitcher Andy Messersmith to resist baseball's reserve clause, and their stand would bring about its fall and usher in the era of free agency.

McNally signed a contract with the Orioles for $105,000 in 1972 and became the American League's first $100,000 pitcher. Three years later, he joined Messersmith in a grievance against Major League Baseball.

McNally and Messersmith, a Los Angeles Dodgers pitcher, argued that the teams holding their contracts couldn't trade them to other teams without their consent.

Victory came on December 23, 1975, when Seitz ruled that MLB players became free agents after playing for one year for their team without a contract. The decision, upheld by the Eighth Circuit Court of Appeals in 1976, effectively nullified baseball's century-old reserve clause and ushered in today's era in which top baseball players command astronomical, multimillion dollar salaries, and even average players draw millions in pay.

All of that was in the future in the early 1950s in Billings and other American cities. Baseball was just one of many recreational programs that youngsters in Billings could choose from to get wholesome summer fun then. By 1952, Dave and about 6,000 other city youngsters could sample dozens of options offered by the city recreation department. It had set up the most ambitious and extensive summer schedule of programs ever offered in the bustling south-central Montana city.

At Pioneer Park, just down the hill from Dave's home, the youngster could sign up for tennis classes, art classes, crafts, or boys' softball. Boys could even pick dance lessons.

Imagine Dave pausing for a minute and basking in the sunshine to once again consider. Then he made up his mind. He had heard that hardball—boys' baseball—was being played on a ball field not far away. So, he and his dog headed to Dave's Field of Dreams.

Dave McNally had started the journey that would bring him fame as a major league pitcher for the Baltimore Orioles. His legacy would grow after he retired and moved back to Billings and became someone who helped future generations of pro athletes gain basic worker rights.

One might assume that Dave's father would influence him and coax him to try out America's summer game. After all, many, if not most, boys growing up in the 1950s could look to their fathers for advice on which sports to play and, later, what careers to consider.

Not so for McNally. The Billings-born star pitcher for the Baltimore Orioles grew up without knowing his father. Jimmy McNally, a junior Navy officer, was killed in a kamikaze attack less than two months before atomic bombs were dropped on Hiroshima and Nagasaki, ending World War II.

Dave, born on October 31, 1942, in Billings, was two when his father died, and thus his mother, Beth, was the most influential adult in his early life. Dave didn't lack for playmates because he lived in a Billings neighborhood filled with children. And he had a role model for athletic excellence in his mother. She had been a star swimmer and tennis player while earning her college degree at then Montana State University in Missoula.

So, when McNally was named the national American Legion graduate of the year in 1971, he used tongue-in-cheek humor to credit his mother for her role in his success.

Interviewed by *Baltimore Sun* beat writer Phil Jackman for an article published in the June 26, 1971, issue of *The Sporting News*, McNally claimed he wasn't an aspiring baseball player as a youngster.

"I never really wanted to play baseball; my mother made me," he said, "Seriously, she always said, 'Have a good time, you'll be working the rest of your life.'

"It was easy to have a good time playing Legion ball in Billings, believe me."

Overcoming the loss of his father, Dave met several influential adult males during his youth, the foremost being Ed Bayne, who became the legendary coach of Billings' American Legion team, the Legion Post 4 outfit. Others who helped mold the man who would become the winningest left-handed pitcher in Orioles history included "Cec" Musburger, the so-called father of Little League baseball in Billings, and two of Bayne's assistant coaches, Joe Pirtz and Les Smith, who helped transform McNally into the top junior pitcher in the country in 1960.

Earl Weaver, McNally's Hall of Fame manager for almost two decades in Baltimore, described the Montanan as an "unbelievable competitor" when McNally died in Billings in 2002. And McNally's trait of being bullheaded when he felt his sense of what was right was challenged was on display in 1975, his last year as a professional athlete.

When the 1974 season ended, Dave was the pitcher with the best record on the team—Jim Palmer later passed him on the team's victory chart—but he wanted a chance to pitch elsewhere.

"I need a change of scenery to see if it'll straighten me out and give me a little extra life," he said to a baseball writer. "I haven't been pitching the way I'm capable, and maybe a trade would wake me up."

The Orioles obliged, shipping him to Montreal. His time with the Expos was historic not because of what he did on the mound—he had a 3–6 record with a pedestrian 5.24 ERA—but for what he did away from the stadium. On June 9, 1975, he announced his retirement, saying his pitching had gotten to "where I was stealing money" and letting down his teammates. He apologized to Expos fans and began preparing to move his family back to Billings.

"I've decided to hang it up. I'm not throwing the ball. I have no oomph on, and there's no ray of hope that it'll get better," he said.

McNally, who was modest yet proud of his big-league performance, said there was "no chance I can do a decent job, and I'm not paid to do that."

Because McNally didn't sign official retirement papers, that opened the way to his historic role in the effort to give major league players the rights other workers enjoyed. Players union chief Marvin Miller contacted McNally after he returned to Billings and asked him to join the case. McNally agreed, and he said "no" when the Expos tried to convince to come back, setting the stage for Seitz's ground shaking decision.

McNally's decision to stand up against the might of the baseball owners may have had something to do with his lineage. He hailed from solid Butte, Montana, Irish stock. His grandfather was James E. McNally, an Irish immigrant who came to Montana's Mining City, became a carpenter and probably worked in one of Butte's many copper mines, shoring up tunnels that honeycombed underground.

James McNally served in the Montana Legislature, was on the Butte school board and ran for mayor. Known as an early activist in the fight against tuberculosis, he died from that disease at age 37 in 1914. His death came four years after his wife, Catherine, died of pregnancy-related complications.

James and Catherine McNally's deaths at relatively young ages left Dave's father, Alfred James "Jimmy" McNally, born in Butte in 1909, and three siblings as orphans. Their aunt, Minnie Greene, Catherine's sister, took in the children and raised them.

Jimmy McNally was a star football player for Butte High School and also was known as a gifted boxer in his hometown. He enrolled in Montana State University in Missoula in the late 1920s and continued to appear in the ring while in college. One of his prize fights occurred in 1929 when a state newspaper listed him as a welterweight entrant in the state amateur boxing tournament. Some records show that, possibly because of limited finances as the Great Depression worsened, Jimmy McNally came home from college in the summer of 1931 and didn't return to Missoula that fall. Other newspaper clips, however, list him as a graduate of MSU.

And Dave may have inherited some of his love for baseball from his father. A 1971 newspaper article that recalled Jimmy McNally included memories of Bill Dixon, a fraternity brother of McNally's, who became a shoe store owner in Missoula.[1]

"He wanted in the worst way to be a baseball player," Dixon said. "He managed our fraternity nine but wasn't quite good enough to hold down his favorite positions, shortstop, and third."

In 1934, Jimmy McNally married Elizabeth Joan Perham. The ceremony took place at the home of Elizabeth's parents, Mr. and Mrs. Arthur Perham, in Butte. The new Mrs. McNally, also a Butte High graduate, earned her degree from Montana State where she was a sorority member, a champion swimmer and tennis player, and, according to her obituary, "a self-acknowledged sports fanatic all her life."

After the marriage, Jimmy McNally went to work as a salesman for the Socony Vacuum Oil Company, and the couple moved to Mandan, North Dakota. Their three oldest children, Dee, Jim, and Dan were born there. In 1941, Socony transferred Jim McNally to Billings, and he and his wife bought a home on Elm Street where Elizabeth lived until her death, at ninety-four, on March 8, 2005.

Jimmy was drawn into combat when increasing demands for manpower prompted the Selective Service to draft even married men with families. When Jimmy was called up in 1943, the couple's four children were barely old enough to form any memory of the event, including a one-year-old Dave. Their father attended Naval Officers Training School in Tucson, was commissioned as a junior-grade lieutenant, and was sent to the Pacific Theater. The Navy assigned him to Okinawa as a port director, and on June 22, 1945, James McNally died in service to his country along with around 160,000 soldiers in the Pacific Theatre.

This left Beth McNally as a single mother of four young children in the summer of 1945. She went to work for the Yellowstone County

Welfare Department in Billings and worked there as a social worker for almost three decades before retiring as assistant supervisor in 1973.

The Billings where Dave McNally grew up in the early 1950s was a city of about 32,000 people. Today, Billings has an estimated population of about 122,000 and is the hub of a metropolitan area with about 190,000 people. In Dave's adolescence, Billings parents had little to worry about with the safety of their children. Magic City youngsters could ride their bicycles, with a sleeping bag and fishing pole attached, on a bridge across the Yellowstone River to the South Hills for an overnight camping and fishing outing.

Youth baseball gave Billings adolescents another outlet for their energy. American Legion baseball was already well-established—high schools in Montana didn't have baseball programs—and adults in the city believed it needed something to give elementary school boys (and later girls) a way to learn summer-game skills. Farsighted local men laid down the first stepping-stone for Dave McNally and others to take a path to baseball excellence in the spring of 1951. That's when Musburger, a local businessman and chairman of the Midland Roundtable, and others outlined plans to bring Little League baseball to Montana.

Grocer Gene Lissa, a longtime Billings resident, donated the use of a lot he owned next to his home at the corner of Virginia Lane and Rimrock Road to the fledgling program, which a *Billings Gazette* headline called "Midget Baseball," the term commonly used then for Little League when that program was just starting. The Roundtable, working with the city recreation department, leveled the site and erected fences that conformed to Little League standards. Base paths and other features of the field measured two-thirds of standard diamonds. Volunteers installed a backstop, bases, and other equipment.

The Little League program got started with twice-weekly twilight games, giving parents a chance to watch their sons play.

Dee Nobles, Dave's sister, graduated from high school in 1953 and began working as a legal secretary for a downtown Billings law firm. Dave's Little League team played its games in the late afternoon, which allowed Dee and their mother to attend them and cheer for Dave and his teammates.

"I used to go to all his games at Lissa Field and Cobb Field (after Dave joined the roster of the Legion Post 4 team in 1957). He was my baby brother."

"We went to all his games. I don't think mother missed a one," Dee said.

When Dave turned 11 in 1953, more than 700 Billings youngsters were taking part in the Little League and a companion Little Bigger League baseball program. Little League included eight teams, with 120 boys, and 90 boys played on six teams in the Little Bigger League. About 500 boys were learning baseball basics in the so-called minor leagues of the two organizations.

Dave took part in local youth activities besides sports. For example, when he was thirteen, he attended the annual Christmas formal dance at Hilands Golf Club, which was near his house and was where Beth played golf.

BACKYARD CIRCUS AND WONDERLAND

There was more to life than just school during the fall, winter, and spring, broken up by the fun and games of the summer. Looming over them, something far more insidious occupied their childhood. As a matter of fact, McNally and his peers grew up when polio, a dread disease that claimed the lives of hundreds of Americans and left others crippled for life, was lessening its grip as a scourge in the United States. Still, it was a serious disease that rarely left the minds of McNally and his boyhood friends.

(Montana had recorded 44 polio cases by late 1950; this was down from 93 cases in 1949.)[2]

One of McNally's boyhood friends, Pete Cochran, later a teammate on the powerhouse Billings American Legion baseball teams of the late 1950s, helped in the fight against polio. The *Gazette* mentioned Cochran for his childhood contribution to the cause.

In August 1950, youngsters in McNally's neighborhood—Billings' so-called tree streets and the adjoining North Elevation neighborhood next to Pioneer Park—put on a backyard circus. They raised $10 in an afternoon, which they contributed to the Yellowstone County chapter of the National Foundation for Infantile Paralysis.[3]

Gazette columnist Addison Bragg wrote about the youngsters' initiative to have fun and to be helpful in the polio fight:

"The money may eventually be used by the foundation for such prosaic items as stamps or typewriter ribbon. It might even place a few bottles of rubbing alcohol in the dispensary of a polio ward. Or it may supply a few vital hours of electricity needed in the operation of an iron lung. Whatever the money may be spent for, it'll be a long time before the chapter forgets how they came to receive the contribution."

Bragg traced the circus idea to a gathering of a "typical neighborhood gang of kids." They were trying to decide on "one last neighborhood summer fling" before school bells rang.

No one knew whether the idea first hatched in the mind of a ten-year-old boy or a thirteen-year-old girl. Circumstances inspired them to do what American kids had been doing for generations: put on a circus.

But not just any circus. They would charge admission and give the "gate" proceeds to the polio fight.

Here's how McNally's peers described their project in the paper:

"The money, all of it goes to polio," said an earnest, blonde, blue-eyed gypsy teller.

A six-year-old red devil, a wide grin crossing his crimson-smeared face, claimed in.

"Yeah, and we got nine dollars and 69 cents already."

One mother, seated in the kitchen chairs that served as bleachers in the backyard of an apartment house at 422 North Thirtieth Street, smiled as she described the irresistible appeal of kids performing in their circus.

"It's surprising how much money these kids took away from us."

Still, a dozen or more parents and grandparents who made up the circus audience seemed to think they had gotten their money's worth.

While they waited for the show to begin, audience members sipped pink lemonade, threw baseballs at a hole in a box (three balls for a nickel) and tried to win gum and candy bars in a penny-pitch game.

Red, yellow, purple, and green crepe paper streamers fluttered in the afternoon breeze. Circus performers bustled to get ready behind the blanket-covered dressing tent. The show was about to begin.

"Ladies and gentlemen."

The ringmaster checked his little black book and lifted his megaphone, made from a cardboard milk bottle to his lips, a mustache pasted on them.

"First act's gonna be a clown act."

Besides the first clown act, the rapt audience watched trap dancers, baton twirlers, more clowns, and a comedy act featuring characters padded with pillows.

The red devil peered out from behind the blanket curtain.

"Hi, grandma."

She waved.

"Tenshun, everybody. Next is gonna be—"

Frantic gestures stopped the ringmaster. He hurried to a conference in the dressing tent.

"She's scared, so the next act will be—"

A friendly, shaggy brown and white dog trotted across the circus "grounds." No one knew whether he was part of the show.

The audience included one especially enthused person, whose applause they could hear for every act. Ten-year-old Sidney Stewart had contracted polio four years earlier. He still walked with a noticeable limp, making him a visible reminder to Billings youngsters of the disease's impact.

When the show ended, Ringmaster Johnny Sheard introduced the fifteen boys and girls whose acts and antics helped fight polio that afternoon. They were Donna Larsen, Marilyn Sheard, Tommy Costello, Nikki Farrell, Jimmy Costello, James Albers, Frankie Thomas, Jo Ann Thomas, Kathy Costello, Patricia O'Leary, Dickie Lewis, Mary Ellen Lewis, Peggy O'Leary, Regina Costello, and Cochran.

Most likely, McNally, seven that summer, saw or at least heard about the circus because he lived in the neighborhood and was part of the tight-knit Billings community, and that may have affected him. Years later, as a retired professional athlete who had returned to Billings, Dave gave freely of his time to help charities such as the March of Dimes raise money to fight childhood diseases.

Memories have faded, and several principal characters, including McNally, are deceased as I write this. But it's likely that Dave McNally and his childhood friends, among them Cochran, Fry, and Bill McIntosh, took part in other adolescent activities in the Billings of the 1950s.

For example, they may have benefited from the foresight of Stella and Don Foote, who established the Wonderland Amusement park on a 32-acre site at the junction of Moore Lane and Laurel Road in Billings.

The Footes had launched KBMY, Billings' second radio station, at the same location in 1946, three years before they opened Wonderland.

The park featured a speedway, thrill rides, pony rides, trout ponds and a train.[4] The park also featured an Old West history museum and a "See 'em Alive Zoo" that pulled in tourists passing through Billings. Children's parties, stock-car races and rodeos attracted locals, according to the 2010 obituary for Stella Foote.[5]

Dave's widow, Jean McNally, said she went to Wonderland while growing up in Billings in the 1950s. Her family excursions to the park occurred years before she and Dave met as students at Billings Central Catholic High School and began dating.

Many Billings youngsters, McNally possibly among them, attended a Kiwanis Club-sponsored Fun Day at Wonderland in the fall of 1952. The service club arranged for youngsters to take over the park on the last Sunday of September. They could enjoy free rides and munch on popcorn while being carried on the rattling train, or they could climb on Shetland ponies for a gentle ride.[6]

The parent Kiwanis organization created National Kids Day to bring adult attention to the problems of youth. However, as the *Billings Gazette* put it, the day meant "an afternoon of entertainment that will not necessitate tapping the piggy bank or asking dad for an allowance."

The *Gazette* later reported that more than 700 youngsters "whooped and hollered in fun" and ate more than 1,200 bags of popcorn.[7]

"The popcorn stand was really overworked," said P. L. Verduin, a Kiwanian in charge of the event.

The smiles on the faces of many youngsters and their exuberance showed that they hadn't visited the park before.

"I believe that many of them were from large families who have not been able to afford trips to the park," Verduin said. Looking at the youngsters' eyes, one could read "a story of enjoyment from which we can conclude the event was successful," he added.

KNOTHOLE GANG

Hey, Dave, Pete, let's join the knothole gang, so we can watch the Mustangs, Bob Fry might have said to his boyhood buddies, Dave McNally, and Pete Cochran, early in the summer of 1952.

The Knothole Gang was a time-honored idea in baseball across the country. It allowed youths to watch games through holes in the outfield fence for free.

Billings got professional baseball in 1947, and by 1949, the Mustangs were using the Knothole Gang plan as a promotion to boost attendance at Cobb Field and help ensure a fan base in the future. A July 22, 1949, advertisement in the *Gazette* beckoned boys and girls to a "Knothole night" when the Mustangs would take on the visiting Boise, Idaho, team.

By June 1952, when Dave was nine—he would turn ten on the last day of October—he was playing Little League baseball on Lissa Field and probably reading the *Gazette* sports section. It was likely that he, Fry, and Cochran all saw a picture in the paper that was a call to action for the trio and other Billings youngsters. It was likely that other kids in the neighborhood, including Bill McIntosh, another of McNally's boyhood friends, saw the same photo and had the same idea.

Hey, you think this might be fun? one of them could have said.

The picture showed Pat Clark from the city recreation department handing out badges to six youngsters, five boys and one girl, good for free admission to four Mustangs games that June. The Billings Optimist Club sponsored the program, which made it possible for about 500 kids to watch action at Cobb Field.[8]

You guys think we should get some Cracker Jacks, hotdogs, or something? a Knothole Gang member might have said during the first game, to which they got in free. They had little reason to cheer, though, for on June 6, 1952, the Mustangs absorbed an 8–3 loss to Magic Valley of Twin Falls, Idaho.

At least we had a 2–0 lead in the first inning, the kids might have said while consoling themselves afterwards. That early advantage, the result of three consecutive singles, evaporated as the Ponies put together two hits only once during the rest of the game.

Teddy Savarese shut us down, the Magic City contingent would have agreed, looking back at how the Cowboys southpaw throttled the home team on eight, well-spaced hits.[9]

It didn't get better three days later when Pioneer League-leading Boise tagged the Mustangs with a 5–4 loss in the second knothole gang game. Louis Vitous punched a tie-breaking single in the ninth inning to cap a Yankees rally that began when they scored twice in the eighth inning to pull into a 4–4 tie.[10]

Let's hope it's not a slaughter this time, the Billings kids could have said to each other as they settled into their seats on June 17, 1952. This time, Idaho Falls furnished the opposition, and it was another night of disappointment for the home crowd at Cobb Field. Right-hander Ken Kimball shut down the Mustangs, 6–2. He gave up two hits in the first inning but settled down and faced only 27 batters in the next eight innings. From the second inning on, Billings couldn't advance runners past second base, and only four Mustangs got that far.[11]

Most youth in American cities in the 1950s had sunny outlooks, but the young Mustang fans were being tested. Were they jinxing the Ponies? They didn't have to worry about that possibility after June 20, 1952, because Billings finally won a Knothole Gang game. The Mustangs nipped Pocatello, Idaho, 3–2, as Don Paulsen's sacrifice fly to deep centerfield plated Ernie Garcia. The knothole kids watched two pitchers turn in solid performances, Billings' Ray O'Connor yielding seven singles, and Jim Howard of Pocatello, which had taken the league lead, giving up six hits.[12]

Dave and his friends had more to do than watching and playing baseball as they grew up in Billings in the 1950s. For example, on Saturday, June 21, 1952, they could go downtown to watch the Billings Historical Parade, known as the Go Western Parade for years before then. The historical parade included mechanized or motor vehicle floats depicting early area scenes or incidents. Current residents, dressed as well-known characters of the early west who came through what was now Billings, such as Buffalo Bill Cody, Calamity Jane, Luther Kelly, and Liver Eating Johnson, rode on parade floats or walked city streets on parade day.

Colorful dress and looks were the order of the day. Maybe handlebar mustaches and other facial flourishes worn by the youngsters' great-grandfathers were rare sights, but the Western motif was clear. Women joined in, wearing jeans, saddle pants, and ten-gallon hats.

Dave and his friends had a way to cool off on hot summer days in 1957, when few if any Billings homes and businesses had air conditioning. They could head to the two city swimming pools, at Athletic Park (next to Cobb Field) or South Park. Younger siblings under ten could splash in wading pools at South, North, and Pioneer parks.

Although swimming, parades, watching the city's minor league baseball team, and other activities were all part of many Billings youngsters' summer days in the 1950s, Little League baseball drew more of McNally's attention than almost anything else. And he was fortunate that a local businessman came across the idea for a youth baseball program that would sweep the country. Little League was born in Pennsylvania just before World War II started, and it became a summertime fixture in Billings and part of the landscape that has lasted through today. The lure of Little League snared Dave.

CHAPTER TWO

FOUNDATION FOR FAME

THE LITTLE LEAGUE IDEA

Two years before he started Little League baseball in Billings, Cec Musburger seemed to have gotten the idea that boys, ages nine through twelve, and later girls in that age group, deserved and would benefit from playing baseball tailored to their sizes, abilities, and skills.

We're left to wonder if he could have envisioned that thousands of Billings youths, starting in 1951 and continuing until now, would play on city Little League teams. Could he have imagined that three boys, his two sons and McNally, who all lived in the same tree-lined neighborhood near the Eastern Montana College campus, would go on from Little League to national fame in sports?

Those boys, touched by the youthful magic of Little League, were Musburger's sons, Brent, who became one of the top TV sports broadcasters in the country, and his younger brother, Todd, who became a lawyer and a top sports agent, and their friend, Dave McNally, who became one of the best major-league pitchers of the 1960s and 1970s as a lefthander for the Baltimore Orioles.

Brent Musburger said in a 2022 conversation with the book author that he thought his father got the Little League from reading an article in a national magazine. The author's research indicates that a 1949 *Saturday Evening Post* article led Cec Musburger to join Lissa and others in bringing the dream of organized youth baseball in Billings into reality.

The *Post*'s May 14, 1949, issue included an article that discussed the history and the structure of Little League ball, then about ten years old and sweeping across the U.S. in the post-World War II years.

Writer Harry T. Paxton wrote the article headlined "Small Boy's Dream Come True." It opened with: "The fastest-growing thing in baseball today is the Little League setup, in which youngsters of eight to twelve play with all the trappings of the major league."

Although Little League started in 1939, the outbreak of war in 1941 halted its growth. Peace came in 1945, and the next three years saw the Little League idea spread from Williamsport, Pennsylvania, through eleven states.

Williamsport was a former lumber town, and now it had a new claim to fame as the birthplace of Little League baseball. Today, it remains the Mecca for Little League, and it's the place where the Little League World series is played, starting in late August every summer. The Musburgers, McNally and hundreds of other talented Billings players never got a trip to Williamsport with a chance to play for what is now an international championship, but another, later group of Billings boys did.

In 2011, the Big Sky All-Stars claimed the Little League West regional championship in San Bernardino, California, and became the first Montana team to reach the Little League World Series. They defeated favored Huntington Beach, California, 1-0, in the semifinals but lost to the same team, 11–1, in the U.S. championship game.

What made the 2011 Little League finale even more special to Billings and Montana was that former Magic City Little Leaguer Brent Musburger was at the mic, broadcasting play-by-play of the championship game for ABC TV.

Sixty-two years earlier, in 1949, a couple of years before Little League ball arrived in Billings, Paxton described the Williamsport field in the *Post* article. It served as the model for all other fields, operating in six states with 157 programs in 1948. By April 1, 1949, 300 leagues were ready to go in eleven states, and others were being organized. The Williamsport diamond was a miniature big-league ballpark, tailored to the size of the players. Features of the park included a "complete outfield fence, built roughly on a 180-foot arc from home plate, over which the boys can hit home runs." Bleachers ran the length of each foul line, and players and spectators could keep track of runs, balls, strikes, and outs by gazing at an electric scoreboard, stationed in a press box behind home plate and operated with a remote-control switch.

Post readers were told that the field was "beautifully graded and leveled, with carefully cropped infield and outfield grass." And on top of that, it was irrigated with its own water system. Teams gathered in dugouts with roofs, and as players came to bat, a public-address announcer told spectators their names and positions. Three umpires, "qualified" volunteers, ran the game.

"The boys themselves cultivate all the professional mannerisms—knocking the dirt off their rubber-cleated shoes, rubbing dust on their hands and then digging in a la Ted Williams or Joe DiMaggio at the plate."

The boys showed a "surprisingly professional" style of play, but not without "a certain small-boy awkwardness." Sure, players made blind swings, bobbled grounders, and uncorked wild throws, but they aimed most throws at the correct base.

Someone watching an early day Little League game would see pitchers who could break real curveballs, fielders who could track down long drives on a dead run, and hitters who could lay down a perfect bunt or blast the ball over the fence. League batting champions almost always hit for an average above .400.

"It's quite a show, and one which appeals to many people who have no interest in conventional ball games," Paxton wrote.

Williamsport, a city of about 50,000, attracted crowds ranging from several hundred to several thousand during the 1948 national championship tournament. Shockingly, Little League games sometimes outdrew the professional Williamsport Tigers, who played in the Class A Eastern League.

Carl Stotz was the father of Little League ball in Williamsport, and once he got the ball rolling, others in the community pitched in to make it a reality. Baseball was the shared American experience, a communal project.

Paxton wrote that it took some time, but Stotz, "no hot-eyed zealot" as Paxton described him but a slightly built man with an "unassuming" manner, eventually made his childhood dream a reality. As a youth, he played baseball on local playgrounds and tried out for his Sunday school league team but always lost out to older young men. Finally, as a young man himself, he got to play a couple of seasons of organized ball.

Then, married, working, with a daughter, his baseball dream faded. However, in the summer of 1938, his nephews, Jimmy, and Harold (Major) Gehron, ages six and eight, "got the baseball bug," restarting Stotz' baseball dream.

They provided the impetus for Stotz to raise the money needed to make his idea succeed. He canvassed local businesses, trying to get them to sponsor youth teams, but the Great Depression was still raging. So, the businesses of the time said no.

After being turned down fifty-six times, Stotz visited Lycoming Dairy and finally got a yes. Floyd Mutchler, the manager, contributed $35. Stotz used the money to buy three dozen baseball-style playing suits at the local five-and-dime store, which is what people in the mid-20th Century called variety stores such as Woolworth's and Kresge's, both now gone from the American landscape. The suits served as uniforms for three teams. Two more businesses, Lundy Lumber and the Jumbo Pretzel Company, got on board, and the fledgling organization could buy shirt emblems and playing-field equipment.

In 1939, the first season featured supervised sandlot ball, but, by 1947, Stotz organized a championship tournament that brought in all-star teams from New York, New Jersey, and Pennsylvania.

Soon, Little League gained national sponsors. They included the United States Rubber Company, which developed baseball sneakers for the Little League players; a leading bat manufacturer, which developed an official Little League bat; and a top baseball manufacturer, which devised the official Little League ball. It was the same size as a regulation baseball but lighter and not as lively.

Williamsport officials credited Little League for helping to bring down the number of juvenile arrests in their city, and it wasn't just boys who grew up without a father like McNally. Thousands of other Billings youngsters, including girls, got a chance to play organized baseball and benefited from Little League in their town, so it really was a blessing for the community, not just for the boys like McNally. Little League also gave men, and later women, a chance to imagine themselves as big-league managers, or in the way that people reading the *Post* article would have thought, as "a Joe McCarthy or a Billy Southworth, manipulating a major-league contender." And beyond all the potential for future careers and financial success, the Little League offered these children, some of whom had fathers who died in the war, an opportunity to form bonds with other kids their age, and by working together as a team, they could learn how to succeed in life while forming blissful childhood memories.

In a few short years, the idea had captivated thousands of boys and men in hundreds of communities. "This is probably only the beginning," Paxton wrote.

And the Billings men who had the vision to start Little League in their city, giving someone like McNally a chance to develop into a major league pitching star, proved Paxton's point.

The Midland Roundtable, a Billings organization that fosters amateur sports in the city and region, worked with the city recreation department to level the Lissa Field site and erect fences that conformed to Little League standards. Base paths and other features of the field measured two-thirds of standard diamonds. Volunteers installed a backstop, bases, and other equipment.

Francis McCord was another Billings person who helped to get Little League started in the Magic City. McCord, who worked at the Billings Conoco oil refinery, and his brother, Bill, an employee of Montana Power Company, had pipes installed to water Lissa Field, and they also got fences built around the field, according to Francis McCord's stepson, Milt Wester.

Francis McCord coached McNally in Little League and, later on, in the Babe Ruth competition. He knew Ed Bayne and, Wester said, gave the Legion Post 4 coach a welcome heads-up: "You've got somebody coming up who's special," Wester quoted McCord, who recognized Dave's talent, as saying.

The Little League program got started with twice-weekly twilight games, giving parents a chance to watch their sons play.

Further evidence of Cec Musburger's support of the Billings Little League program appeared in advertisements for his business, the Appliance Mart, along with the James Automatic Dishwasher Company, in 1953. The ads, which ran five times that summer in the *Gazette*, invited readers to tune into the KBMY radio station every Sunday from 8:45 a.m.-9:30 a.m. for the Little League Clubhouse program. Musburger interviewed several of McNally's Little League teammates along with future

American Legion baseball teammates, including Jim Michel and Jerry Narum. On August 21, 1953, he interviewed players in town for the Midland Roundtable Little League tournament. A week later, he brought boys playing in a Babe Ruth tournament into the radio station's studio for interviews.

The ads didn't list McNally, who was ten years old then, but he might have been interviewed. If such an interview did occur, it's likely that the value for such information would have aged well like old baseball cards or fine wine.

Dick Harte remembers McNally from his days as a Little League star. Now retired and living in Bozeman, Montana, Harte was a few years younger than McNally.

His connection to McNally came from playing on the same Little League team, Q's Sports Shop, as McNally and having his father, Don Harte, coach both him and the future Orioles star. In a 2023 interview, Harte recalled a Q's team anchored by McNally, Bill McIntosh and Dick Letwak.

"They were really good," he said of the trio, and McNally was especially versatile as a baseball-loving youngster.

"He'd pitch one game and catch the next," Harte said. That presented a challenge for the senior Harte.

"My dad had to find a left-handed catcher's glove" for southpaw McNally, so he could take a turn behind the plate. When league officials asked his father to coach at Lissa Field, "he inherited these three incredible players," said Dick Harte, who got to play on the same diamond as the trio of future Legion stars.

Most youths in the 1950s and 1960s—generally boys before Title IX prompted interscholastic competition for girls—played several sports in junior high school and in high school. This was a time before parents sent their children to specialized sports academies, hoping that top instructors would mold their progeny into top prospects for college competition—or even professional athletes.

Typical of his time, McNally as an all-around athlete at Billings Central High School, the city's Catholic high school, made the rosters of two Rams athletic teams. By November 1957, when basketball coach Ed Hummel was assessing his team, he included McNally, a then 5–10 sophomore, among his top young players. McNally's name also showed up on Central's football roster during September 1956. McNally was a freshman at the time, and the Rams traveled 50 miles to Hardin to face the Bulldogs. As a sophomore, he was a team manager for the Rams football program, but he never played high school football seriously.

Dave was a good enough basketball player to earn post-season honors; however, he got far more acclaim for his baseball skills, as shown by coverage in the *Billings Gazette* and recollections to this day from those in Billings who knew him as a teenager. It had become clear that baseball was the sport that would make McNally a household name in his hometown, in Montana, and even far beyond the Treasure State.

RIGHT TIME AND PLACE

McNally was growing up when Billings was becoming one of the premiere baseball towns of its size in the United States. The Billings Mustangs joined the Class C Pioneer League in 1947 and competed against another Montana team, Great Falls; four Idaho squads, Boise, Lewiston, Pocatello, and Twin Falls; and a Utah outfit, Salt Lake City.

Mustangs' management showed awareness of the potential for developing youth baseball players in the Magic City. In 1951, Mustangs manager Larry Shepard complimented the Midland Roundtable for leadership in fostering local Little League competition.

"Billings youngsters are most fortunate to be able to play on such a diamond as Lissa Field," he said.

That year, the Billings Boosters defeated Miles City, 18–14, to win the first Midland Empire Little League baseball tournament at Lissa Field. The Boosters played error-free ball and won all five games they played, including shutouts of Miles City, Shepherd, and Lovell, Wyoming.

McNally, Cochran, Fry, McIntosh, and other younger Billings baseball players could use older Little Leaguers as role models, if not heroes. Particularly, they could look up to the tournament's home run champs: Dick Lamb of the Boosters and Fred South of Miles City. Lamb hit two home runs, and South clubbed five four-baggers.

That same summer, brothers Brent and Todd Musburger played for a Braves team that captured the city Little League championship. The Braves won 42 games and lost seven.

By 1952, Butte joined the ranks of Treasure State cities with Little League teams. Tournament brackets in those early years were based on geographic proximity instead of adherence to state boundaries. Thus, leagues in Billings and the far northwestern Montana town of Libby, which began Little League play in 1955, faced teams from neighboring states in early tournament games instead of having in-state competition.

Dave, as a Little Leaguer, began showing the pitching skills in 1954 that, developed more, would make him a major league star. He was the winning pitcher in the Lissa League All-Stars' 11–4 win over the Mustangs in the city playoffs. The triumph gave Lissa third place.

As a twelve-year-old in 1955, he showed he carried a potent bat. He displayed his threat as a hitter by clouting a three-run homer for Q's Sports Shop in a 7–5 win over Reporter Printing at Lissa Field.

LITTLE LEAGUE ENDS FOR DAVE

1955 was Dave's last season of Little League play. He was a 12-year-old that summer, the age limit for Little League, and he turned 13 on October 31 that year.

The season opened on June 11 with 16 teams that included more than 200 youths. Dave and his Q Sports team played at Lissa Field, where they saw Billings Mayor Earle Knight throw out the ceremonial first pitch. The mayor performed the same function at Billings' other Little League fields such as Sugar Field, Veterans Park, Central Park, and Little Giants Field.

Dave's mother, Beth, and his sister, Dee, may have seen him and his teammates play that Saturday. Thus, they could have witnessed the antics of spectators and parents described by *Gazette* sports editor Roy Anderson.

"My boy was safe, you–you robber," a husky woman in a blue dress yelled at the umpire.

A girl in pigtails next to her was just as agitated.

"Kill the umpire," she shouted.

The base runner, the woman's son, however, displayed better sportsmanship.

"Ah, mom, I was out (by) a mile," he said.

It was, Anderson said, "the first time of the many that the boy, and his hundreds of Billings brothers, will show their elders that good sportsmanship is one of the more important parts of playing Little League baseball."

The games were "strictly big league," and featured players in uniform, umpires at home plate and on the bases, announcers, and scorekeepers.

Fans showed the same behavior they displayed when attending games that involved the professional Billings Mustangs at Cobb Field. They applauded youngsters for good play and offered advice to pitchers and batters that everyone could hear. Spectators directed some of their best razzing at the mayor. The lanky right-hander threw the first ball to the league president, forcing the "rather portly gentleman" to reach for the high, outside pitch.

"Ball one," blurted a youngster in the stands. Someone asked His Honor to throw another pitch so photographers could get a better picture.

The youngster, however, wasn't satisfied.

"My grandmother could have hit that one," he declared, seeming to say the ball needed to have some zip on it to qualify as a Little League-quality pitch.

Pride in the program by both adults involved in Little League and players was in the air.

"After all, all but two of the boys on the fine Legion ball team that is now representing our city on a tour of midwestern states got their start in Little League baseball," said a league official.

As for Dave's team, Q's Sports Shop lost to the team sponsored by his Little League mentor, Cec Musburger, Appliance Mart, 5–3, that day.

Billings gave Dave the foundation he needed to succeed as a professional athlete–and ultimately in life. The building blocks included the community where he lived, the experiences he and his childhood friends had, and the strong, influential athletes who shaped his character. They prepared him for the next step: stardom and national acclaim as a pitcher for one of the country's top American Legion programs, the Billings Legion Post 4 team.

MOVING UP THE LADDER

By 1957, the year he turned fifteen, Dave was playing at the next level in the Babe Ruth program. He was on the National Division team that played Laurel's American Legion team, which was preparing for the state Babe Ruth tournament in Libby.

McNally was a teammate of other Billings boys who would form the nucleus of the powerhouse Billings Royals, who dominated Montana and Northwest American Legion play at the tail end of the '50s. McIntosh and Narum were among his National Division teammates.

Another Billings Babe Ruth team, the American Division squad, was also Libby-bound. It warmed up by playing Cody, Wyoming's All-Star team. Several American Division players would go on to become stalwarts of Eddie Bayne's Royals, among them Wayne Bell, Cochran, and Rich Fox.

The Billings teams were scheduled to leave later in the week on a 530-mile bus trip to the tournament in Libby. McCord, president of the Billings Babe Ruth program, expressed confidence in the Magic City squads' prospects at the state tournament.

"We're going to Libby to win the tournament, and with two teams such as these, we feel we can get the job done," he said.

Glendive won the 1957 state tournament by defeating Butte, 5–4, sending the Eastern Montana city to the regional tournament in Kellogg, Idaho. Billings' American Division team claimed third place with a 2–1 win over Libby. In that game, Cochran started the winning rally with a single in the top of the eighth inning.

Montana didn't have high school baseball, so the only opportunities McNally and other Billings adolescents had to play baseball were Babe Ruth and American Legion competition in the summer. Typical of youths his age, McNally tried—and excelled—at other sports once the school year began. He enrolled in the city's Catholic high school, Billings Central, where he would graduate in 1960. He soon became known as a basketball star and a baseball standout.

McNally started his time as a basketball player for the Rams with games on the freshman C squad. He started at guard and scored a basket as the team defeated Laurel in December 1956.

A year later, as a 5–10 sophomore, Dave had blossomed into a forward who scored 13 points for Central's B team in a 43–34 win over Belfry. Coach Ed Hummel was expecting good things from McNally and teammates Ed Batt and Don Dubuque. The Central skipper said at the beginning of the season that he hadn't settled on a specific offensive scheme, but "we will do a lot of running."

McNally made his mark on the hardwood during his junior year in high school. The Rams traveled to Sidney to play the Eagles, who won three straight state championships under the eye of Toby Kangas, a legend in Montana coaching circles. Sidney needed a basket from Al Mann with 28 seconds left to hold off the Rams, 58–56. McNally scored 17 points, second to John Link's 21 in the Rams' scoring column. Players for the Rams that day who would join Dave on the powerhouse 1960 Billings Royals American Legion team included McIntosh and Tom Costello.

At the end of that season, in March 1959, Montana's state Class A basketball tournament took place in Billings at the Shrine Auditorium, where Central won a consolation game against Lewistown, 54–45. McNally received credit for helping the Rams win that tournament game. He scored 21 points and was "deadly" at the free throw line, where he sank all seven of his shots. Dave also contributed to the win with a strong rebound that complimented work on the boards by 6–3 center Paul Weber.[1]

By then, Jim Thelen had taken the reins as Central's coach. McNally and his teammates experienced Thelen's efforts to make the Rams competitive in Montana's tough Class A league. For example, in December 1959, when Dave was a high school senior, Thelen prepared the Rams for a long road trip. They rode the team bus about 230 miles to Great Falls to face another Catholic high school, Great Falls Central, on Friday night. Then, they traveled east to play the Havre Blue Ponies before making a long trip home that would bring them back into Billings late Saturday night or early Sunday morning, completing a journey of about 700 miles. McNally scored 36 points in the two games, both Central losses.

"DAVE CERTAINLY CAUGHT OUR ATTENTION"

A man who saw McNally in Billings during the 1950s and was aware of his potential later rose to the top tier of Montana politics after Dave's death. That was John Bohlinger, who served as the Treasure State's lieutenant governor from 2004 to 2012 as the No. 2 man in the Brian Schweitzer administration. Bohlinger, who grew up in Billings a few years ahead of McNally, not only knew about McNally as a junior player but also probably learned about a future Baltimore Orioles' teammate of McNally before Dave did. That individual, who would become one of Dave's best friends in Baltimore, was future Hall of Fame third baseman Brooks Robinson.

It was McNally, however, to whom Bohlinger paid the most attention almost 70 years ago.

"David certainly caught our attention during his Legion days," Bohlinger recalled in a 2023 interview.

"He was a dominant pitcher. People couldn't hit his stuff. He had a good curve and fastball."

As a New York Yankees fan all his life, "I was disappointed when Dave signed with the Orioles," Bohlinger said.

Even before Dave signed with the Orioles, Bohlinger learned about Brooks Robinson, a native of Little Rock, Arkansas.

Bohlinger, born in Bozeman, Montana, became a Billings resident when his parents moved to the city when he was a youngster. Then, after his father died when Bohlinger was fourteen, "My mother was going to send us (Bohlinger and his sister) to a foster home." But his grandmother in Little Rock intervened.

She offered to take in John and his sister. John was already a licensed driver, so Bohlinger's mother and her children loaded the family car. And the two siblings drove to Little Rock and stayed for a while with his grandmother. An aunt and uncle, sister and brother, lived nearby and frequently stopped in to visit with his grandmother.

His grandmother's vision was so bad that she needed a magnifying glass to see newsprint, but she was an avid reader of the local newspaper. Through her, Bohlinger learned about a local American Legion baseball sensation, a third baseman who would become an Orioles teammate of McNally.

"Brooks was already a legend, like Dave (would become) in Billings," Bohlinger said.

A PRODIGY SERVES NOTICE

McNally was only 15–he would turn 16 on Halloween Day in 1958– when he served notice to Montana baseball fans of his potential greatness. That declaration occurred during the 1958 state American Legion tournament in Helena, where Dave struck out a state tournament-record 19 Missoula batters and limited the Garden City club to three hits in a 5–0 win.

The victory sent Billings' Yellowstone Legion Post 4 squad, the defending state champions, back to the finals with a shot at winning the state title for the fifth straight year. Ed Bayne's team had won the state championship seven times in the previous eight years, a string interrupted by Butte's state title in 1953. Pitching in the game that sent Billings to the title contest, McNally found himself in a duel with Missoula pitcher Mike Dishman, who held Billings hitless until the sixth inning. The Magic City team then scored all of its runs on three walks, an error, a wild pitch, and two singles.

Despite his record-setting performance, McNally didn't get to cruise to a win. His wildness gave Missoula its only hope for a rally. He walked eight batters, but whenever the western Montana team sensed the potential to rally, Dave reared back and recorded "one strikeout after another."

For example, Missoula had its best scoring opportunity in the third inning when Dave walked two batters and gave up a bunt single. Then, with the bases loaded, McNally struck out the next two batters and got the final out of the inning on a pop-up.

Dave helped his cause in the fourth inning by picking off a Missoula base runner who had reached on a walk. The next batter lined a double to the fence but was stranded. Billings only collected three hits, but Bayne's team proved opportunistic in scoring all their runs in the sixth. McIntosh walked, and Russ Powers singled to second. After an infield fly out, Narum's sacrifice fly plated two runners. Ray Haroldson walked to load the bases, and Bell walked to force in a run.

The final three Billings runs scored on a wild pitch, Frank Pirtz's RBI single, and a mishandled line drive scored as an error.

Just before Dave caught the eye of major league scouts, Legion Post 4 produced another pitcher who got a chance to show his skills at the game's top level. That was Jerry Walters, who spun a masterpiece to give Billings the 1958 Montana state championship.

He blanked Missoula on one hit for a 2–0 victory that advanced Billings to the regional tournament at the team's home park, Cobb Field. Walters had a no-hitter until the ninth inning when, with one out, Dishman slashed the ball to third base. Narum made a masterful backhand stop, but he had no chance of getting Dishman who was racing to first. The next Missoula batter grounded into a double play to end the game.

IMAGINING THE BIG LEAGUES

Did McNally ever imagine a future where he would pitch for a major league team and have the game nationally broadcast on TV? It's possible, given that Billings residents got their first look at the new medium in 1953.

Two television stations went on the air in the Magic City that year: KOOK-TV, now KTVQ, and KGHL-TV, now KULR-TV. At about that time, Beth McNally got a TV set, according to her daughter, Dee Nobles. Thus, Dave may have joined millions of Americans who occasionally watched major league baseball games on the small screen. Many big-league teams played day games then, and Billings fans would have known when to turn on their TVs by checking the program listings in the *Gazette*.

It's impossible to say if, when, or how often he watched TV games, possibly picking out heroes as sources of inspiration. They might have included New York Yankees slugger Mickey Mantle, New York and later San Francisco Giants star Willie Mays, or Detroit Tigers pitcher Jim Bunning, all future Hall of Famers. Or, possibly, future Baltimore teammates such as Brooks Robinson, just starting his sensational career with the Orioles, and Frank Robinson, then a young slugger for the Cincinnati Reds. Those baseball greats and others became names that the people of Billings could get familiar with from the comfort of their own homes.

By 1958, Security Trust and Savings Bank was sponsoring a daily TV log that ran in the *Billings Gazette*. Weekend broadcasts included the "Game of The Week," broadcast late Sunday mornings. Thus, on June 22, 1958, sports fans, teenagers and others, McNally included, could have watched the Baltimore Orioles play the Chicago White Sox at Comiskey Park. For variety, in May that year, KOOK broadcast the Yankees versus the Kansas City Athletics and the Senators versus the Yankees.

Ed Bayne, Jr., one of McNally's close friends, recalled that time period 65 years later. He said Dave and McIntosh, another member of

McNally's circle, came over to the Bayne house several times. The Baynes lived in the same neighborhood near the Eastern Montana College campus, so they probably walked over.

"They'd come to the house and talk to Dad (Ed Bayne, their coach), then watch or listen (to baseball games)."

The Yankees and the Dodgers were baseball's top teams at this time, especially during the 1955 World Series between the two New York teams just before the Dodgers moved to Los Angeles. That was the Series when the Dodgers finally beat the Bronx Bombers, an outcome sealed by Johnny Podres' shutout victory in Game 7.

"That was a big deal because the Dodgers never beat the Yankees," Bayne said.

Bayne said Dave "initially patterned himself" after his hero on the Yankees, pitcher Whitey Ford. "He looked up to him." And Dave's admiration of the future Hall of Famer was understandable because both were southpaws, their build during their playing days (Ford, 5–10, 178 pounds; McNally, 5–11, 185 pounds) was almost identical, and both relied on cunning and a tricky curveball rather than blazing speed to retire batters.

Thus, long before McNally became a hero to hundreds of aspiring baseball players, in Billings, in Montana, in Baltimore and across the country, he could find his own diamond heroes on a TV set in his hometown.

Another memorable event then was when Legion Post 4 scrimmaged with the baseball team from Eastern Montana College. Bayne recalled McNally struck out 12 EMC batters, and his Legion team won "something like 20–0."

"McNally's curveball baffled the EMC batters so completely that one pitch he threw caused the batter to swing before the ball hit him in the stomach," Bayne said.

Probably influenced by TV and what they read in the *Billings Gazette*—and maybe in the "Bible of Baseball," *The Sporting News*, McNally and his Billings baseball buddies imagined a future in the big leagues. It was something that he, along with several other Billings players, all signed by major league teams in the late 1950s and early 1960s, got a shot at.

"We always talked about that," Bayne said, remembering conversations he and his teenage friends had about making "the bigs." Using Topps baseball cards and dice, the youths played a baseball simulation game.

"I always wanted to play for the Yankees," Bayne said. McNally, though, said, "I just want to play ball. If I don't get that, I'll get a job," according to Bayne.

McNally's talent spared him from that course. It allowed him to develop his skills to where he was able to play ball at baseball's highest level.

CHAPTER THREE

PRELUDE TO GLORY AND A LIFETIME MATCH

LITTLE WORLD SERIES IN BILLINGS

In 1957, Billings became the second Montana city to play host to the American Legion Little World Series, following Miles City which was the site of the 1943 Little World Series. Although Billings didn't qualify for the tournament in 1957, that wasn't because of a lack of excellence by the Magic City team.

Ed Bayne's Legion Post 4 team tasted success throughout the 1950s by winning the 1952 state championship and then starting a string of fourteen straight championships from 1954 to 1967. That run made the Billings squad the New York Yankees of Montana American Legion baseball.

Legion Post 4 also won the 1954 regional tournament. It's almost certain that McNally and his companions on the team, who would gain fame across the land in 1960, watched the 1957 national tournament at Cobb Field. In the following year, they reached the Legion Series.

FIRST LITTLE WORLD SERIES APPEARANCE

Bayne's crew firmly established itself on the national scene in 1958. That's when Billings reached the American Legion national championship tournament in Colorado Springs. The Magic City youths got there by first winning the state tournament, defeating Missoula in the finale in Helena.

His team's excellence prompted Bayne to praise the squad regularly, an example being this accolade in the *Gazette*:

"The people of Billings should be proud of these young kids. This young ball club had to come back and get the job done in the state tournament."

Billings defeated Helena in the opener but then lost to Missoula, forcing Billings to rally and win three straight loser-out games. The victories came over Helena, once, and Missoula, twice. Bayne said three Billings' pitching rotation members, Jerry Walters, Dave McNally, and John Houson, performed extremely well.

Billings progressed from Helena to the regional tournament at Cobb Field. The host team won the title by beating Centralia, Washington, 2–1, and advanced to the sectional tournament. A newspaper photo showed the local outfit getting ready to fly to Hastings, Nebraska. This was when air travel had just become affordable as a means of transportation for regular Americans. At the sectional, tournament favorite Ontario, California, drubbed Denver, 20–4, and Billings eliminated Denver with a 5–0 victory. Billings then nipped Ontario, 3–2, in eleven innings to become sentimental favorites at the tournament. McNally pitched into the ninth inning, beads of sweat cascading down his skin as he powered through with a distinct fire within. He gave up three hits and struck out fifteen, but he tired in the ninth when Ontario got to him for a single and a walk, prompting Bayne to replace him with Walter, who got credit for the win.

"Our kids are real fine. I think we can win this tournament," said an upbeat Bayne.

Billings took a 47–5 season record into the showdown against Ontario, which the Montanans won, 3–2. That sent Billings to Colorado Springs, where their appearance at the Little World Series was the first by a Montana team. The Legion's national championship tournament included four teams. Besides Billings, they came from Ohio (Cincinnati), Massachusetts (Everett), and South Carolina (Greenwood). Billings drew Cincinnati in the second first-round game.

Legion Post 4's trip to the Legion World Series was a big deal in its hometown. About 500 Billings people trekked to Colorado Springs for the tournament. The Billings contingent included about 300 persons who were in town for the opener, which was rained out. Those cheering for Bayne's team included Mayor Earle Knight. He carried honorary memberships in the Billings Chamber of Commerce that he planned to present to the city's players and coaches at the tournament.

A rainout didn't dampen Bayne's optimism. "We have come to Colorado Springs for one purpose–to win the Little World Series," he said before taking his team to a movie instead of a baseball game. He tapped Jerry Walters to pitch against Cincinnati. The righthander compiled a 21–1 record through the Hastings sectional, and he had won seven straight games in state, regional, and sectional play.

The Billings standout caught the eye of major league scouts that year, including Yankees' talent hunter Tony Robello, who watched the sectional tournament. Although Walters was the Billings pitcher headliner that season, Robello said he was keeping an eye on more than one of Bayne's pupils. "This Billings team is a good one because it has one of the best Legion coaches in the nation. They make very few mistakes," he said.

But Billings' winning ways ended against Cincinnati. The defending national champions posted a 5–2 win over Billings, behind a four-hit, eight-strikeout performance from southpaw Scott Seger, who went on to have a ten-year professional career (1959-1968), all in the minors where he had a 59-65 record.[1] Billings started a rally with one out in the ninth inning but a strikeout, and then a ground ball out by Dave, pinch-hitting, ended the game. The game at Colorado Springs' minor-league park, Memorial Field, attracted about 1,250 spectators, including about 500 from Billings.

Billings' 1958 season ended when Everett eliminated the Magic City team with a 7–0 win. Again, Billings had hitting trouble, getting five safeties against three Everett pitchers. Dave pitched all but the first third of the first inning.

It was then that professional baseball came knocking, but it was not for Dave . . . at least not yet. Walters, eighteen then, signed with the Cleveland Indians. He received a $25,000 bonus when Carl Mays, a former Yankees pitcher turned Indians scout, presented the contract to him in Colorado Springs. Walters had graduated that spring from Billings High School. In his first year of playing Legion ball, 1957, he went 13–1, and he finished with a 21–2 record in 1958.

"I started playing baseball when I was 3 years old," Walters said. "I've always been a pitcher. They tried to make a catcher out of me at one time, but it didn't work out good."

Walters pitched for six seasons, 1959 through 1962, in the minor leagues, but he never reached the majors. His 35-41 won-loss record included a 15-4 record at Selma of Alabama-Florida League in 1961, his best season as a pro. He also made stops at Burlington in the Carolina League and Minot in the Northern League.[2] Sadly, a sore arm shortened his career.[3] Having had to give up his pitching mitt, Walters became a car dealer in California.[4]

Walters said his fastball was his best pitch, and he used his curve ball and change-up as needed.

Bayne heaped praise on his ace that year.

"He really did a good job for us; he was the workhorse of the ball club," Bayne said, pointing out that Walters "started to concentrate" after he realized that pitching was a lot of work.

"I think he's one of the outstanding Legion players in the country. I think he had more potential than any pitcher in the Little World Series," Bayne said.

Cincinnati claimed the 1958 American Legion national championship, defeating Everett, 12–1, in the last game. It was Cincinnati's fifth junior championship.

FIRST DATE: A MATCH THAT LASTED

One Sunday during the 1958–59 school year, the phone rang at Jean Hoffer's home in Billings. When Jean came to the phone, Jim Scarborough, a friend of hers as well as Dave's, greeted her. Scarborough said that Dave, a junior at Billings Central Catholic High School, wanted to take Jean, a sophomore at the school there, out on a date that night.

"I knew he wanted to take me out," the future Jean McNally said more than a decade later, "but I hadn't heard a word from him. I told him (Scarborough), one, if Dave wants to take me out, he can call himself; and two, I happen to be busy tonight."[5]

Jean was seeing someone else then, but if Dave knew that it didn't stop him. "He called me the next day," Jean said.

She remembered their first date: "Would you believe we went to the Big Boy Drive-In and had a Buzz? It's like a 7-Up, with some other things in it. We laugh about it now."

When Jean recalled her first date with Dave, they both had moved far beyond eating burgers and fries at a Billings drive-in. By then, during her 1971 look-back interview, nine years had passed since her husband's spectacular major-league pitching debut in 1962.

In 1959, Dave and Jean experienced a first date that was as much an All-American experience as any teenagers in the country in the 1950s could have had. They broke the ice by going to the Big Boy Drive-In. Don Campbell operated the eatery at Rimrock and Airport Road, just below the Rimrocks and along the main route to the Billings airport. In 1959, Campbell advertised a Sunday dinner special that probably was typical of the menu that Dave and Jean looked at. For one dollar and ten cents, patrons could choose from *World Famous Kentucky Fried Chicken*, fresh jumbo shrimp, or bar-b-q ribs. For seventy-five cents, a customer could get fish and chips.

(The restaurant, a Billings small business that survived the pandemic, still operates today. It was renamed Jim's Southside Drive-In in the 1960s, and it became King's Hat in the 1970s. Located on First Avenue South, the drive-in's signature burger is the Flying Burger—a saucer-shaped all-beef patty sandwich placed between two pieces of toasted white bread. King's Hat employees use a cast-iron press, similar to a waffle iron, to create the burger.)[6]

Their date at the 1950s Big Boy Drive-In started Dave and Jean's romance of almost forty-three years, till death did them part. "I thought he was really neat, and we started dating pretty steady after that," Jean said.

1959: EXCELLENCE AGAIN BUT NO SERIES

Excellence on the baseball diamond was becoming the standard for Billings' American Legion team, and 1959 was no exception. Still, Legion Post 4 was denied a return trip to the Little World Series and would have to wait until 1960 for a triumph at the national championship tournament. A highlight of the 1959 season occurred in June that year when Bayne's team wrapped up a three-state tour. Facing Scottsbluff, Nebraska, Dave fired a no-hitter to pace his squad to a 10–0 victory.

Dave gave up four walks in the shutout. He got in trouble only once, in the second inning, when Scottsbluff took advantage of three Billings errors to load the bases. Dave got out of the jam when Scottsbluff tried a suicide bunt, but its batter missed the ball. That allowed his team to trap a runner trying to score from third, ending the inning.

Scoreless through four innings, Billings broke through with four runs in the fifth and added three runs in the sixth and three in the eighth.

Billings lost an earlier game to Scottsbluff on that trip, and that game lives on in the memory of Billings Legion players from that time who are still alive. Teammate Bill McIntosh (who passed away in 1989), one of Dave's best friends, engaged in youthful shenanigans with Dave while they played Legion baseball. On this occasion, however, it was Wayne Bell (who passed away in 2016), who mostly played catcher for the squad, who was Dave's partner in mischief.

McNally and Bell's most notable misadventure took place in June 1959 when the Billings team played Scottsbluff in a two-game series during Legion Post 4's annual spring "big trip." Billings, coming off its first Little World Series berth in the 1958 at Colorado Springs, was favored. Scottsbluff, however, proved to be a scrappy underdog. As the hometown newspaper described the game, the home team "scored one of its biggest victories in the history of the sport here in an 11–5 upset of touted Billings, Montana."

Dave took the mound in the fifth inning when the Montanans held a 3–1 lead, but Dave, the "fire-balling pride of the Billings mound corps," who won nineteen games and lost just twice in 1958, saw his pitching unravel in the seventh inning when he was literally "bunted to death." He hurt his cause even more by throwing three wild pitches and committing two errors. When the inning ended, Scottsbluff had scored ten runs, and the home team cruised to victory.

Dave and Bell left Scottsbluff with more than hurt pride. They also felt Bayne's ire after a prank they pulled during the game. An elderly man was the plate umpire. He kept putting his weight on Bell's back and was missing call after call. Bell walked to the mound, talked briefly to Dave, and returned to his position behind home plate. Then he put his catcher's glove in front of the umpire's mask. Dave threw a fastball right at the target. At the last second, Wayne dropped his glove, and the ball hit the ump in the middle of his mask. He stumbled backward and landed on his rear end.

As Ed Bayne, Jr., recalled, "We all thought it was funny, but Coach didn't. He came out of the dugout in a sprint and pulled both players. Then sent them to the right-field bullpen with orders to run. When the game ended, the umpire entered the Billings dressing room under the grandstand and apologized for missing so many calls." He said he was getting older, and Dave threw so well he couldn't follow the ball, according to Ed Bayne, Jr. His father and the ump shook hands, and the team left to have dinner. Midway through the meal, Bayne got a phone call from the groundskeeper at the Scottsbluff baseball park. He wanted to turn off the lights, but two players, Dave and Bell, were still running. Bayne, who had forgotten about the two mischief-makers, sent Bob Glasgow, the team bus driver, to get them.

The 1959 season set the stage for 1960, when Dave would achieve renown as the best junior pitcher in the United States. And when he would lead Billings' Legion Post Four team to a pinnacle never before or since achieved: an appearance in the national championship game of the Little World Series.

EGO WILL TRIP YOU.

Parents of children growing up in the 1950s, as well as other adults influential in the lives of young people, often issued timeless warnings. The clichéd phrases they used included "Don't get too big for your britches" or "Don't get a swelled head." And they applied to Dave McNally and his Billings Legion Post 4 baseball team in the summer of 1959.

Their lesson in humility occurred in the small Nebraska town of Central City, and it became a story told by Ed Bayne Jr., in the 2015 book about his father, *Coach: Baseball and Life—Ed Bayne Style*. The incident happened during Legion Post 4's annual "Big Trip," when, with Bob Glasgow at the wheel, the team bus made a swing throughout the Midwest, playing teams in Nebraska, Kansas, Minnesota, Wisconsin (and sometimes in other states). Bayne's plan was to have his team face the best competition possible, so it would be ready to contend for a state championship in Montana and, frequently, a regional championship and even for a berth in the Legion World Series.

Thus, Central City, a town then of about 2,400 people, which isn't much bigger nowadays with a population of a bit over 3,000, furnished what seemed to be token opposition for Billings. With a few hours of spare time before the game, the Billings players asked Bayne if they could go swimming at the city pool. He said, yes, and after swimming, "we hit the DQ (Dairy Queen) for ice cream sundaes, shakes, ice cream cones and other snacks," Ed Bayne Jr., recalled.

When game time came, the Billings players saw a field with gopher holes in the outfield, and a snow fence surrounded the diamond. "We felt like this was going to be an easy game and played like it," Bayne said. The Billings pitcher, who the book quoted Bayne as saying was LJT Miller, threw sixteen straight balls. Chuck Stroup, who normally was the Billings catcher, played left field and muffed three fly balls. As Ed Bayne, Jr., put it, "the ten-run rule was in effect, and we got our butts beat." Billings, which held a 1–0 lead going into the bottom of the third inning, gave up seven runs to Central City in that inning, and the home team rolled to a 16–2 win.

Afterward, Coach Bayne said, "Now what do you think about ice cream, swimming, and small-town teams?" As his son put it, "We got the message big time!"

CHAPTER FOUR

BEST IN THE LAND

1960: GLORY YEAR

Although the 1960 season ended with the disappointment of losing the Little World Series championship game, Billings and Dave McNally could look back at a summer filled with highlights. Legion Post 4's play vaulted the team and its star pitcher into national prominence. Notable games were:

June 3.   Dave, Chuck Miller, and Jim Olsen combined to no-hit Miles City in an 11–5 win.[1]

June 8.   The Billings squad stopped in St. Paul during a lengthy tour of the Upper Midwest. Dave tossed a no-hitter, struck out fourteen, and walked four in an 8–0 win.[2]

June 12.   Billings won for the ninth time in ten road games by defeating the Oshkosh, Wisconsin, Fuller Post No. 70 team, 8–4. Dave went the distance and got the win. He helped his cause in the seventh, stroking one of three singles plus three walks and two Oshkosh errors that yielded five Billings runs.[3]

June 17.   Billings whipped the visiting Cheney Spuds of Tacoma, Washington, 9–0. Dave pitched a two-hitter and struck out twenty-three. He also tripled and then scored Billings' final run on a wild pitch.[4]

June 24.   Dave pitched his second no-hitter of the season during an 8–0 win at Minot, North Dakota. Dave struck out twenty, prompting Bayne, his manager, to say he "was at his best" that night.[5]

June 29.   Billings outlasted visiting Sheridan, Wyoming, 2–0. Highland got the win with pitching help from Dave and Miller. The win boosted Billings' record to 25–2.[6]

July 2.   Dave struck out twenty-seven and allowed one hit, a bunt single, as his team whipped Glendive, 22–2. Dave got the high strikeout total thanks to passed balls by his catchers. Four Glendive batters struck out in one inning and five in another because of the miscues.[7]

July 12.   Billings notched Win No. 32, 7–0, over visiting Worland. Dave teamed up with fellow southpaw Paul Highland to no-hit the Wyoming squad through six innings. Dave struck out nine and walked three to get the win.[8]

August 9.   Dave fired the only no-hitter in the country at a state tournament in 1960. He threw a near-perfect game against Butte in the Miles City tournament. Billings won, 11–0. Dave faced only twenty-nine Butte batters, two more than he would have pitched to in a perfect game. He struck out twenty-three and walked two.[9]

August 13.   Dave followed up his no-hitter against Butte with another one against Miles City in the state championship game. Dave struck out twenty-two Miles City batters and walked five in the 10–0 win. It gave Billings its seventh state championship in a row.[10]

Now it was on to the Legion regional tournament on their home diamond, Cobb Field, for Bayne's crew. It wasn't all seriousness for the Billings team that week in August 1960. The Montana Open golf tournament was underway at Hilands Golf Club in Billings, and Dave joined outfielders Dick Letwak and Bill McIntosh to watch the opening round.[11]

Earlier that summer, Ed Gorilla, coach of the Fargo, North Dakota, Legion team, got on board the Billings-McNally bandwagon. Billings defeated Fargo three times in four games they played that year, leading Gorilla to call Bayne's outfit "the best team in our area."[12] "Billings is better than any Minnesota team I've seen this year, and Dave McNally is the best pitcher we've faced. He's faster than anyone we've seen," Gorilla said, adding that Billings took advantage of every break it got.

Butte sportswriter Frank Quinn said that Dave, who "has major league scouts buzzing around Billings," exhibited "the same spirit as that of his father who displayed that give it all quality in athletics and in service to his country."

Amidst his rise to national fame, Dave kept a streak of mischief going. Antics that he and his best friend, McIntosh, engaged in included a memorable incident in the summer of 1960. As related by Ed Bayne, Jr., several Legion Post 4 players were sitting in the first-base stands at Cobb Field, watching the Billings Mustangs play. The contingent included Dave and McIntosh. "Suddenly, there was a loud bang from under the grandstand in the men's restroom," Bayne said.[13]

Dave, McIntosh, and a couple more boys, who had been away from their seats, came running up the stairs and sat down with the team, but their reappearance didn't escape the notice of veteran Billings police officer Blackie Johnson. Johnson, a Legion baseball booster and friend of Coach Bayne, monitored the Legion players during their activities, sanctioned or not, around Billings. Johnson, standing on the opposite third-base side of Cobb Field, rushed over to where the Legion players were seated. Apparently singling out Dave and McIntosh as the ringleaders of what had happened, he grabbed them, and the story of what had happened spilled out.

A fan had gone into the men's restroom, entered a stall, closed the door and sat down on a toilet. McNally and McIntosh came up with the idea to roll a cherry bomb under the stall door toward the unwitting individual answering nature's call. When the bomb went off, "the man came roaring out of the stall, pants down, (toilet) paper in hand, and smoke all around," Ed Bayne, Jr., said. After the smoke cleared, literally and figuratively, Johnson told Ed Bayne, Sr., what had happened. The Legion skipper suspended McNally and McIntosh, and they missed the team's road trip to play Sidney and Glendive.

"MORE FLIES AROUND THE HONEY"

"More flies around the honey," was the phrase *Billings Gazette* sports editor Roy Anderson used to describe the major-league scouting attention focused on Dave when the Northwest Regional tournament began in Billings. The August 1960 event at Cobb Field drew eighteen pro scouts, likely all or most all of them trying to get a good enough assessment of the star southpaw to decide if their club should offer him a shot.

Anderson reported that the latest scout to arrive in the Magic City was Walter Shannon, farm director of the St. Louis Cardinals. Other teams that sent scouts were Detroit, San Francisco, Cleveland, Pittsburgh, the New York Yankees, the Chicago White Sox, Philadelphia, Kansas City, and Milwaukee. Baltimore sent a four-scout contingent, including Jim Wilson and Jim Russo, who would figure significantly in Dave's signing with the Birds that September. The Los Angeles Dodgers, who became a leading choice for McNally as he pondered his future, sent Pat Patterson.

Someone who warned against overbidding for Dave showed up in Billings. Mays, a pitcher for four major league teams between 1915 and 1929, was a sixty-six-year-old scout for the Cleveland Indians. He had signed Billings pitcher Walters to a deal with the Tribe in 1958. While at the Billings regional, he contacted three members of the Great Falls Legion team.[14]

Mays said Cleveland wanted Dave, but not at the asking prices being bandied about: "He might be worth about $50,000 on a bonus, but not the $80,000 to $90,000 they (other teams) are mentioning."

Billings showed itself able to compete with the large-city competition at the regional. On August 21, 1960, Legion Post 4 blasted Denver, 16–2, in front of 3,500 hometown spectators. Highland, Huntsberry, and Miller teamed up to limit Denver to eight hits. Huntsberry got the win.

Cochran, Letwak, Huntsberry and McIntosh led Billings' attack with three hits apiece. Cochran smacked two triples to go seven-for-twelve in his batting at the regional. Two days later, an even bigger crowd, 3,904 fans, swarmed to Cobb Field and saw Dave lead Billings to a 2–0 win over Seattle with his pitching and batting. Dave was so effective that he didn't allow a Seattle batter to hit a ball out of the infield. He allowed two hits, struck out nineteen, and walked four. He clinched the win in the eighth inning when, with Billings ahead, 1–0, he blasted a pitch over the left-field fence.

Seattle brought a 32–4 record to the tournament, and its brilliant defense kept the game close. In the seventh, Billings loaded the bases with no one out, but Seattle squelched the threat with a double play and a pickoff at second base.

Billings punched its ticket for its second trip to the Legion World Series in three years on August 25, 1960, with a 9-0 win over Denver. Denver came back through the loser's bracket to reach the championship game. Bayne's club blanked the Mile High City crew, 9–0, behind right-hander Steve Hunt's three-hitter, assisted by excellent fielding. He got into bases-loaded jams in the sixth and eighth innings but escaped without allowing a run each time. Chilly winds buffeted the 3,071 fans who attended the game. That brought attendance for the ten tournament games to 15,243.[15]

As Billings prepared to leave for Nebraska, the Legion squad got a pat on the back from one of the big-league scouts who attended the regional tournament. Shannon said Billings showed a more professional look than any other young baseball club he watched in 1960. "They do things the way the pros do," said Shannon, whose Cardinals were the parent club of the Billings Mustangs. "You can see in this young club what a professional team in Billings has meant. In addition to providing professional facilities, the youngsters show by their play they have profited by the 'inside baseball' example set by the Mustangs," Shannon said.[16]

If Dave and his teammates needed an example of what a player coached by Bayne could do in the pros, they didn't have to look far that summer. Elwood "Woody" Hahn was a star pitcher for Legion Post 4 in the mid-1950s. He received a baseball scholarship to Washington State University, earned a degree from the school, and the St. Louis Cardinals signed him to a big-league contract. St. Louis sent him to his hometown, and he was pitching for their farm-team Mustangs.

On Saturday, August 27, 1960, while Billings was traveling to Hastings, Hahn notched his eighth win of the season as the Mustangs topped the Great Falls Electrics, 11–3. Hahn went the distance and gave up nine hits and two earned runs. At that point, Hahn had appeared in thirty-one games and had struck out 84 batters in 126 innings. He had a 4.64 earned run average, fourth on the Mustangs' staff.[17]

Hahn pitched for four seasons in the minor leagues, from 1960 through 1963, and rose as high as AA with Tulsa of the Texas League in 1962. In his final year as a pro, 1963, he again pitched for his hometown Mustangs. He compiled a 24-31 win-loss record in the minors.[18]

After he left the pro ranks, Hahn took on a variety of roles in Billings, including serving as elementary physical education supervisor for School District 2,[19] director of the Billings softball leagues,[20] assistant athletic director for District 2, general manager for the Mustangs, athletic director for Eastern Montana College (now Montana State University-Billings), and Pacific West Conference Commissioner. MSU-B inducted him into its Hall of Fame in 1998.[21]

DISAPPOINTMENT IN HASTINGS

A disheartened Dave McNally walked off Duncan Field, the baseball diamond in Hastings, Nebraska, on September 4, 1960, after the national championship game. Dave's shoulders slumped, but he cheered up when he heard words of praise from some of the several hundred Billings people who had traveled to the American Legion Junior World Series. They had hoped the Legion Post 4 team would bring home the first Little World Series title to the Magic City and Montana, but they tasted disappointment instead.

Billings' prospects looked good for the first four innings because Dave pitched in a way befitting his reputation as the best young pitcher in the country—someone who big-league scouts at the tournament had followed for two seasons. Sportswriters around the country touted McNally as tops in the land, including one writer who had had a front-row seat to watch top Legion pitchers several times. That was Robb Madgett, sports editor of the *Hastings Daily Tribune*. A couple weeks before the 1960 Little World Series started in Hastings, Madgett asked who remembered a 1959 game at Duncan Field, when a left-handed pitcher from Billings struck out twenty-one Hastings batters and pitched a two-hitter but lost, 5-4.

"This corner does, and so does the entire Hastings Junior Legion program. He is fireball Dave McNally, perhaps the best Junior Legion pitcher in the United States," Madgett wrote.[22]

With that kind of hype surrounding him, the prevailing wisdom was that it would take a large sum of money to get McNally.[23] And he lived up to that acclaim by holding Tulane Shirts of New Orleans scoreless while Billings built a 3–0 lead.

Then astute observers spotted fatigue in Dave's body language. Pitching his third game in a week, he lost his pitching control in the fifth and sixth innings. He walked a batter, threw a wild pitch, walked another batter, and threw another wild pitch. Dave uncorked a pitch that got by Bell for a called passed ball, and another wild pitch allowed New Orleans to score its first run.

The floodgates opened. By the time Ed Bayne removed Dave and sent him to right field, he had walked in three runs. McNally had struck out eleven New Orleans batters, but he had walked ten. New Orleans scored seven runs in the decisive sixth inning, and the Louisiana team notched a 9–3 victory. That put them atop the 33,000 Legion ball clubs vying for a national title in 1960.[24]

Afterward, it came out that New Orleans had Dave McNally's number from the beginning of the second inning and simply had to sit back and wait for the right chance to take advantage. *Hastings Daily Tribune* Sports Editor Madgett shared this tidbit in the paper's September 5, 1960, issue. Here was how the signal theft worked, according to Dale Boudreaux, New Orleans utility catcher. He watched Bell and quickly deduced the pitch that he was signaling Dave to throw. When Bell wanted a fastball, he held his mitt face-up. When Bell wanted a curveball, he held the mitt face-down.

After the game, Dave asked New Orleans catcher Joseph McMahon to verify what Dave suspected was going on. "You knew every pitch I was going to throw, didn't you?"

"Yes," McMahon said. "Bell gave it away with his mitt."

Dave told McMahon that he thought New Orleans was sniffing out his pitches, but he wasn't sure how. "I think that this sort of upset me. I knew that something was wrong, when someone in the dugout would yell the batter's first name on the fastball and his last (name) on the curve." Dave said that he paid little attention to New Orleans' communications from the dugout to the batter's box until it became obvious that his pitches were being telegraphed.

It was Dave's turn to show that he, too, could adapt to the opposition's tactics. "I really had you stumped, though, when I started throwing that side-armed stuff, didn't I?"

"Yes, you did," McMahon said. "That's when we quit yelling anything. Baseball's a great game, isn't it?"

The two players shook hands and walked away as friends. It was Dave's first loss after eighteen straight wins that season, including five no-hitters.

BOB FRY REMEMBERS HASTINGS

Bob Fry, another friend of Dave's and teammate on the 1960 Legion Post 4 team that reached the Little World Series, has fond memories of that time. "One of the things I remember is how well all the people in Nebraska treated us," said Fry, a retired dentist in Billings who earned a baseball scholarship to Washington State University and played for the Cougars in the 1963 College World Series. From the welcome Bayne's team received after landing at the airport, through the time it spent at the tournament in Hastings, "They really took good care of us," Fry said.

He recalled the fatal fifth and sixth innings in the championship game against New Orleans. Dave had won eighteen straight games, but a streak of wildness allowed New Orleans to rally and take the lead. That prompted the team's pitching coach, Pirtz, to pull his ace southpaw for a reliever but, possibly thinking that he might need Dave to pitch again later in the game, Bayne sent Dave to the outfield. A New Orleans batter connected against Highland, the Billings relief pitcher, and the ball got past Dave. It flew all way to the wall in Hastings' cavernous field, which had foiled Fry's hopes that the team would play on a diamond with a short right field fence.

Although Fry thought "what beat us was Dave's lack of control," having Bob Chilton, a Helena man, serving as home plate umpire may not have helped. "I was in center field, and I could see the plate. He tightened the strike down to about the size of a basketball," Fry said. "There's they no way they should have put a Montana umpire behind the plate." Fry speculated Chilton had overcompensated in New Orleans' favor to avoid possible accusations of favoritism.

When Billings Legion Post 4 qualified for the 1960 Little World Series in Hastings, Nebraska, it no longer was a novel experience for several of Ed Bayne's players to have a national spotlight shine on them. That seasoning, with a shot at being the best in the land, had happened before to Dave. McIntosh and Bell also had a previous Legion Series under their belt. All three had been on the Billings team that traveled to Colorado Springs in 1958, where they lost two games and finished fourth in a four-team field.

As Dave and his teammates warmed up in Hastings, they undoubtedly noticed a crowd of big-league scouts—more than two dozen of them—in the stands.[25] The gathering of bird dogs included ones from the Orioles, who had Dave in their sights but faced plenty of competition for the star pitcher.

SWARM OF SCOUTS FOLLOWS MCNALLY TO BILLINGS.

Dee Nobles, Dave's sister, remembers the buzz about her brother. She and their mother, Beth, drove to Hastings for the tournament. School had already started in Billings, and Jean Hoffer, Dave's girlfriend and later his wife, had started her senior year at Billings Central High School and couldn't attend. After Billings lost the championship game, Beth and Dee drove home. It was a long trip, lengthened in late summer heat when few cars had air conditioning and freeway speed was a rarity because only short sections of the interstate highway system had been built.

Dave, although "crestfallen" after the loss, remained the major player of interest to the big-league representatives, Dee said, and there was good reason for their excitement since he had allowed just two earned runs and had struck out 259 batters in 119 innings during Legion play that summer before post-season tournaments.[26] During the tournament, she recalled, "All these scouts were approaching him. We drove home, and it was like a parade."

"All of these scouts were following him. When we got to Billings, my mother, who was very smart, contacted her CPA and our family attorney, Cale Crowley."

Crowley, Beth McNally, and her late husband, Jimmy, had been friends since the days when they grew up together in Butte. Crowley's home in Billings was on Pine Street, a couple of blocks from where the McNallys lived on Elm Street. Crowley and the accountant helped Beth set up "headquarters" at her house where scouts could make their pitch. Dave wouldn't turn eighteen until October 31 that year, so he needed adult help in signing a contract if he made a deal to play for a big-league team. Such guidance proved valuable to a young pro prospect like McNally because he didn't have an agent when he considered his signing options.

Neighbors of the McNallys on Elm Street must have wondered what was going on in early September 1960. Reportedly, at least ten major league scouts knocked at the door, hoping to get a chance to sign Dave. Competition soon boiled down to the Dodgers and the Orioles, who made the highest bids, and the Orioles got the upper hand and ultimately signed Dave because he liked their scouts.

Three decades later, Russo detailed the successful attempt to get Dave in a 1992 book, *Super Scout: Thirty-Five Years of Major League Scouting*. A Billings American Legion program that was "one of the best anywhere," coached by a "good baseball man," Ed Bayne, impressed Russo. He saw the "first-class" trappings of Legion Post 4's program, including an air-conditioned bus that took players to games, providing the same comfort on road trips as rock groups and country-western musicians experienced in the 1980s and 1990s.

"McNally was a hot name," Russo said. "Every club in baseball knew about him." The thinking was that McNally would sign for a high number—maybe $100,000.

Wilson, a former pitcher for the Orioles and other major league teams, was in his first year as an Orioles scout and already proving to be a good one. Wilson liked Dave a lot, and so did two other Baltimore scouts who had seen him pitch: Byron Humphrey and Burleigh Grimes, the last legal spitball pitcher in the majors. Russo heard from Jim McLaughlin in the Orioles front office, who "told me to join the other three guys at Hastings, Nebraska, to see McNally (pitch) . . . and decide whether he was worth pursuing at the price it was going to take."

Before Russo got to Hastings, Dave pitched and won twice. He struck out nineteen in his first outing and seventeen in the second one, yielding six hits altogether. In the championship game, however, "McNally looked tired to me—not as fast as I had been led to expect. But, damn, it was his third game in a week; he surely was tired."

Russo witnessed "one of the best curveballs I had ever seen on a seventeen-year-old." A full-time scout since 1951, Russo remembered "an old baseball truism": that southpaws didn't have to throw as hard as right-handers. And occasionally, Dave would "pop a live fastball."

Russo was sold on Dave. He had shown enough pitches combined with "great poise and polish" to convince Russo that he and Wilson needed to get to Billings. They would have to "go hard" to get him. When Russo and Wilson got to the McNally home, they met Crowley, considered the top criminal lawyer in Montana. "This will not be easy," Russo said to Wilson.

Russo learned Crowley had been a good friend of Dave's father, a bond deep enough that Crowley said he cried only once in his life, when he heard that Jimmy McNally had been killed at Okinawa. Realizing that Dave would make the final decision about the team he would sign with, Russo made a direct pitch at the seventeen-year-old. "Dave sat across the room and never said a word or asked a question, yet I had no doubt he was absorbing everything I said."

The Dodgers dickered with Dave, his mother, and Crowley before the Orioles representatives got their turn. Los Angeles' offer of $75,000 "thinned out the table," sending other clubs packing—including the Yankees, which was especially satisfying to Russo.

Baltimore, one of the original major league franchises in the late 1800s and the early 1900s, lost its original Orioles in 1903 when they ceased operation. Two New York City businessmen bought the franchise rights to the original Orioles and used them to establish the New York Highlanders, who were renamed the New York Yankees in 1913. Baltimore, meanwhile, didn't have a big-league club for almost fifty years. The absence of a major league team in the city that produced Babe Ruth ended in 1954 when the St. Louis Browns moved to Baltimore. From then on, the Orioles had the Yankees in their sights as the team to emulate. CBS had purchased the Yankees, and, as Russo said, "Some genius of broadcasting had put a new operating rule into effect: from that day forward the Yankees would give no pitcher a bonus over $50,000, because a pitcher could come up with a bad arm and the money would be wasted."

Knowing that, Russo believed the Orioles could beat the Yankees in the bidding for Dave's services. "No club can have a rule that dumb and stay where the Yankees had been," as kingpins of baseball, he said. The Yankee bonus rule must have been real because when bidding for Dave reached $75,000, the Yankees were among the clubs that bowed out.

McLaughlin and Russo had discussed money and felt $80,000 was a fair offer to Dave. Grimes, however, came to a different conclusion after watching Dave in Hastings. "Whatever it takes," said the old spitballer.

"Burleigh, we have to stop somewhere," Russo replied, but he also had to consider what he was hearing from the Orioles' front office. "McLaughlin's last words to me from Baltimore were, 'Don't lose him.'"

Russo offered McNally an $80,000 bonus and a negotiable salary. Crowley said the Billings people would consider the offer and get back to Russo. On Wednesday that week, Crowley called. He said that the Orioles were "in the ballpark, but they still had clubs to talk with." The next day, Crowley and the accountant came to the hotel where Russo and Wilson were staying. They were told the Dodgers had upped their offer to $90,000.

Russo spent an hour selling the Orioles. He told Crowley that his team would not get into a bidding war. Plus, taxes would swallow much of the $10,000 difference between the Orioles and Dodgers offers.

"Dave will decide tomorrow," Crowley said.

Russo was feeling pressure from his boss, too. McLaughlin was calling, sometimes twice daily, telling the scout not to lose Dave. "If it takes more money, we have it," McLaughlin said. Russo responded he didn't want to get into a bidding contest.

Writing decades after he worked for the worst team in baseball history, Russo added a parenthetical note in his book: "Now, let's stop right here and get something straight. I wasn't that protective of Orioles money. I just felt very strongly that whatever bid we made, the Dodgers would top, so we weren't going to win if things went that way. We had to fight this one out on different grounds, and I felt if I could do that, I had the edge. After all, I was an old (St. Louis) Brown."

By Friday, decision day, Russo was sick, "really sick—diarrhea, nausea, vomiting, the whole thing." He struggled to a pharmacy to get medicine that would help. That's when he fully grasped the frenzy that

Dave's pitching ability had triggered, both in his hometown and in big-league circles.

The pharmacist looked at a wan Russo and asked, "Are you a baseball scout?" That comment shocked Russo a bit, but he felt too sick to think of a witty comeback. "Yes," he said, and the pharmacist laughed. "I thought so. Two other scouts have been in already this morning complaining about the same thing. The only thing wrong with you guys is you're feeling the pressure."

The pharmacist handed Russo some Kaopectate to ease his symptoms and shook his head. "Damnation. I knew Dave was a hell of a pitcher, but I didn't know he was that good."

A bit later, Crowley and the accountant came to the hotel for what Russo knew would be the Orioles' last shot. "After the morning I had gone through, I was glad it was. But by the time we had our meeting, the pharmacist's Kaopectate had done its job, and I was beyond worrying about having to interrupt negotiations to make an indelicate but quick exit."

Crowley asked Russo to increase the bonus. Russo replied he felt the offer was sufficient. He repeated his reasons but didn't mention his unwillingness to get into a bidding war with the Dodgers. Russo thought he was audacious to use "the taxes-will-eat-up-the-difference" ploy in front of an accountant. The argument may have worked, though. Maybe the extra $10,000 *would* push Dave into a higher income-tax bracket; whatever the accountant was thinking, Russo got away with the tactic.

The numbers guy didn't explicitly agree with Russo's tax comment, but he didn't say, as Russo thought he might, "Bullshit. You pay the money, and we'll worry about taxes."

Russo wasn't sure what he would have done if negotiations got derailed at that point. That morning, McLaughlin had called. "Don't you lose McNally," he repeated to Russo, and those words rang in his ears as he negotiated with the Billings delegation. He thought to himself that his "good buddy Jim" was making the bidding for Dave uncomfortably personal. Crowley listened to Russo, said he would call with Dave's decision, and prepared to leave.

This is it. Give it your best shot, Russo thought. He walked across the room, stood directly in front of Crowley, and looked straight into his eyes. "You told us the only time in your life that you ever cried was when you learned Dave's father had died. I'll tell you how strongly I believe in what we've told you. If you let Dave go with any club other than the Orioles, his dad will turn over in his grave."

Crowley gave Russo a strange look, got up, walked to the door, and said he would get back to Russo and Wilson. Russo's dramatics didn't impress Wilson. "Well, we've lost him. How in the hell could you say something like that?"

Russo sensed Wilson might be right, that he had totally turned Crowley off. But Russo told Wilson what he had told himself. "This man is a trial lawyer. He has to appeal to a jury when he is trying to save a client from the gallows or the electric chair or the rope on a tree branch or whatever the hell Montana uses for ultimate justice now. I tried to speak his language."

Russo knew Dave would make the final decision, but he also knew that his lengthy discussions with Crowley would affect the outcome. Dave would listen to Crowley's last words of advice.

Thirty minutes later, Crowley knocked on the hotel room door. "He's yours," the lawyer said. "He wants to go with the Orioles. But couldn't you search your heart for five thousand more?"

By then, Russo said, he "loved" the Billings kid, whose name appeared everywhere in newspaper sports sections that summer. Still, Russo said no to Crowley's request because "old Brownies never die," a reference to when he had to find talent for the bedraggled and poverty-stricken St. Louis Browns. But Russo made sure that Dave got a salary that was larger than it might have been at an earlier point in the negotiations. Thus, "he got his money—after the bidding."

Russo and Wilson attended a party that night at the McNally home. Russo said Dave was a member of "a beautiful family, just truly delightful." During the evening, Russo remarked to Crowley, "By the way, if I'm ever up for murder, I want you to defend me."

Crowley laughed. "We'd both hang," he said.

It was official now. Dave was a Baltimore Oriole. By the time he turned eighteen, on October 31, 1960, he had been told where to make the first stop in his professional career: the Arizona instructional league in Phoenix.

And that bonus? Three years later, Dave still considered the signing amount a personal matter, although "I've seen it estimated everywhere between $20,000 and $120,000," he said, smiling during a conversation with a Baltimore writer.[27] When the Orioles signed Dave, team brass may have felt like high rollers playing craps at a Las Vegas casino. They had just rolled the dice after making a high house edge bet, with poor odds of winning. Now they wanted to see if their purported $85,000 wager—the bonus given to Dave—would pay off or would the house of failed major-league prospects win.

Finding baseball players who could make the grade in the major leagues was far from a science when Dave was a still unproven phenom. As a Baltimore sportswriter described the gamble that the Birds were taking on all their prospects, "There is a resemblance between developing major-league ballplayers, mining diamonds and picking beauty queens. The waste product, the also-rans are abundant."[28]

McLaughlin, the Orioles farm team director, provided figures to back that assertion. Since 1954, when the St. Louis Browns moved to Baltimore and the organization rejoined the major leagues, the Orioles had signed 895 players. Only 153 were still playing professionally at the end of the 1960 season, and only eleven were regulars in the big leagues, ten with the Orioles.

Baltimore was signing fewer players than in the past, but its farm team expenses kept rising. "Everything is higher," McLaughlin said. Despite attempts to curb the size of signing bonuses, those payouts kept getting bigger, and it cost more for working agreements between the Orioles and their farm teams.

With Dave, though, the Orioles would recoup their investment several times over. The next step in their project to develop him as a big-league pitcher was to have him play in the southwest.

CHAPTER FIVE

LEARNING IN THE BUSHES

PLAYING IN ARIZONA

Like almost all rookies in an era before massive media exposure, Dave started his pro baseball career in relative obscurity. Two months after he signed with Baltimore, he joined the Orioles team in the Arizona Instructional League, sometimes called the Cactus League, and played there in October and November 1960.

One of his teammates in Arizona, and later in Baltimore, was a fellow bonus baby, Boog Powell. Arizona also was where Dave first experienced playing for Earl Weaver, who began managing in the minor leagues in 1956 and was managing the Bird youngsters in the fall of 1960 in between managerial stints at Aberdeen, South Dakota, in 1959, and Fox Cities, Wisconsin, in 1961[1] And he met another youngster, a bonus baby who would become his most frequent battery mate and a lifelong friend, catcher Andy Etchebarren.

By early November, Dave had become the top pitcher in the Cactus League. His record was 2–0, he had struck out eleven in fourteen innings and had a shiny 0.64 earned run average.[2] McNally improved his record to 3–0 by beating the Los Angeles Dodgers' squad of youngsters, 4–3. He held the Dodgers to three hits over eight innings. McNally was, however, in constant trouble; he walked nine and hit two batsmen. He was behind, 3–2, when Weaver pulled him for a pinch-hitter during the Baby Orioles' winning rally.[3]

One of Dave's best outings came on October 27, when he gave up one earned run to the San Francisco Giants. Baltimore errors, including one by Dave, allowed the Giants to score two unearned runs against him. John Miller, a Baltimore native, pitched the last three innings and got credit for the Orioles' 10-inning, 4–3 win.[4]

After instructional league play finished, Dave went home to Billings, where he chatted with *Gazette* sportswriter Don Zupan and shared his impressions of instructional league play.[5] "The hitters were different down there. They're better," he said. Dave added he "learned a lot about baseball" under the tutelage of Weaver and coach Harry Brecheen. He was unsure of whether the Birds would assign him to a Class B or Class C team in the spring. Whatever happened, "I know I'm going to like playing for the Baltimore organization."

Dave said he planned to find a job—he found work with a local wholesale florist[6]—and stay busy while he was in Billings that winter. Going to college and enrolling at Gonzaga University in Spokane, Washington, was a possibility, too, he said. It wasn't just baseball talk that occupied Dave's time when he returned home for the winter of 1960–61. He played pickup basketball with friends from his high school days as a participant in the annual "casa clambake" at Central High in December 1960.[7]

The event featured a basketball game pitting a team of "old-timers," who had graduated from Central from 1949 to 1956, against the "Kids," made up of Central grads of the previous four years. Dave played for the Kids, coached by Kerry Feldman, another 1950s product of the Billings Legion Post 4 baseball program.

1961

Details of how the Orioles planned to develop their prized bonus baby were unclear and kept changing as the 1961 season began. While the wheels turned in the Orioles front office, Dave enjoyed his first spring spent basking in the south Florida sun and splashing in ocean waters. He did this while living temporarily in Miami for his initial round of spring training with the Orioles.

First, Dave was told to report to the main Orioles training camp in Miami, under the overall watch of Birds manager Paul Richards.[8] Because Dave had been a late arrival in Miami, Richards kept him out of inter-squad competition on an early March weekend. Then, in April, just before the major league season started, the Orioles cut him from their main roster and told him to report to their farm club in Appleton, Wisconsin.⁹

Back home in Billings, his mother wished she'd hear more often from her now-famed son. "He doesn't write often," Beth McNally said in March. She said her mail brought a Miami newspaper, which contained an article about Dave. It said that Orioles manager Richards had helped him learn how to throw a better curve ball.¹⁰ "Dave still doesn't know where he may play ball this summer, but he's having quite a time in Florida." She said this even though it seemed her son knew where he would play, illustrating the old maxim that children don't always communicate well with their parents.

Dave had learned to love ocean fishing, but while going through drills and enjoying a new form of recreation, he hadn't forgotten the young woman in his life who was finishing high school and would become his wife, Jean Hoffer. "He doesn't write much, but he called his girlfriend in Billings the other day and was happy with the way things were going for him in Miami," Beth McNally said.

St. Patrick's Day had just passed, and the McNallys in Billings plus Dave in Miami celebrated their Irish heritage and their seeming good fortune.

Although the Orioles had signaled their intention to have Dave play in Appleton in 1961, they sent him on a roundabout route to the Wisconsin city. In April, the Orioles reduced their roster to thirty-three players by sending him and two other young pitchers to their Thomasville, Georgia, farm club.¹¹ A few days later, Dave had to pack his bags again and head to another farm club. He would make the next stop in his career playing for Victoria in the Class AA Texas League.¹²

Victoria got McNally from Appleton under a deal that Victoria had with the parent Orioles. Its limited working agreement with the Birds gave Victoria the choice of five players on the Foxes' roster; Dave was one of those chosen. Foxes manager Weaver, though, already liked what he saw in the Billings southpaw and said there was a good chance that Dave would return to Appleton soon.[13]

Just a year after he dominated American Legion competition in Montana and across the nation, Dave learned he couldn't feast on batters in the Class A Texas League. He lost three of four games in Victoria in which he was the pitcher of record. He pitched nineteen innings, striking out nineteen and walking eighteen.[14] It was a far cry from his 1960 Legion finale when he won eighteen straight games before losing in the national championship game.

Dave's troubles in Victoria prompted Derrest Williams, general manager of the Rosebuds, to say: "He's a good boy, but he's just not ready for the Texas League."[15] Thus, it was best for the Orioles to drop him down to Class B Fox Cities so as not to ruin his confidence, Williams said.

Playing for the Foxes didn't prove to be the tonic that Dave needed. He got the starting nod when they played at Lincoln, Nebraska, on May 13, and he "looked tough" in the beginning. In the second inning, however, he walked four, and he gave up two singles, each bringing in two Chief runs. That was all for Dave, and he absorbed Fox Cities' 6–1 loss.[16]

Dave had been a winner in the 1960 instructional league in Arizona, but he didn't win as a professional in the higher-level minors until May 25, 1961. That night, he threw five innings and struck out nine to defeat Cedar Rapids. The Foxes needed a five-run sixth inning to top the Braves, 7–4. McNally got relief help from Dick Tetrault and Miller, who preserved his win.[17] Next, on June 3, he pitched seven solid innings against Lincoln, giving up two runs. The Foxes won, 3-2, but Dave was lifted for a pinch-hitter and didn't get the win.[18]

Dave was an even-keeled person, but he shared exciting news with his Fox City teammates in early June. His mother and his finance were driving from Billings to Appleton to watch him pitch professionally for the first time. And Dave rewarded them by going the distance, ten innings, in a 5–4 win over Cedar Rapids on June 16. Wild at the start, he recovered to whiff seven. He gave up eight hits and walked five batters.[19]

Dave was just a shade below 500 the rest of the way—six wins against seven losses—to finish with an 8–10 record with the Foxes. He struck out 155 batters in 140 innings and walked 96. He still needed more development, as evidenced by his 4.18 earned-run average in Appleton. Still, that represented improvement over the 6.16 ERA he compiled during his troubled stay in Victoria. Dave updated his mother after he completed the season at Fox Cities. "He finished up much nicer than he started," Beth McNally said. Indeed, his mark with the Foxes was impressive given his winless start with Victoria in the Texas League and his early troubles in Appleton.

Dave, a representative of Fox Cities on the all-star team of the Three-I league, came back to Billings for a few weeks before his next stop in Phoenix, to get more seasoning in the Arizona Instructional League.[20] Again, Weaver managed the Orioles' Cactus League team, and he touted the amenities the Baby Birds were getting in Phoenix.[21]

His players got a special rate while staying at the Days Apartments in Scottsdale, and the youngsters got more than a roof over their head and a bed to sleep in. "It works out real good," Weaver said of the arrangement where twenty players shared five two-bedroom apartments, rented at $30 per month per player, utilities included. "The place has two swimming pools—one heated—plus a shuffleboard, a putting green and driving range for the golfers, and kitchenettes in each (apartment)."

Highlights of Dave's second season in the Cactus League included a five-hitter when the Baby Birds beat the San Francisco Giants, 10–1,[22] and a complete-game win over the Pittsburgh Pirates.[23] Dave finished the 1961 instructional league season tied for first place in complete games pitched and was 5–1 with a 3.91 ERA.[24]

Then it was time for a matter of the heart. Dave wedded Jean Hoffer on December 30, 1961, at St. Patrick's Catholic Church in Billings.[25]

As 1961 wound down, better days were on the horizon for Dave. He and Jean started 1962 as newlyweds. And a bright season playing in Elmira, New York, lay ahead. Before that, however, McNally needed to overcome more challenges on his road to becoming a major-league pitcher.

CHAPTER SIX

SERVING NOTICE

1962

The Orioles welcomed Dave to their spring training camp in Miami with ample optimism. They were counting on McNally to pay dividends on the team's sizable investment in him. Billy Hitchcock had taken over as the Birds manager, and he gushed over the Billings southpaw. "He's an outstanding prospect. He's got a good chance. He could come (on) fast," Hitchcock said.[1]

Although Hitchcock had seen little of Dave's pitching, Orioles pitching coach Harry (The Cat) Brecheen had while working with the nineteen-year-old in the Cactus League. "He has as good an assortment of pitches as any kid I've ever seen," said the veteran baseball man. "He's got 'em all—fastball, slider, curve and change. And like Billy says, he's around the plate with all of 'em."

Dave acknowledged his spotty 1961 record, which he said was caused by control problems, but he knew why he improved as time went on: "In the first twenty innings, I walked thirty-five. Finally, my control improved by pitching regularly." He credited Brecheen for noticing that he was throwing sidearm too much. "He tried to get me not to drop my shoulder when I threw. I've got to get used to throwing overhanded instead of sidearm," he said.

Dave was not expected to stay with the big club after spring training.[2] But, as spring went on, the Orioles saw more and more potential in him. On March 12, he threw three scoreless innings against Kansas City against the A's. That outing reminded Orioles' coaches of what they had seen two years earlier, when pitcher Steve Barber in 1960, just like Dave in 1962, worked himself out of a jam. Barber "refused to be stampeded," then-manager Richards said.[3] Likewise, for McNally.

Speaking of McNally's performance against the A's, Hitchcock said, "He showed good stuff, threw a real live fastball, and was cool and poised in getting out of that jam." His manager thus affirmed that the Billings youngster was displaying the skills and tenacity he would need for s successful major-league career.

FINDING THE GROOVE IN ELMIRA

The 1962 season, McNally's second full one as a professional player, started with him having to prove himself at the top level of play. He received middling praise at the start of the season. *Baseball Digest*, for example, said this about him at the start of spring training: "Displays good speed and balance. Curveball fair but should get better with control."[4]

He showed promise at Class A Elmira, New York, where he threw thirteen complete games and logged a 3.08 ERA. Control remained an issue, though—he led the Eastern League in walks and wild pitches. When Dave arrived, he caught the city's attention like a windstorm racing across the plains of his native Montana. On April 23, 1962, opening day for Elmira, Dave made his first start for the Pioneers and shut down the visiting Binghamton Triplets, 11–3, in their Eastern League contest. Dave struck out fifteen batters, which was believed to be a modern record for a Pioneer pitcher in an opener at the home park. McNally gave up seven hits and walked five. The only sour note in his performance, on a frigid evening, was a solo homer he yielded in the seventh inning.

Serious baseball fans, those who read the sport's "Bible," *The Sporting News*, would have had an idea of what to expect when Dave strode to the mound that April night. The publication quoted George Staller, who managed McNally briefly in Ardmore, Oklahoma, in 1961:[5] "I didn't have McNally very long, but I liked what little I saw of him."

Staller said that Dave, who turned nineteen after the 1961 season ended, was in "a little over his head." But that was because of Ardmore being a "bad ball club, and it wasn't so much a question of him hurting the club as it was of the club hurting him."

One game stuck in Staller's mind, and it spoke to Dave's character. "He's got courage, this boy. I remember one day (when) I walked out to the mound, not intending to take him out. Before I said a word, he growled, he growled, 'You ain't taking me out. I'm going to beat those guys.'" Dave didn't win, but he "did get out of the jam nicely. I liked the way he reacted. He didn't start walking off the mound when he saw me coming and meekly hand me the ball."

Dave's success at Elmira—he had a 15–11 record there—continued, capped by his being named to the Eastern League All-star team in July. He pitched two innings in his team's 5–2 win over the league-leading Williamsport Greys, giving up two hits, one run, and struck out while walking two.[6]

Then came Dave's breakthrough moment as a pro, when the Orioles called him up to the big club late in the 1962 season. After Elmira's season, the Orioles told Dave to report to Baltimore, and on September 26, Hitchcock tabbed McNally to start against Kansas City.

A mere 2,840 dedicated fans saw Dave's major league debut at Memorial Stadium. Other people in Baltimore had little incentive to attend the doubleheader between the Orioles and the Kansas City A's. Both teams languished in the bottom half of the American League. Plus, a constant drizzle fell during Baltimore's last home stand of the season.

Tens of thousands of Orioles fans thus missed a pitching highlight of the season. Dave was on the verge of turning twenty, and Jean was nineteen, when one of the most exciting things in their young life happened: he threw a two-hit shutout to beat the hard-hitting Athletics.[7] After the 3–0 win, Dave sat in the Orioles locker room at Memorial Stadium, probably still in a daze as he pondered what had happened. Especially since he threw six straight balls to the first two A's batters he faced as drizzle provided the backdrop for the twilight opener of the doubleheader. "I was nervous, plenty nervous," he said.[8] "After I threw a couple of strikes, I was all right, though. I feel real happy. I guess that's one of the best jobs I've ever done."

Dave settled down after throwing the early balls. He gave up a double and a single that caused no damage, struck out four and walked three in the first four innings. Fellow "bonus baby" Andy Etchebarren interrupted Dave. The pitcher wasn't giving himself enough credit, Etchebarren said. "One of the best? That was the best," said Etchebarren, who had caught Dave throughout the 1962 season when both played for Elmira.

"One hundred pitches and one hour and thirty-two minutes to shut out one of the hardest hitting teams in the league. How can you pitch any better than that?" Etchebarren said. Dave got all the offense he needed to win in Baltimore's half of the second inning. The uprising included a Jim Gentile single, Pete Ward's double, Bob Saverine's groundout that drove in a run, and Etchebarren's RBI single.[9]

After the game, *Baltimore Sun* writer Doug Brown's story spoke of Dave's rising stock with the Birds. "Dave McNally may be the only boy from Montana who doesn't know how to ride a horse—as his buddy, John Miller says—but he's a whale of a pitching prospect," Brown said.[10]

Up in the press box sat one excited spectator, Earl Weaver, Dave and Etchebarren's manager at Elmira. Weaver was in Baltimore to join the Orioles' coast-to-coast team of scouts and minor-league managers at the annual season-ending seminar for farm team personnel at the stadium. Plainly proud, Weaver said, "I've got a lot of company." He nodded toward Jim Wilson and Jim Russo, who teamed up to sign Dave to his Orioles contract in 1960 in Billings after Dave led his Legion Post 4 team into the championship game of the American Legion Little World Series. "I thought McNally pitched a real smart game—not like a lot of rookies who just try to blow the ball past the hitters."

Dave had thrown a better fast ball than he showed against Kansas City, according to Weaver. "One thing I've always felt was in his favor—when he didn't have a real good fastball, he could get his breaking stuff over."

Probably more than any other pair of Orioles, Dave's and Etchebarren's careers progressed on a parallel track. So, it's interesting to compare Weaver's final report on those two players on his Elmira club. It said Etchebarren might be a year away from playing in the majors. He finished with a .240 batting average, boosted by the .325 pace he batted at from June 15 on, after starting with a .179 average. Dave also seemed to need at least part of a season playing for AAA club before he would be ready for the big leagues, Weaver said in his report.

But he changed his assessment after seeing both youngsters in action against Kansas City. "When you see them both play the kind of baseball we just saw them play, you just don't know. You've got to say, yes, they've both got a chance next season." And Dave had another believer in Brecheen, Baltimore's veteran pitching coach. "You've got to give McNally a real good chance (of playing in the majors in 1963 based) on the stuff he showed Kansas City."

Brecheen pointed out that Dave threw sinking balls and rising ones, too. "When a nineteen-year-old kid wins fifteen games in his second year as a pro and then shuts out a team that hits the ball as hard as Kansas City, you've got to like his chances. He's got all the pitches. All he needs is work." Brecheen gave Dave useful pointers that helped him end his early wildness against the A's. "My curve and my slider were breaking low the first five innings, and Harry noticed that I was dropping my arm too much to the side," Dave said. Brecheen told Dave to throw more overarm pitches, and he started getting the ball over for strikes from then on.

Hitchcock too, like something else about Dave's style. "He keeps the ball down. If you're going to be wild, that's the place to be wild," he said. Although Dave was nervous, he didn't show it, Hitchcock said, and after Brecheen gave his tip, Dave started throwing breaking balls. "He pitched quite a game," Hitchcock said.

Sixty-one years later, Jean McNally remembered the game as being "very exciting." She, Dave, Etchebarren, and his wife got a blast of excitement from the game. The couples were staying in a small motel on the outskirts of Baltimore. "We were just floating high," she said.

A "nice restaurant" across the street from the motel beckoned. The McNallys and the Etchebarrens stopped in and ordered steak and champagne to celebrate the triumph. "We just were like in a daze, like what the heck happened?"

Dave and Jean McNally had just gotten a taste of the excellence Dave would display during his 13-year career with the Orioles.

Dave's icebreaker in The Show didn't go unnoticed in his hometown. On September 30, 1962, *Gazette* Sports Editor Don Zupan's *From A to Z column*, headlined "LEFTY MCNALLY DRAWS RAVES," mentioned that "a lot of Billings people were elated" by his showing.

Billings residents got a sample of what Baltimoreans were reading about the shutout in their newspaper, the *Baltimore Sun*, thanks to a Billings-Baltimore connection. That was through Will Foy, producer and manager of the Ferde Symphony Pop Orchestra in Baltimore. Foy, who had worked in Billings as a bellhop several years earlier, shared the *Sun's* writeup with the *Gazette*.

Closing his column, Zupan wrote, "We'll be scanning the Baltimore box scores in 1963, Dave, hope we see your name there often."

Orioles farm director Harry Dalton cautioned that 1962 was just Dave's second as a professional. Sill, Dalton thought Dave had an "outside chance" to make the big-club roster in 1963. "He's young and short on experience but certainly has the emotional and mental maturity to pitch up here," Dalton said.

After the win, Beth McNally probably was the proudest mother in Billings. "I'm thrilled to death," she said.[11]

And if a mother knows her children better than anyone, Beth was onto something. She would be even more thrilled in 1963 because a spot on a big-league team, the Orioles, awaited her son.

CHAPTER SEVEN

BUILDING TOWARDS GREATNESS

1963: ACCLAIM IN BALTIMORE

Dave said he progressed "quite a bit" in 1962. He pointed to control as his major early-season problem. McNally expected to report to camp weighing 198 pounds, the same weight he carried at the end of the 1962 season.

McNally had accumulated an arsenal of pitches which included his fastball, slider, curve, and changeup. "I'm working on all of these pitches. My slider has improved a lot," he said.

He planned to concentrate his curve ball that spring to reduce the variability of its effectiveness: "Some nights it's good, and some nights not so good."

Dave assessed his chances of making the Orioles roster during his third season as a pro. "It all depends on what I do in spring training," he said, noting that the Birds picked up two lefthanders, Mike McCormick and Pete Burnside, in the off-season.

Dave didn't let his head swell when he heard Hitchcock say that he had a bright future. To Dave, that meant he had a chance of making the club–nothing more, nothing less—and if he didn't stay with the big club in 1963, Dave said he would like to pitch for Rochester. He apparently admired Rochester manager Darrell Johnson, who had been a catcher for Cincinnati in the 1961 World Series.

Despite some uncertainty, Dave's eye-catching big-league debut late in the 1962 season gave him stature with Orioles brass and team-watchers when the 1963 season dawned. On April 30, two days after Dave's win over the Angels, *Baltimore Sun* sports editor Bill Tanton reflected on his future with the Orioles. Using quotes from Hitchcock and general manager Lee MacPhail, he looked back at Dave's rise to fame, from a Billings wunderkind to a prospective anchor of the Orioles' pitching staff. The headlines in his column summarized the gist of what Tanton wrote about: McNally's Legion Ball Record Drew Scouts, Dodgers Bid High, Too, But Dave Liked Oriole Scouts, and Chances of McNally Being Sent Down Are Remote: MacPhail.

When the Orioles brought up McNally from Elmira, Hitchcock gave him some advice. "Just pitch the same way you've been pitching all year," he said.

But Dave had already shown himself capable of pitching better than he had done in the Eastern League. MacPhail also left no doubt about his belief in Dave's future. "I'd say the chances are very remote that McNally will be sent down at the cutoff date," MacPhail said. "I think Dave's first game would have won him a job, much less his second one. He seems to have licked his control problem."

For those *Baltimore Sun* readers who didn't know about Dave's upbringing, Tanton reminded them he had lost his father in World War II, leaving his mother to raise Dave and his three older siblings as a professional working woman in Billings.

"Right now, the world looks mighty rosy to Dave," Tanton said, comparing the youngster from Billings with two already famous Baltimore pro sports athletes. They were Al Kaline, who had gone straight from the city's Southern High School to the Detroit Tigers, and Big Daddy Lipscomb, who never played football in college yet became an all-pro tackle in the NFL. "But Dave McNally, the Orioles' 20-year-old lefthander, is threatening to outdo them all," Tanton wrote.[1]

Tanton reminded his readers that Dave didn't play high school baseball because it wasn't an interscholastic sport in Montana. Interviewed in late April 1963, Dave pointed out that spring back home was usually too late and short for baseball. That made American Legion competition in late spring and summer the only realistic outlet for high school boys who wanted to play organized baseball in the Treasure State. "I got a letter from home the other day, and my mom told me they had snow there the other day," he remarked in late April.

Hitchcock boosted Dave's chances of staying in The Show after two years of development in the minor leagues. Asked if Dave's performance so far was a fluke, Hitchcock said, "A fluke? How could it be a fluke? The boy has pitched three games, and he's allowed three runs. That's no fluke. That's good, solid pitching."

Dave had followed up his September 1962 two-hitter win against Kansas City with two more regular-season victories to start 1963. He beat Cleveland, 8–1, on a seven-hitter, and he notched a 4–2 victory over the California Angels in which he went eight innings with six strikeouts and one walk while giving up four hits. McNally also pitched once in relief in that time span. He faced the New York Yankees and retired three batters in order.

Dave made the Orioles' Opening Day roster in 1963, but as a rookie what had happened the year before wasn't something he had experienced first-hand. Still, he probably sensed that the Orioles were playing with a chip on their shoulder. An unnamed national sports magazine said the 1962 Orioles did "too much gay living and not enough ball playing."[2] That resulted in the Birds finishing seventh in the ten-team American League. MacPhail didn't allow the slam to go unanswered. He wrote a note to the magazine calling the article "embarrassing and damaging to the Baltimore team."

Then the Orioles proved that 1962 was in their rear-view mirror, and they had the makings of a pennant contender in 1963. By April 23rd, they were in first place, one-half game ahead of New York, Chicago, and Kansas City, all tied for second.

Although Chuck Estrada was out with an injury, Baltimore's pitching stayed strong. Dave showed he could contribute when he pitched an 8–1, complete-game win over the Cleveland Indians on April 20th. As Zupan wrote in the *Billings Gazette*, "If the Billings boy can take up the slack while Estrada's out, the Orioles might have the last laugh on the magazine that ridiculed them."

Dave showed his Montana mettle early in the season. The Minnesota Twins were in town for a game on April 23rd, and Memorial Stadium seemed like an icebox that night to spectators, players, and umpires accustomed to spring days by that time of the year.

The temperature at game time hovered in the forties. Wind gusts that peaked at 30 mph made it a game where some in attendance wished they had brought along thermal underwear. A newspaper story and photos captured the misery in detail. As Associated Press writer Gordon Beard described the scene, even umpires discarded their proprieties during the 1–0 game won by Baltimore.[3]

Base path umpires Joe Paparella and Hank Soar put their hands in their pockets for most of the game. Fellow man in blue Al Smith kept his arms folded.

Orioles coach and later team manager Hank Bauer took off his jacket when he strolled onto the field for coaching duties, but Bauer, who had been a Marine during World War II, evidently knew how to stay warm. He wore thermal underwear, two sweatshirts, and a dickey half-shirt, all layered over his uniform shirt. He also tucked a hand warmer in his hip pocket.

Memorial Stadium workers didn't raise team flags that normally rimmed the upper deck. Four flags that were flying looked freshly starched as they rippled in the wind.

One sportswriter in the press box griped that his ballpoint pen was freezing between innings. Instead of catching foul balls with their bare hands, most spectators let the balls roll. One brave spectator blew a bugle during the game, ignoring the risk that his lips would freeze to the mouthpiece.

What softies, Dave may have thought to himself as his eyes scanned the stadium on a night when he didn't pitch.

"This is the same kind of weather we have at home," he said.

Aparicio, however, took a different view. "When it gets this cold at home, people start dying," said the native of Venezuela.

"When the temperature drops to 80 degrees, my father uses blankets,"

Earlier that month, on April 15, a day after Yankees beat the Orioles, Hitchcock, concerned about when Estrada would return from his injury, thought about using Dave as his fallback pitcher before his team next faced the Bronx Bombers. The Orioles skipper, however, expressed no qualms about turning to his prize rookie southpaw. "I wouldn't be a bit afraid to pitch McNally," he said.

Dave was far from an established member of the Orioles pitching staff that April. Still, he had created enough buzz in Baltimore to be featured in a newspaper real-estate advertisement. The ad beckoned potential homebuyers to an open house at 1610 Division Street in Lutherville. The McNallys—the family then included Dave, Jean, and their infant son, Jeff, born earlier in 1963 in Billings, where the McNallys lived in the offseason during the early part of his pro career—resided in the Baltimore area during the major-league season. They would become Lutherville residents, but not until 1965, two years later. What was billed as the "Dave McNally Special," was a four-bedroom Cape Cod "with exceptionally large rooms." It sat on a half-acre lot, and it had two full bathrooms and a walkout basement.[4] Asked about the ad in 2024, Jean McNally said she had never seen it or heard of it.

April also saw Dave "survive" a roster cut that actually didn't happen to him. His hometown newspaper contributed to the confusion when it reported that the Orioles had optioned Dave and another pitcher, John Miller, to their Triple A Rochester farm club.[5]

Oops. Wrong. Nine days later, the paper reported that Dave was still with the big club. This news came from Jean, who was in Billings and was getting ready to leave for Baltimore with Jeff.[6] "Dave is with the Orioles in New York City and is really fascinated by the big city," Jean told the *Gazette*.

Manager Hitchcock explained what had happened. Miller, "while very promising," wasn't quite ready for the majors. Another pitcher, Buster Narum, was staying with the Orioles because of his experience, and Hitchcock was keeping Dave because he needed his left arm. That need became acute because Baltimore shipped southpaw Steve Dalkowski to Rochester and the Birds would have been short of lefties if they had not kept Dave.[7]

The contradictory reports probably didn't surprise Dave. Back in February 1963, he said, "They don't tell you anything," as he packed his bags in Billings and prepared to leave for spring training in Miami.[8]

Dave turned out to be more than a spectator gawking at the sights of the Big Apple. On April 14, Hitchcock gave him a shot against the Yankees, in relief. He pitched one inning and retired Tony Kubek, Bobby Richardson, and Joe Pepitone in order. None of them hit the ball out of the infield. As the *Gazette's* Don Zupan put it, Dave's performance meant that "the former Billings Legion hurler, although only 20, isn't afraid of the Bronx Bombers.[9]

Dave's fan base in Billings, already large because of his American Legion stardom, kept growing when he wore an Orioles uniform. The *Gazette* noted that the Magic City had more Baltimore Orioles fans than ever because of Dave's presence on the team. "The Billings southpaw looks like he's going to be a satisfactory 'Saturday' pitcher. He's won both starts on this particular day of the week."[10]

It wasn't all smooth sailing for Dave in the early weeks of the season. On May 2, the Chicago White Sox torched him for seven runs in 3–1/3 innings, but he escaped defeat when the Orioles rallied late to win. Hitchcock had yanked Dave, so his record remained 2–0.

Despite that shelling, Dave drew praise from an opposing team that he had pitched against. Here's what a story in the *Detroit Free Press*, part of which the *Billings Gazette* reprinted on May 5, 1963, said: "Take it from the Los Angeles Angels, young Dave McNally is worth every cent of the $80,000 bonus given him by the Baltimore Orioles."

"He's as good as any lefthander in the league," said the Angels' Leon Wagner, who had seen Dave hold his team to four hits before faltering in the ninth inning.

Dave impressed LA with his poise and control. Though he possessed only average speed, he displayed a fine curveball. He had shown an impressive control, according to several players on the West Coast team who batted against him. "I didn't think he'd be that good, but after the first time I faced him, I knew I was going to have trouble," Wagner said.

Orioles teammate Ken Hunt said, "Dave's got an idea of what he's doing out there. He's not overpowering, but he can throw to spots. He gave me only one ball to hit all night."

The *Gazette's* Don Zupan added a sardonic comment: "You're not washed up yet, Dave!"

Through 21-1/3 innings, Dave had allowed 10 earned runs. That mound work included nine innings against Cleveland, one against New York, eight against the Angels and 3-1/3 against Chicago. He, Steve Barker, and Mike McCormick gave the Orioles three lefthanders, none older than twenty-four.

By June, with his record at 2-1, Dave had tasted relief duty. He initially thought it would be better for his career to return to the minor leagues and be a starting pitcher rather than to come out of the bullpen in the major leagues. But he changed his mind and decided he would rather stay in the majors, even if it meant being used as an occasional reliever. Hitchcock said that Dave could handle either long or short relief work, and Dave was aware that his options with the Birds were open. Estrada was still on the injury list, so Dave could expect spot-starting assignments as the season went on.[11]

By September, Dave's performance in his first full season as a big leaguer earned him recognition as baseball's best rookie southpaw rookie pitcher. The acclaim came from the Topps Chewing Gum Company. Two other players on the all-rookie team were Rusty Staub of Houston, who was on the New Orleans team that defeated the Billings Legion Post 4 team in the 1960 American Legion Little World Series championship game, and Pete Rose, starting his career with the Cincinnati Reds, a future World Series opponent of Dave and the Orioles.[12]

The Orioles faded after their early-season lead. They finished in fourth place with an 86-76 record, 18-1/2 games behind the pennant-winning Yankees.

Dave didn't set the American League on fire in his first full season in the major leagues. He had a winning record, 6–5, as of August 22 after a five-hit victory over the Los Angeles Angels, but he lost three of his final four games to finish with a 7–8 record. He pitched 125 innings, gave up 133 hits, struck out 78 batters, and walked 55.[13]

In October, as he reflected on the year, Dave's baseball smarts undoubtedly left him puzzling over his 4.58 earned-run average. Yet, on several occasions, Dave showed he hadn't lost the mound mastery that first made him a nationally renowned junior pitcher in 1960. For example, on April 27, he went eight innings and gave up four hits in a 4–2 win over the Angels. Relievers Dick Hall and Dean Stone gave him late-inning help to preserve the win. Jackie Brandt got three hits, including a second-inning homer that put the Orioles in front for good, and Joe Gaines hammered the ball into Memorial Stadium's right field seats for the second Baltimore run.

The Angels rallied in the eighth inning, getting their two runs on an Ed Sadowski home run, which spoiled Dave's hopes for his second major-league shutout. The Angels continued their threat in the ninth inning when Albie Pearson singled, and Orioles manager Billy Hitchcock decided Dave's mound duty was over for the day. He sent in Hall, who got one out, and then Stone finished up by getting Angels' cleanup hitter Felix Torres to slap a grounder to second baseman Dave Johnson, who completed the game-ending double play.

"If yesterday's brand of pitching continues much longer, McNally may become something more than a weekend employee," the *Baltimore Sun* account of the game told readers.

Sitting in the locker room afterward, Dave showed the ability, at age twenty, to take a big-picture outlook on how the game affected his prospects. "I was real happy to get this game in before the cutdown date. . . . These days are important–damn important," he said. Dave knew the Orioles had to cut three players to get down to the 25-player limit, and he didn't want to play in the minors again.

"He's a pretty smart lad," Hitchcock said. "He pitched an outstanding game."

Hitchcock sensed Dave was tiring in the eighth inning, but the southpaw didn't realize it until he got into the clubhouse and sat down. "You never feel tired when you're pitching. It's only when you get out of there and sit around a while that it catches up with you," he said. "But I'm very happy the way everything turned out. We won, and that's all that counts. I would have liked to have finished—naturally." McNally said he thought he made only two mistakes in the game, both in the eighth inning, on a curve he tried to get up in the strike zone and a fastball he tried to get down. "Other than that, I had my pitches where I wanted them."

Dave helped a teammate on the Orioles unexpectedly that season. He offered hitting advice to normally hard-hitting Jim Gentile, who was mired in a slump but broke out after a few words with the rookie pitcher. "You'll never guess who changed my stance," Gentile said. "Dave McNally. He said I was holding my hands too close to my body. I got 'em out and you saw what happened."

Late in the season, Dave's Billings fans learned he wouldn't be spending much time in his hometown. Instead, he was heading to Puerto Rico to play winter ball, along with Boog Powell. Word of Dave's off-season plans came from Ralph Nelles, a leading light in Billings' sports community. "Dave said he's likely to spend but three days in Billings after the American League season ends," said Nelles after visiting with Dave in Minneapolis.[14]

Winter leagues had been part of the professional baseball landscape since the late nineteenth century when some players, trying to supplement their low salaries, opted to play year-round, possibly in preference to barnstorming and working a "real" job during the offseason. Also, the leagues that developed in warmer climates encouraged business in those regions.

Early winter leagues tended to have a mix of players: big-league stars, benchwarmers, minor leaguers, amateurs, and semipro players competing head-to-head. Some leagues, including the California Winter League and the Cuban Winter League, gave Black players (or Negro players as they were called then) an opportunity to play against white major leaguers—an option not available in the majors until the Brooklyn Dodgers broke the color line by putting Jackie Robinson on the field in 1947.

That historic event caused the composition of winter league team rosters to change. Because Black stars could play in the majors, and salaries increased for professional players, winter leagues became dominated more by developing prospects and international players.[15] Besides the Puerto Rican Winter League, big-league teams could send their prospects to the Panama League, the Venezuelan League, the Mexican Pacific League, the Nicaraguan League, the Columbian League, the Occidental League, the Veracruz League, or the Dominican League.

The heyday of winter ball occurred in the early 1960s, and this was the backdrop for McNally and Powell's playing days in Puerto Rico.

Dave believed he could use extra work to sharpen his pitching. He had become established in Baltimore's pitching rotation, but Hitchcock used him sparingly during June and July. "Most of the top men in the Baltimore organization are of the opinion that McNally will win his share of ball games for them in the future," *Gazette* readers were told. And with a pitching coach like Harry (The Cat) Brecheen mentoring him, Dave was "likely to justify their faith."

Competing in the Puerto Rican League, Dave and Powell played for the Mayaguez Indians. Powell slugged three home runs and drove in ten runs in a three-game stretch. Dave pitched hitless ball for six innings and struck out 11 on October 19, when he walked nine and was taken out for a reliever.

His time in Puerto Rico gave Dave his first look at Roberto Clemente, a budding star for the Pittsburgh Pirates and the player who would spark them to victory over the Orioles in the 1971 World Series. On November 13, Clemente drove in three runs with two hits in San Juan's 11–1 rout of Mayaguez on a day when Dave wasn't pitching.[16]

When the Puerto Rican season ended in November, Dave owned the second-best pitching record. He owned a 4–1 record, had a 1.41 ERA and had struck out 37 batters in 45 innings.[17]

Back home in Montana, Dave still had a solid fan in his former battery mate, Bell, from when they played together for Legion Post 4. In the fall of 1963, someone asked the former catcher how many no-hitters Dave had thrown during his Legion career. "Hundreds of them," said Bell, by then a top receiver for the Montana State University (Bozeman) football team. Though exaggerating, he still captured Dave's dominance of junior baseball in the Treasure State.[18]

CHAPTER EIGHT

NEARING THE PROMISED LAND

1964

Dave gained insight in the 1964 season that carried over and improved his pitching in the future. He was far from a polished pitcher, ready for everything he would face in the major leagues, during his early years with the Orioles. Particularity in 1964, his pitching was erratic, and his record was subpar. He needed work to become a player at the top level.

Dave won three of his first four games in 1964, his second full season in the majors. Then he lost ten of fourteen games through September 7 before winning his last two outings of the season. What was going on?

A possible explanation can be found in what happened on a hot summer evening during the second half of the season. Dave was playing catch with teammate Russ Snyder in the outfield, when the Orioles outfielder mentioned something that he picked up on. "I can tell whether you're going to throw a curve or a fastball," he said. "I can't tell you why, but I can tell almost every time."[1]

This guessing game continued for three weeks. Snyder kept studying Dave's delivery, and finally he deduced the answer: Dave was tipping his pitches. "It was my hands," he said. "You see, I have short fingers and arms. As I brought my hands over my head on the fast ball, the heel of my bare hand, or the fleshy part, was touching the heel of my glove, but on the curve, which I have to grip (the ball) differently because of my short fingers, the heel of my hand was not touching the heel of my glove."

This was obvious to hitters, who didn't need a signal from their coach or someone in the dugout to know what was coming from Dave. "A player on another team tipped off one of our guys that I was telegraphing my pitches. Cleveland was picking them up, I think, and maybe Kansas City. There probably were others, too." Someone on the Orioles might have gotten a hint of Dave's giveaway sooner, but they were sitting in the dugout, where it was hard to see a pitcher's hands. "The hitter has a perfect view of them, though," Snyder said.

On July 11th, 1964, Dave experienced a lightbulb day when Cleveland shelled him for thirteen hits in eight innings. That loss convinced him that poor pitching was not to blame for his troubles; instead, opposing hitters knew what to expect from him. "Looking back, I think that was the game. They were getting the pitches when I went into my windup but not when I pitched from the stretch position."

Dave needed to change his windup. That wasn't easy. Brecheen worked with him, and teammates helped by trying to call his pitches during batting practice. The Orioles' brain trust figured out that Dave's short arms caused his hands to come apart. The remedy was to bring his hands up to the side instead of bringing them directly over his head. "This worked," Dave said. "I was able to keep the heel of my bare hand in contact with the heel of my glove until it was too late to do the hitters any good."

Still, the season was almost over before Dave felt confident enough to use his new windup in a game. He used it just once, in a one-hit, ten-strikeout win against the Washington Senators on October 1. Dave didn't expect the new windup to be a panacea in future seasons. It did, however, boost his confidence. "I don't know whether it will make any difference in my record, but it'll make a one hundred percent difference in my confidence. It's got to. If the hitters know what's coming, it's impossible to beat 'em."

In February 1964, the Orioles put former Yankee Hank Bauer in charge of the team, in place of fired manager Billy Hitchcock. On February 18, Dave signed his Orioles contract. Bauer saw one aspect of Dave's game, which didn't involve pitching, that needed improvement.

"I'll tell you one pitcher (that) bunting practice helped last spring—Milt Pappas. He moved up eight runners last season," Bauer said.[2] "I'll tell you one boy who's gonna work on it this spring–Dave McNally. He bunted up three runners in ten tries. A pitcher's gotta do better than that. A pitcher who can bunt has a better chance of staying in a close ball game than a pitcher who can't."

Back home in Billings, people got a chance to see and hear from a pitching legend, who praised Dave's prospects of becoming a standout pitcher. Hall of Famer Bob Feller, who starred for the Cleveland Indians in the 1940s and 1950s, came to the Magic City as a guest of the Midland Roundtable in May.[3] Addressing the Roundtable during a luncheon at the Northern Hotel, Feller said, "McNally will become one of the top pitchers in the American League as soon as he becomes thoroughly acquainted with the league. It takes a pitcher a few seasons to get to know the hitters he faces."

The Iowa-born Feller found time to share pitching tips with almost 200 Little Leaguers at a Billings West End parking lot. They took away memories of a legendary pitcher that linger to this day.

Dave caught the eye of another future Hall of Famer that spring. Henry Aaron, the Milwaukee Braves' slugger who then owned the highest batting average of any active major leaguer, said quality pitchers made it likely that baseball wouldn't see another .350 hitter. "I just don't see how anybody can hit for that high an average anymore, with the kind of pitching we've got to hit against today," Aaron said while in spring training at West Palm Beach, Florida.[4]

Reviewing the crop of outstanding young pitchers, who came up to The Show almost together, he said, "These kids have been well schooled. They know how to pitch. They had more and better instructors. They come up with sliders and screwballs as well as different changes of speed. It's remarkable how they know so much." Aaron ticked off a list of six "fine rookies" who broke in during the 1963 season; among them was Dave McNally.

Dave's stock with the Orioles jumped upward on April 3, when he was one of three pitchers who blanked the defending champion New York Yankees on two hits during a spring training game.

Dave used curveballs, fastballs, and changeups to befuddle the Yankees. He struck out one and walked two. Afterward, Dave took a deep breath when writers asked him if he thought his chances of being on the Orioles pitching staff had improved. "I was definitely worried, but now I definitely feel that I can make it. I originally thought I might last the first thirty days, and then I didn't know. Now I'm pretty confident," he said. "I used mostly my fastball down. That seemed (to be) the (best) pitches, although I had control of my curve, too."

The Yankees were swinging at his first pitches, so Dave threw fastballs down. "That seemed the quickest way to relieve my worries—shut out the Yankees." And Dave used his slider for the first time since June 1963. He threw that pitch twice, getting Bobby Richardson on a groundout and allowing Mickey Mantle to walk on a 3–1 count. "I threw five or six in the bullpen tonight. Pappas showed me how to throw it the other day, and I decided to use it."

Brecheen approved of Dave's using the slider, which he said went well with his fastball and curveball. "If he's now getting the curve across, he can use the slider. As long as he gets the ball over (and) throws strikes, he's got a helluva shot at making our staff. He's always had good stuff. Off what he did for us last year, he should improve."

1965

Dave's third full year in the major league turned out to be a season of frustrations mixed with accomplishments. By the time he turned twenty-three in October that year, Dave had compiled an 11–6 win-loss record for the Orioles, whose 94–68 record left them third in the American League, eight games behind the Minnesota Twins, who became the World Series runners-up that year. He pitched 198 2/3 innings and struck out 116 batters while walking 73.[5]

Dave and his teammates had to watch the Fall Classic on TV, but they were setting the table for the triumph of 1966 that would make them the toast of Baltimore.

Dave and Jean and their young family spent part of the 1964–65 offseason in Billings, where two sets of grandparents—Jean's mother and father, and Dave's mother, Beth—got to share spoiling two grandchildren: two-year-old Jeff and infant daughter Pam, born in Baltimore in June 1964.[6]

Then McNally headed to Miami for spring training. Before he began workouts in earnest, he had time to play the other sport he loved: golf. Dave played in the 25th National Baseball Golf Championship in Miami and finished eighteenth, with a four-round total score of 405.

Besides improving his pitching delivery, Dave got another boost in 1965. It involved the vice he battled throughout his life—smoking, a common habit among adult and young men at the time and increasingly seen among women in the 1960s—and his temporary victory over it. Which led to something expected—a weight gain—and something not expected from that—more pitching victories.

During the second half of the season, Dave quit smoking, but as many smokers will attest, he was enjoying food more. His weight went up and, in what defied logic for baseball people, so did his victory total.[7]

Dave weighed 188 pounds when the season started, and by July 4, he had a mediocre 3–4 record. Then, after he quit smoking, both his appetite and the quality of his pitching rose. Dave, who weighed 202 pounds at the end of the season, finished with an 11–6 record after winning eight of his last ten decisions. That confounded traditional baseball wisdom, which held that a pitcher with a big belly would have trouble bending properly at the waist when he threw a fastball.

Dave couldn't explain the apparent contradiction. "All I know is that the more I gained, the better I pitched. When I'm heavy, I don't feel as good, but I pitch better, maybe because I'm stronger and don't know it," he said.

It wasn't the first time that Dave had experienced this puzzler. In 1962, his best year in the minors, he went 15–11 for Elmira, New York, and weighed 205. Considering that, Dave probably expressed surprise to Jean when he received a letter from the Orioles at their home in Billings before the 1965 season. It told Dave to report for spring training in February at 190 pounds. Although Dave said he would accede, "if I don't get off to a good start, I'm not going to let it worry me if I gain weight."

The tussle over the best weight for Dave was a relatively minor matter, but it showed that Dave already planned to obey his own sense of the right path in life as he progressed toward stardom.

Dave's 1965 record seemed a solid performance for a pitcher who didn't turn twenty-three until after the season's play ended, yet that record obscured marked swings in his play. He didn't go over .500 until July 20 when he pitched a complete-game, 6–1 win over Cleveland in which he held the Indians to six hits. That victory made him 5–4. After two no-decision outings, Dave shut out the California Angels on August 4. He went the distance and allowed five hits to go with six strikeouts and four walks. But four days later, he lasted only two innings against Kansas City and took the Orioles' 4–3 loss to the A's, a game that was winnable because he gave up four hits, struck out one batter and walked two. Dave bounced back to beat Washington on August 12. He pitched six innings, gave up five hits, struck out six and walked one, to improve his record to 7–5.

An earlier pattern, though, repeated itself. Two no-decision games preceded Dave's loss to Chicago in Comiskey Park. Bauer pulled him after 2-2/3 innings, during which Dave allowed five White Sox hits and four earned runs. The home team won, 6–5. Once more, Dave endured two no-decision games before he ended the season with a flourish: a four-game winning streak.

It started on September 7 at Yankee Stadium, where Dave yielded eight hits in 6-2/3 innings but just one earned run as the Orioles topped the Yankees, 4–2. Next, on September 15, he threw a complete-game, 3–2 win over visiting Detroit, holding the Tigers to five hits. Minnesota was headed to the World Series as the AL representative, but Dave handled the Twins in Minneapolis on September 22. Again, he went the distance and turned in a six-hitter as Baltimore won, 5–2.

Finally, on October 1, Dave threw his best game of the year, a two-hit shutout on the road over Cleveland that lifted the Orioles to 2–0 victory. After beating the Indians for his eleventh win, Dave said the reason for his late-in-the-season success was less about how he was throwing than where he was throwing. "I've been worrying less about keeping the ball low and away and have been throwing as hard as I can while trying to move it in and out on the hitters," he said.[8]

Meanwhile, the Orioles were floundering, too. They crept within two and a half games of first place on May 9 and again on May 14th, then got within one game of the lead on June 24th and again two days later. But the Birds soon started slipping and finished eight games behind the Twins.

In early August, when his team was trying to hold on to second place, Orioles skipper Bauer and pitching coach Brecheen bemoaned the sorry state of their pitching staff.[9] "I'll tell you, the way these starters are going, it's really sucking up our bullpen," Brecheen said on August 8. At that point, Baltimore's starters had lasted fifty-six innings during a road trip then eleven games along. McNally pitched the only complete game in that span, the shutout of the Angels.

The result was that relievers Stu Miller, Hall, Harvey Haddix, and Don Larsen got a lot of work—too much work. Further aggravation: Hall was pitching with a sore arm.

Bauer admitted the situation "(didn't) "look so good right now."

Speaking after Kansas City won three of four games, Bauer pointed out a 4–3 loss to the A's as especially troublesome. The A's built a 4–0 lead and got the winning run when Orioles shortstop Bob Johnson bungled a routine grounder in the sixth.

The Orioles rallied for three runs, but it was in vain because, as Bauer said, his outfit was "sleeping on the bases." Larsen, pitching because of Dave's exit after two innings, led off the sixth with a double but failed to advance on a dribbler to the right side of the infield. Snyder followed with a long fly to center field that would have scored Larsen if he had been on third.

When the season finished, the Orioles could play the "wait until next year" tune. Little did they know they would reach baseball's promised land in 1966, and Dave would become the toast of Montana and Baltimore.

CHAPTER NINE

BEST IN THE AMERICAN LEAGUE

BAUER'S CONFIDENCE

After finishing third in 1965, the Orioles entered 1966 with plenty of confidence—and a manager who believed in their potential. In early January that year, Hank Bauer wrote a newspaper column in which he talked about the trade, made famous in a timeless monologue from Susan Sarandon in the opening moments of the film *Bull Durham*, that landed future Hall of Famer Frank Robinson.[1]

"Even though I don't have (Milt) Pappas anymore, I still have some pretty good pitchers on my staff—guys like Steve Barber, Dave McNally, and Wally Bunker," Bauer said. Barber and McNally started slowly in 1965 but finished with fifteen and eleven wins, respectively. And Bauer expected Bunker, who won ten, to return to his form as a rookie when he won nineteen in 1964.

Although Dave became known as an advocate for baseball players' labor rights, he wasn't eager to take on that role early in his major-league career. He was supposed to take over as the Orioles' player representative to the union in the 1966 season. "I think I may decline the job," Dave said. "There are other guys on our club who would really like it."[2] Dave had served as an alternate rep under Dick Hall. His hesitation in becoming the liaison between players and management was based on what he had seen: when an Oriole became a player rep, he was traded.

That pattern started in 1961 when Gene Woodring, then an Oriole and the player rep, headed to Washington after being picked by the

Senators in the expansion draft. Other Orioles who had been player reps and then were traded included Walt Dropo, Ron Hansen, Wes Stock, Mike McCormick, Pappas, and Hall. One exception to the trend was Brooks Robinson, a former rep still with the Orioles.

Besides Bauer, Billy Hunter was bullish on the Orioles. "Baltimore will win the American League next season (1966)," said the Orioles' third-base coach, a former shortstop with the Orioles and the Browns, among other big-league teams.[3] Hunter predicted that Frank Robinson would provide the power Baltimore needed to capture the flag. His batting would complement the Orioles' strong pitching, exemplified by Dave, who could become the best pitcher on the Orioles staff that year, Hunter said. "I'll be surprised if Dave doesn't win fifteen games for us this year. He was terrific the last two months of last season."

Dave accepted invitations to speak at sports banquets both close to home and in Orioles country during the off-season. He and Brooks Robinson were head-table speakers at the Sportsman's Dinner in Lethbridge, Alberta, on February 4.[4] He also got a chance to play the other sports he loved, basketball and golf, before spring training started.

And it was contract time. According to his hometown paper, Dave signed a 1966 contract for $16,000, which Harry Dalton, Baltimore's director of player personnel, called a "good raise" over McNally's 1965 salary.[5] In inflation-adjusted terms, Dave's pay for 1966 would be worth $154,238 in 2024.

The *Billings Gazette* got its story about Dave's salary from the United Press International. Papers throughout the U.S. using the Associated Press account, however, gave his estimated 1966 salary as $15,000.

Regardless, Dave was making decent pay for the time, but if he had picked up a paycheck in 2024, that 1966 inflation-adjusted amount was a rounding error in the salaries that even average players draw nowadays.

In late February, after the day's drills finished, Dave sat down with a Baltimore sportswriter and discussed two subjects possibly related to his performance. The topics: his smoking, or lack of it; and his weight gain. After he quit smoking in the previous season, Dave had started again, and that vice was in direct violation of a formula which, although stumbled upon quite by accident, proved to be highly successful last year for him.[6]

Here's how that worked. In 1965, when Dave gave up smokes, he gained fourteen pounds. He also logged an 8–2 record during the no-cigarettes, more-pounds time. Dave conceded that other factors may have been at play. Perhaps his strong finish was due to improved control and less use of his sinking fastball. But he didn't think it was a coincidence that his win total went up when he stopped smoking. And he was ready to start his method of winning again.

"I started smoking again after last season, but I'm going to stop again, too," he said resolutely after finishing the third workout of spring training.

The workout had been brief—an hour and a half—but it was stiff, in sunshine after a bout of rain in humid south Florida, and sweat was trickling across Dave's freckled face.

"I'm going to stop ... Well, I'm going to stop as soon as I make up my mind to stop." He took a drag on his cigarette and smiled as he admitted the control that cigarettes had on him, something smokers can relate to. "I've stopped five or six times before, once for as long as six months."

1965 offered a contrast in terms of his smoking or lack of it in regard to his weight and record. He started the season smoking and weighed 188 pounds, and his pitching record on July 4 was 3–4. After he quit smoking, he experienced something common for people who give up the habit: he saw his appetite soar in "ungodly" fashion. He put on eight pounds in the first ten days after putting away his cigarettes.

But like someone who accepts the challenge of scaling a high mountain peak back in Montana, his pitching soared during that time. He won eight of his last ten decisions, finished with an 11–6 record and weighed 202 pounds. "All I know is that the more I gained, the better I pitched. When I'm heavy, I don't feel as good, but I pitch better. Maybe because I'm stronger and don't know it." By gaining this weight, he was unintentionally bulking, giving him more energy to burn for the game. This was what allowed his pitching to improve as dramatically as it did.

Despite his fine finish in 1965, the Orioles told Dave to trim down to 190 pounds when he reported to spring training in 1966. He tried but still was at 196 when he checked in, only six pounds short of his goal. But that didn't bother Harry Dalton, director of player personnel, who said he was willing to accommodate Dave's theory until it was proven wrong.

Dave looked at himself. "I'll tell you; it's a real struggle for me to keep at one-ninety. Look at these legs. Must be almost one hundred and ninety pounds in them alone."

Dalton, however, thought something else caused Dave's improved pitching: better control. "I've got the figures right here," he said. "In the first half, he gave up thirty-nine walks in eighty-five innings. In the second (half), he gave up thirty-four in one hundred and fourteen innings."

Newspapers in Baltimore and elsewhere in the country regularly mentioned Dave's Montana background, sometimes as if that made him a character out of a Western movie. For example, in February, United Press International's Milton Richman, writing from the Orioles' spring training camp in Miami, gave people a tongue-in-cheek description of the Treasure State pitcher:

"You figure a guy from Montana would be at least a bit bow-legged, wear Western boots, roll his own cigarettes, possibly play the guitar, and certainly be at home on a horse. Well, if you figure that about Dave McNally, you figure all wrong even though he was born in Billings, Montana."[7]

Here's how Dave defied the stereotype:

- His legs were "as straight as a pair of foul poles"
- He wore conventional dress shoes
- He smoked filter-tip cigarettes
- He didn't play any musical instrument; and
- He "holds on for dear life anytime someone manages to coax him atop a horse."

Instead, think of Dave as a pitcher, maybe the best on an Orioles' staff that topped the American League in efficiency in 1965. "I guess not many major-league ball players ever came from Montana at that," Dave said, adding that the only ones he knew about were Herbie Plews and Curt Barclay.[8] Then he gave Richman and newspaper readers across the country a tip about another Billings pitcher who was coming up and who would star, although briefly, in the major leagues. "The New York Mets have a good-looking young pitcher coming up from Montana. His name is Les Rohr. I'd keep an eye on him."

Some baseball experts, both in Billings and elsewhere in the country, thought Rohr had the talent to surpass McNally. The big southpaw stood six-foot-five and was a starter on the first state basketball championship team at his high school, the 1963 Billings West Golden Bears. Baseball, though, was his ticket to fleeting fame.

The New York Mets, then baseball's sorriest team, drafted Rohr in 1965, and he broke into the majors in spectacular fashion. On September 19, 1967, he defeated the visiting Los Angeles Dodgers at Shea Stadium. He earned the victory, a 6-3 win in which he pitched six innings, allowed six hits, three runs (two earned), walked three, and struck out six.

Eleven days later, on September 30, 1967, Rohr went one better at Dodger Stadium. He beat Drysdale with a 5-0 shutout in which he went eight innings, allowed six hits, walked two Dodgers, and struck out seven.[9]

Injuries cut Rohr's career short. He hurt his pitching elbow during a 2-1/3-inning stint against Houston in the Astrodome in 1968 and was tagged with the Mets' 1-0 loss in a 24-inning marathon. That injury led Rohr to retire early, after the 1970 season when he pitched for the Mets' AAA (Tidewater) and AA (Memphis) affiliates. He went 8-7 that year with a 4.60 ERA. He compiled a 2-3 record with a 3.70 ERA during his three years in the majors, including 1969 when he was on the bench when the Mets topped McNally's Orioles in that year's World Series.[10]

Rohr died in Billings on November 6, 2020. He was 74.

It was not as if Dave hadn't already caught the eye of savvy baseball observers, not with his 11–6 record in 1965, along with 116 strikeouts in 199 innings and a 2.85 earned run average. Pappas, the anchor of the staff, was gone in a trade to the Reds, and the Birds needed a second strong arm to complement that of Steve Barber. Dave seemed the logical choice. "If I can pick up where I left off last year, I think I can help the club," Dave said.

Thinking back to his growing-up years in Billings, McNally said he never aspired to being a cowboy. "I never did any cow-punching, and I never was much for riding horses," he said. He recalled his start in professional baseball, playing in the Arizona Instructional League in the winter of 1960 after signing a contract with the Orioles. There, he encountered players from the east and south who all, he said, "rode much better than I did."

Orioles players said Dave had the makings of one of the top AL pitchers, but he wouldn't toot his own horn. Talking about opposing batters, he said, "Bill Skowron and Don Lick are real tough, but Tom Tresh kills me consistently."

"Don't believe that," Richman wrote. "No one kills Montana's Dave McNally, even if he isn't the fastest gun in the West."

Dave got off to a sparkling start in 1966. He won his first three games of the season, starting with a 7–2 home-park decision over the New York Yankees. He followed that with a 4–3 win over the Yanks at their house and then added a 3–2 victory over the Detroit.

Beating the Tigers, though, wasn't easy. The Orioles needed two Dave Johnson home runs off Denny McLain plus Curt Blefary's dinger to edge the Tigers at their place. McNally went 6 1/3 innings and gave up six hits and both Detroit runs before yielding to Stu Miller. "I'm just a lucky Irishman," Dave said afterward.[11] "I didn't have it today, the first two innings especially. I felt dead in the third inning." His remedy: taking smelling salts "to wake me up a bit. I felt a little better after that."

But some issues remained. "The more I tried to kick myself, the worse I got," he said. "It seems my better pitches they hit the hardest. Their line drives were caught, though, and their ground balls were base hits."

Thus, Dave continued a pattern that would mark his career. He may not have been the most elegant player on the mound, but he got the job done. He finished the regular season with a 13-6 record and a 3.17 ERA.

Jubilation and cheering for the Baltimore Orioles swept the Treasure State on September 23, 1966, the day after the Birds clinched the American League pennant. Thirteen stories in Montana's major newspapers carried the news, and it rated front-page mentions in the Helena *Independent-Record*, the *Billings Gazette*, the Missoula *Missoulian* and the *Great Falls Tribune*.

Baltimore's first AL pennant, and with it the city's first World Series berth, was a long time coming. When that happened in September 1966, Dave had played a key role in the accomplishment, something celebrated throughout Montana and especially in Billings.

Jim Palmer got the Orioles into baseball's promised land when he pitched a 6-1 win over Kansas City. The right-hander limited the homestanding Athletics to five hits, while the Birds pounded a dozen hits. It was the fourth straight win for Baltimore, which had led the AL since June 14, and it eliminated second-place Detroit from contention.

The Series still awaited a National League representative. The Los Angeles Dodgers and the Pittsburgh Pirates were battling for the flag, and the San Francisco Giants were a dark horse in third place. Los Angeles ultimately won and earned a second straight trip to the fall classic.

For Baltimore, there had been no fall glory since 1896 when the "old" Orioles won their third straight National League championship. That was seven years before the World Series started. Baltimore briefly played in the American League, in 1901–1902, but the Orioles were non-contenders then. They finished fifth and eighth before the franchise moved to New York, where the team became the Yankees. Baltimore then spent fifty-two years in the minor leagues. The city regained major-league status in 1954 when the inept St. Louis Browns moved to the Maryland metropolis.

Dave's hometown paper, the *Billings Gazette*, trumpeted the Orioles' triumph atop the front page of the September 23, 1966, issue. Beneath a headline that read BIRDS BUBBLE . . . AND BILLINGS HAS A WORLD SERIES PITCHER, people in the *Gazette*'s widespread circulation area were told, "There is finally joy in 'Mudville.' The city that gave birth to 'Casey at the Bat' as well as a more mortal hero, Babe Ruth, won its first American League pennant Thursday and celebrated in traditional baseball style, waiting to welcome home the heroes."

The Baltimore dressing room in Kansas City was "only a notch below a full-scale riot . . . and literally afloat with celebration champagne," the *Gazette* account said.

All-star third baseman Brooks Robinson, one of Dave's best friends among the Orioles, got into the clubhouse first and stood at the doorway greeting teammates.

"I got cold chills when there were two out in the ninth inning," Robinson said. "I just didn't believe we were finally going to win."

His concern stemmed from the fact that Baltimore finished second in 1960 and was even closer in 1964, claiming third place but with a two-game gap between the Orioles and the first-place Yankees, compared with being eight games behind the Yankees in 1960.

"After those two near misses, this party seems even better now," Robinson said.

Gazette sportswriter Roy Anderson conveyed Billings' excitement about Dave's ascent to Series play in a front-page story beneath the headline, "He's Our Boy!" Anderson pointed out that Billings was normally a National League town because its minor-league Mustangs had been a National League farm team affiliated with the Brooklyn Dodgers and the St. Louis Cardinals. On September 23, 1966, however, the Billings buzz was all about Dave and his climb from Little League ball to American Legion stardom to being a World Series pitcher at age twenty-three.

Someone who expressed surprise that Dave and the Orioles clinched the flag well before the season ended was Bayne, McNally's Legion coach. "I didn't realize we were that close. This is just wonderful. It's something I've dreamed about," Bayne said. Bayne said that Dave had longed to play in a World Series, now was going to, and he is "still so young." The legendary coach said all of Billings was pulling for Dave. "This is real fine for Billings and for the whole state—a Montanan in the Series. I sure would like to see Dave pitch in the Series. I'll bet there will be a lot of people going."

CHAPTER TEN

SHAKY SERIES START

BUILDUP

When the Orioles flew to Los Angeles before the Series with the Dodgers, they landed in familiar territory. The City of Angels gained an American League team in 1961 when the Los Angeles Angels took the field. The team name changed to the California Angels in 1965 and stayed that until 1996. The following season, the team became the Anaheim Angels, a name that stuck until 2004 when the franchise became the Los Angeles Angels of Anaheim, its name through 2015 when it regained the name it has today, the Los Angeles Angels.

Divisional play hadn't started in 1966, so Los Angeles played against the entire American League field. The Orioles visited the Angels nine times that season, and Bill Roney's outfit came to Memorial Stadium nine times.[1]

For the Series, the Orioles stayed at the Continental Plaza on Sunset Boulevard, a hotel owned by cowboy actor Gene Autry, who owned the Angels.[2] How young and naïve were many of the Orioles, including Palmer and possibly McNally, too? When they were having breakfast on the morning of the first game, several of the players, including Jim Palmer, then twenty, read complimentary copies of the *Los Angeles Herald-Examiner*. The coverage puzzled the Orioles.[3] "The *Herald-Examiner* called us the junior league. They said the junior league loop leaders were in town to play the Dodgers," Palmer said. "Are they insulting us? I didn't realize that's what they (newspaper sportswriters) called the American League."

Dave wasn't much older, himself. He was twenty-three, and he would turn twenty-four on October 31, 1966. We don't know if he was any more worldly-wise than Palmer. Probably not.

There was good reason to feel intimidated. The Dodgers' track record of postseason success included beating the Yankees in the 1963 Series before they passed the baton of NL representation to St. Louis in 1964. The Cardinals, led by the pitching of Bob Gibson, defeated the Yankees for that year's title. The Dodgers were back in 1965 when they topped the Minnesota Twins for the Series title.

Palmer, Dave, and the rest of the team got a laugh out of what they saw when they boarded the bus that would take them to the Dodgers ballpark for the biggest game of their lives. Palmer recalled the event almost six decades later. "There was a real estate sign on the side of the road on Sunset Boulevard. It said, 'WOULD YOU BELIEVE FOUR STRAIGHT,'" referring to the widespread belief, not just in Los Angeles but just about everywhere in the country but Baltimore (and maybe even Billings) that the defending world champion Dodgers would whip the Orioles.

Some Orioles, notably Palmer, remembered that sign, which they would see again on the return trip to the hotel after the game.

MCNALLY'S MOMENT

Hank Bauer tapped Dave to be his Game One starter. As he prepared for his start against the Dodgers in Chavez Ravine, he knew his hometown and his state of Montana stood firmly behind him. He asked his teammates to look at the bulk telegram that had arrived in the visitors' locker room. The telegram contained more than 7,000 signatures from well-wishers in Billings and throughout Montana.[4]

Dave's first taste of World Series competition proved ironic because, when the field of major-league teams bidding for his pitching arm in 1960 came down to two teams, the Dodgers were in the running. In fact, they actually outbid the Orioles, Dave recalled in October 1966.[5]

Dave said he chose the Orioles because he wanted to join a younger team.

"Dave has wanted this all his life and now he has done it," said Bayne, who as Legion Post 4 coach, with the help of his assistants Les Smith and Joe Pirtz, had groomed several pitchers who signed big-league contracts. Dave, however, was the first pitcher from Billings and Montana to pitch in a World Series.

All the hopes and prayers of his Montana fans didn't keep Dave from enduring a troublesome, no-decision outing. Moe Drabowsky got the win after pitching one of the most masterful relief jobs in Series history. Dave lasted only until the third inning. By then, he had thrown sixty-three pitches and issued five walks.

Bauer turned to Drabowsky, a 31-year-old Polish-born pitcher the Orioles had gotten from Kansas City for $25,000 in the 1965 draft. And Moe, whose given name was Myron and who was known as a free spirit, delivered.

He held the Dodgers to one hit the rest of the way and struck out eleven, a Series record for a reliever. He whiffed six Dodgers in a row at one point, matching a Series record set in 1919.

"This was one of the best relief jobs I've ever seen, if not the best," said bullpen colleague Eddie Fisher after the 5–2 win.

Maybe thinking the Orioles were too tight before the game, Drabowsky brought a transistor radio to the Orioles bullpen before the game and hung it on the gate. He turned on the radio and said, "Let's have a little music, boys."

Dave tried not to be blue afterward. "The ball just kept taking off on me," he said.[6] He said he wasn't nervous about his debut on baseball's biggest stage. "I was very calm and confident," he said. "I was surprised how confident I was. But I couldn't get the ball over the plate, and all they had to do was stand there and get walks."

He traced his control problem to his difficulty in adjusting to the mound at Dodger Stadium. "It has a bigger slope than what I'm used to," he said.[7] "The front of the mound was steep, causing me to drop too sharply when releasing the ball."[8]

CHAPTER ELEVEN

CHAMPS OF THE WORLD

After their first-game win in the 1966 Series, the Orioles boarded the bus again for a jubilant ride back to the hotel. And would you believe it? Palmer, and perhaps others, saw the same real-estate sign on the side of the road they had seen going to the game. It now read: *Would you believe the Orioles in four straight?*

To this day, that message has stuck in Palmer's head. Here, you had a real-estate company touting the Birds instead of, say, trying to attract buyers for a three-bedroom house, two baths, a pool, for $39,950, or something like that.

GAME FOUR

Baltimore became bird-crazy when the Orioles flew back from Los Angeles in early October 1966 following two more World Series victories over the Dodgers, behind great starts by Palmer and Wally Bunker.

The frenzy reached the point where Baltimore police were hard-pressed to get a handle on ticket scalping. They arrested twenty people on charges of scalping World Series tickets before the third game, including nineteen people picked up during the three hours before game time.

Scalping was fast and furious, is how one cop might have described what was happening.[1]

Captain Joseph E. O'Donnell, of the vice squad, said that ticket scalping for an Orioles game was new in his city. "They usually turn out for the Colts," who with quarterback Johnny Unitas had become the idols of the Maryland city.

Twenty plainclothes policemen, drawn from the vice squad and the Northeastern district, mingled with the crowd before the game, hunting for scalpers, but so-called "signifiers" lessened their effectiveness. Signifiers were persons familiar with Vice Squad officers and were paid to point them out to scalpers.

Fifteen to twenty more officers strolled through downtown bars and hotel lobbies, looking for scalpers. Among those caught was a man who sold two $8 tickets to a policeman for $50. Police said most of those arrested appeared to be amateurs, some of them from as far away as Mexico and Canada.

Police used marked currency and waited on the stadium grounds for ticket offers, or, if they saw people selling tickets, they tried to buy them with the marked money. Ticket prices ranged from $15 to $25 for an $8 seat, although in some hotel lobbies, a ticket could be purchased for as little as $9.

Now, on October 9, Baltimore—and much of Montana, including Dave's hometown of Billings—awaited McNally's second World Series outing. This time, for the sweep and the championship.

Pregame workouts were underway, and Dave saw teammate Paul Blair beaming after hitting the game-winning homer a day earlier. He also saw Jerry Hoffberger, principal owner of the Orioles and owner of the Baltimore brewery where Dave worked in the offseason.

Jerry is one happy guy, Dave probably thought to himself as he continued warming up for a rematch with the Dodgers' Don Drysdale.

A record crowd of 54,458 people, thirteen more than the day before, stood for the playing of the National Anthem and then settled into their seats. Vice President Hubert Humphrey, a Minnesotan and a fan of the Twins who lost to the Dodgers in the 1965 Series, threw out the first pitch.

"Play ball," the plate umpire yelled, and the Dodgers came to bat.

Maury Wills popped to Dave Johnson on Dave's first pitch, and Willie Davis grounded to Powell, who made an unassisted putout at first base. Lou Johnson fouled out to Etchebarren to end the Dodgers' half of the inning.

The Orioles also couldn't get anything going in the bottom of the first. Aparicio fouled out to John Roseboro, Snyder was out when he was hit by his own bunted ball, and Frank Robinson flied out to Tommy Davis.

The scoreboard continued showing goose eggs for both sides in the second and third innings as Dave threw no-hit ball, and Dodgers pitcher, Don Drysdale, gave up just a single to Brooks Robinson in the second. The Dodgers finally broke through in the top of the fourth on a one-out single to left, but a double play snuffed their hopes for a rally. Dave, certainly pleased by his pitching that day, had to be wondering if his Orioles would deliver just enough offense for him to win, and as a matter of fact, they did, via a solo home run by Frank Robinson.

Snyder opened the Orioles' fourth with a popup to Jim Lefebvre, and Robinson took his usual aggressive stand at the plate against Drysdale, a pitcher Frank knew well from his days as a National Leaguer. Robinson connected on Drysdale's first pitch and blasted the ball 410 feet into the left field stands. 1–0 Baltimore.

That power hitting was something Orioles fans had grown used to in 1966, after Robinson won the AL Triple Crown with 49 home runs to go with his .316 batting average and 122 RBIs.

Robinson, the first AL Triple Crown winner since the New York Yankees' Mickey Mantle achieved the feat in 1956, trotted around the bases and then into the Baltimore dugout. There, he got a hero's welcome to go with the huzzahs that rocked Memorial Stadium.

The Orioles failed to generate more offense after Robinson's blast. John Kennedy threw out Brooks Robinson, and then Willie Davis made an almost unbelievable catch of Powell's shot to deep center field. The Dodgers outfielder gauged the ball's trajectory, saw that it was going to his right, took five steps laterally along the fence, and then leaped to pull in the ball with his arm extended backward. The ball was over the fence when Davis snared it.

As Dave returned to the mound, he might have been wondering if that one-run lead would hold up. Sure, the Orioles had now shut out the Dodgers for twenty-eight straight innings. Still, he might have been thinking, *I'd sure like to get an insurance run or two.*

Despite a single, Dave got some heroic defensive help from Brooks Robinson, and by the end of his fifth inning, the Dodgers owned a World Series record of twenty-nine straight scoreless innings.

Dave was still on the mound in the eighth inning with the lead. Then in the Dodgers' eighth, a defensive move by Orioles' skipper Hank Bauer paid off. He sent Paul Blair in to play center field. Lefebvre came up, and Dave got him to a full count before the Dodger second baseman smacked Dave's pitch deep into center field. Blair raced backward and climbed the fence to make a catch that robbed Lefebvre of what seemed a sure home run.

Dave had already thanked Brooks Robinson for his defensive game, and he probably gave Blair at least a handshake, and maybe a hearty pat on the back, for his game-highlight catch.

The Orioles went hitless in the bottom of the eighth, and it was now the Dodgers' last chance to win and keep the Series going.

Pinch-hitter Dick Stuart struck out, and Dodger manager Walt Alston sent Al Ferrara to the plate in place of Drysdale. Ferrara lined a single to center, and Luis Aparicio, a veteran player, strolled to the mound for a word with Dave to calm him down. Ferrara returned to the dugout after Alston sent in Nate Oliver as a pinch runner.

Next up was Wills. Dave got a 3–1 count on him and then walked him with a pitch that was high and outside the strike zone. The Orioles got Willie Davis on a high fly ball that Frank Robinson easily caught, forcing both Dodger runners to hold their bases.

Now it was time for Brecheen to have a word with his young pitcher. When the Cat got to the mound, he cautioned Dave against making a mistake at this crucial time.

The Dodgers' hopes had come down to Lou Johnson, who led the team in RBIs that year. Dave fired two quick strikes, then got Johnson to hit a fly ball to center field. Again, Blair made it look easy. He parked underneath the ball, gloved it, and the Orioles reigned over baseball as World Series champions for the first time in the city's history.

As the stands exploded in shouts of joy, Frank Robinson and Russ Snyder joined Blair for an outfield celebration. Simultaneously, the infield became a mad, swirling mass of Orioles. Face lit up in a grin, Brooks Robinson seemed to take flight as he leaped toward the pitching mound where McNally and catcher Andy Etchebarren gazed at him, perhaps wondering who should catch their do-it-all third baseman—a moment captured by photographer Bob Daugherty in what became one of baseball's most iconic celebratory images.

The jubilation on the field, in the stands, throughout Baltimore, back in the state of Montana, and back home in Billings celebrated the Orioles completing the first American League World Series sweep since 1950. The Orioles were supposed to be short on pitching, yet they set a Series record of holding their opponent to thirty-three straight scoreless innings. Drabowsky started the string in Los Angeles when he relieved Dave and pitched six scoreless innings, and youngsters Palmer, Bunker, and McNally finished the job.

The city that produced Babe Ruth finally had a world championship baseball team. "There's no way to express my feelings," Dave said afterward, above the din in the locker room. "Give plenty of credit to Andy Etchebarren. He caught a beautiful game. And don't forget Frank Robinson's home run—without that one, we're still playing."[2]

Afterward, Dave's deadpan sense of humor kicked in. "If only we had some starting pitchers, we would've wrapped up earlier," he said.[3]

McNally said he had no idea what Aparicio said to him during their mound conference. When Lou Johnson came up in the ninth inning with two outs, prompting Brecheen to stroll to the mound, the pitching coach advised him to throw low breaking balls to a dangerous right-handed hitter. "I got him with three breaking balls," Dave said. Etchebarren agreed: "Dave threw some great breaking balls."

The Orioles scouting report on the Dodgers said their weakness at the plate was a good fastball—a suggestion that Dave couldn't fully follow. "I don't have a fastball like the other guys on our staff," he said, "but my curveball sets up my fastball."

Dave tried to temper the praise he was getting by pointing out one area where he was mediocre in the game: his hitting. Drysdale struck him out once, and he popped out to Wills at shortstop in his other at-bat. "How can that guy get me out?" he asked, not expecting anyone to take him seriously.

Dave made his way through bedlam in the winners' locker room. Reporters and fans, including Humphrey, crowded in the space. Humphrey told Dave that Orioles' owner Jerry Hoffberger had predicted Robinson's home run when Frank faced Drysdale in the fourth inning.

Then Dave joined Jean and looked for a delegation of Billings people who had flown in for the game. They included his mother, Beth; his sister, Dee; his brother, Jim; and Ed Bayne. "I haven't got a button left on my shirt," said a beaming Bayne. Dave saw a stub of a cigar in his former coach's mouth and, knowing Bayne as well as he did, didn't have to ask what had happened to the rest of the stogie. Bayne had chewed up much of it in the tense ninth inning before Johnson's game-ending out.

Dave took his time to thank other special fans who had rooted for him that day. Besides his mother, sister, and brother, Jim, three aunts having their first reunion in thirty-three years saw him: Mrs. John Suhr Hobbins, of Madison, Wisconsin; Mrs. Herbert Weed, of Scarsdale, New York; and Mrs. Robert Herndon, of Larchmont, New York. Dave's grandmother, Mrs. Arthur Perham, however, decided against being in the stadium because "I just couldn't stand the excitement of actually being at the games," she said.[4]

Mrs. Perham, though, watched the game on television at the home of her granddaughter, Mrs. Jack Johnson, in Madison, and left no doubt that she was one of the top fans of the winning pitcher. "Dave's a wonderful boy," she said.

Asked what he would do next that October, Dave said, "We're just gonna sit quiet here at home for a week, relax and talk about the Series."

With the Baltimore celebration over, Beth McNally needed to return to her job as a social worker with the Yellowstone County Welfare Department. She got on a plane back to Billings and found herself almost as much a hero as Dave. When her flight landed at Billings' Logan Field on Sunday, October 16, 1966, a delegation of friends was waiting to greet her. The greeters included Billings Mayor Willard Fraser, who presented Beth with a bouquet on behalf of the city. "Every city needs a hero, and Dave is one of ours," Fraser said.[5]

It seemed that everyone who came to the airport wanted to talk to Beth, shake her hand, congratulate her and ask what it felt like to have a son whose pitching won the deciding game of the World Series. Beth was "radiant" as she greeted her friends. Then, a police escort, with well-wishers parading behind, took her to her home.

Dave's mother said she was disappointed that control problems led Orioles manager Bauer to pull him out of the first Series game, which Drabowsky won in relief. "But he said it was his fault. He just couldn't seem to get the ball over. But his team won, and that's always most important to Dave."

Growing up, Dave always dreamed of playing in the major leagues and in the World Series, Beth said, "but he didn't really think he'd do it someday."

Beth had seen Dave pitch twice in the 1964 season, both times against the New York Yankees, once at their stadium and also in Baltimore, but those regular-season games couldn't compare to the excitement of the World Series. Asked if Dave was nervous before pitching the first game or the fourth game of the Series, Beth said, "Well, he didn't look it, but I'm sure he was." She fully realized how nervous he had been when she saw a newspaper photo of Dave after the fourth game finished.

Dave's share of the World Series payout amounted to about $12,000, but Beth didn't think he'd have time to spend much of the money. He needed to stay in shape for the 1967 season, and he was getting requests to speak at functions around the country. Beth shared Dave's optimism about the Orioles' prospects for 1967. "He expects them to be right up there again," she said.

THE FRIEND WHO BET AGAINST THE ORIOLES

McNally's friendship with Pete Cochran, which began when both were growing in Billings in the 1950s, survived even having his former Legion teammate bet against him and the Orioles during the 1966 Series. Cochran's play for Legion Post 4 got him a look from the Dodgers. They signed him, and he played in the Dodgers farm team system for three years. He left baseball, served in the Army, earned a business degree from the University of Denver and become a Billings banker, a position he held for thirty years.

In early October 1966, after the Orioles had won the first two games of the Series and just before the matchup was set to resume in Baltimore, Cochran was home, sipping a drink in a Billings bar. Someone else at the bar, caught up in the Orioles frenzy in Billings, blurted out, "I bet Baltimore wins in four straight." Cochran, true to his Dodgers ties, responded, "Not a chance. I'll bet you forty dollars that doesn't happen."

Then came the Orioles' four-game sweep, the closer being Dave's shutout performance. Cochran and the boisterous Baltimore fan settled up. Did he tell Dave about the bet? "Oh, yeah, I let him know," Cochran said. But the wager didn't damage the bond between Cochran and Dave. After Dave retired from baseball and returned to Billings, he had lots of time to play the other sport he loved: golf. He and Cochran frequently played together in foursomes at Yellowstone Country Club.[6]

Besides Bayne and family members, Dave had two more individuals from the Magic City cheering for him in Game 4, and both brothers were part of Billings' growing presence on the national baseball scene. They were Tom and Joe McIntosh; Tom was the oldest child of a family of four, and Joe was the youngest. In between was their brother, Bill, a Legion Post 4 teammate of Dave's and a member of the 1960 national runner-up team.

Tom played for the Billings Legion post in the early 1950s and earned a baseball scholarship to the University of Arizona. After finishing his undergraduate work, he enrolled in medical school and became a physician. Joe, meanwhile, received a baseball scholarship to Washington State University—Bayne's alma mater—and was drafted by the San Diego Padres, for whom he played two seasons, 1974 and 1975, before earning a law degree and becoming a lawyer who has spent most of his career in Seattle.

Well before that, in 1966, both got to watch Dave's mastery in the Series finale. Tom McIntosh had started his career in a Washington, D.C., suburb and when the Orioles reached the fall classic, "My mom said, you get to go to the Series," Joe recalled. She bought her youngest son a plane ticket for the trip from Billings to Baltimore, where he joined Tom, and together they saw Dave's triumphant day.

CHAPTER TWELVE

A PRESIDENT TAKES NOTICE

A few days after Dave's triumphant World Series-clinching win over the Los Angeles Dodgers in October 1966, he and Jean made a short drive from their Baltimore home to suburban Woodlawn. Their destination was the Social Security headquarters.

Both Dave and Jean were far from Social Security age—he turned twenty-four that month, and she was twenty-three—so the reason for the trip requires explanation. Social Security officials had invited the young Montana couple to the facility to join President Lyndon Johnson on a speaker's platform. Together, Johnson and Dave touted a provision in the federal government-run retirement program that benefited Dave and other young people like him, children of service members killed in World War II who were receiving early Social Security survivor benefits.

If it hadn't been for Social Security, he might not have been able to help the Orioles reach the pinnacle of major league baseball, Dave said. Dave, the youngest of four children, and his three older siblings, sister Dee, and brothers Jim and Dan, became entitled to early Social Security benefits, starting in 1945. Each of the McNally youngsters received monthly benefit checks, drawn in their deceased father's name, until they turned eighteen. For Dave, that meant getting a check through the fall of 1960; he turned eighteen on October 31 that year.

So, on this October 1966 day, Dave expressed thanks for the program to help lift older Americans out of poverty that President Franklin Roosevelt pushed through Congress during the Great Depression. According to an article in his hometown *Billings Gazette,* Dave conversed with Social Security Commissioner Robert M. Ball, who quoted the Magic City ace: "Those Social Security checks coming in every month made it possible for me to play American Legion ball in my hometown of Billings, Montana. The year I was eighteen, Billings reached the finals of the American Legion tournament. We lost to New Orleans, but it brought me to the attention of the Orioles, and I was signed up."

There's no record of Johnson's reaction to Dave's remarks, but the ebullient president was undoubtedly thankful for them. A wire service picture of the occasion, published in the *Gazette*, shows Johnson giving Dave a congratulatory handshake. Next to Dave, Wilbur J. Cohen, undersecretary of the Department of Health, makes an imitation pitch. But he gets it wrong. He uses his right arm—Dave was a southpaw.

It wasn't just Johnson, at the highest level of the federal government in nearby Washington, who took notice of the Orioles and Dave. Vice President Hubert Humphrey, a Minnesotan and a Twins fan, did, too. After Dave bested Dodgers' ace Don Drysdale with a two-hit shutout in the Series finale, the Dodgers locker room got a visit from Humphrey, who had thrown out the first pitch in the game. He worked his way over to where Drysdale was sitting. "You pitched a real fine game," said Humphrey, described as a good baseball fan. "The ball was working good. You had a lot on it."

"Thank you, sir," Drysdale said, rising to his feet. "Dave McNally pitched a great game for Baltimore."

"Yes, he did," Humphrey said. "I thought it was a well-played game for both sides."

CHAPTER THIRTEEN

POST-WORLD SERIES FUNK

The Orioles and Dave needed to prove that 1966 wasn't a fluke. Unfortunately, in 1967 it looked like they were one-year wonders. The Birds finished with a mediocre 76–85 win-loss record and sank to sixth place in the ten-team American League: fifteen and one-half games behind the pennant-winning Boston Red Sox. Dave, bothered by a sore elbow and shoulder, notched a 7–7 record, a major falloff from his 1966 record.

Now in the national spotlight, Dave assumed new postseason roles, both at home in Billings and in Baltimore. He found himself much in demand on the "rubber chicken" circuit, giving dinner speeches. And back in Baltimore, the company that owned the Orioles, the National Brewing Company, brought Dave in for management training. Company executives worked to improve one aspect of his delivery–not how he pitched, but how he spoke.

Knowing Dave better than anyone else, his mother appreciated the value of the voice coaching he was getting. "Dave does well in the questions-and-answers sort of a program. He thinks well on his feet, but he has trouble keeping from talking too fast. Everyone kids him about the speed of his talking," she said.

Billings would soon learn how well the voice coaching had worked. Dave was coming home to the Magic City for what Mayor Fraser had proclaimed as Dave McNally Day. The day, February 6, 1967, included a banquet put on by the Midland Roundtable, the city's premiere sports organization. Dave joined teammate Brooks Robinson as featured speakers for the event.

A HOLDOUT FOR HIGHER PAY

That day in his honor happened amidst one of the first instances in which Dave stood up against his employer, seeking workplace improvement. Years before he helped overturn baseball's reserve clause, he began a method for resisting the sport's entrenched establishment, especially Orioles executives and their allies within the press corps that covered the team. Starting in 1967, his tactic was to be a regular holdout from the Orioles spring training camp. That gave him the only leverage he had to seek higher salaries from the franchise that owned his contract and prevented him from finding another team willing to give him a better deal.

Dave's first holdout occurred while he got his first taste of national glory, which spilled over into Montana, where he already was a famed athlete. This came a few months after the 1966 World Series. Dave, home in Billings for the day proclaimed in his honor, joined a crowd of about 800 well-wishers at the Billings Central High School gym for the breakfast event.[1]

In his remarks, Brooks Robinson lauded Dave, his mother, and the city of Billings. He said his biggest thrill so far in what became an illustrious career was beating the Los Angeles Dodgers in four straight games in the 1966 World Series. Robinson credited manager Hank Bauer for the triumph, calling him "a good baseball man who is great at handling players."

Amid the bonhomie, however, Dave said he was prepared to take a stand for his belief that he deserved a pay raise. "It doesn't look like I'll sign before going down to Miami for spring training," Dave said before the dinner. "We're still talking, but we haven't gotten together on any figures yet." The *Gazette* article didn't mention the salary that Dave was seeking. He reportedly was paid $18,000 in 1966. Robinson, who broke into the big leagues a few years before Dave, was set to report to training camp with a $75,000 salary for 1967 after signing his contract a few days earlier.

Although Dave referred to plurally "we", apparently he was handling salary negotiations by himself then, when sports agents were almost unknown.

Still, an overall aura of good feelings ruled at the dinner. Robinson chimed in with words of exaltation. Addressing Dave, the all-star third baseman quipped, "I thought the whole town of Billings was out to meet you yesterday. You'd think you were something special."

It was a heady time for Dave, who had just turned twenty-four, but he didn't let the praise sideline him from battling for the pay he believed he deserved.

WIMPY NEEDED HIS HAMBURGERS

Dave ended his 1967 holdout in short order on February 26. His decision to sign may have come down to getting free hamburgers in the clubhouse on Sundays. Dave's contract was believed to be for $25,000, a $7,000 raise over his 1966 pay.[2] "We both gave a little," he said after his negotiations with Dalton. "I didn't want to sit it out any longer. As far as I'm concerned, a pitcher's spring training ought to be a little longer than it is. I never feel ready when the season opens."

Etchebarren watched Dave jog across the outfield soon after he came to terms. The Orioles catcher couldn't resist a wisecrack. "Wimpy couldn't stand it any longer. He had to sign to get those free sandwiches and milk in the clubhouse every day." Hamburgers were locker room manager Clay Reid's specialty, and Dave probably missed only a few bites because of his holdout.

As then-Montana journalist Norm Clarke learned, Dave picked up the "Wimpy" nickname early in his Orioles career. In 1963, Clarke quoted teammate Wes Stock's explanation: "You know that Wimpy in the *Popeye* comic strip. He's always eating hamburgers by the dozen. Well, that's Dave."[3]

Dave didn't deny his love of hamburgers and what they had done to his physique. Faking a punch at Stock, he said, "I've gained ten pounds since I joined the club, and Wes knows why."

Less happy was Palmer, who topped the Orioles in their 1966 World Series championship season with a 15–10 record. He signed for an estimated $15,000, representing an educated guess that his pay rose $5,000 after he had become the youngest pitcher to throw a World Series shutout, on October 6, 1966, nine days before his twenty-first birthday. "I gave in," Palmer said. "It wasn't exactly what I thought it should be, but there'll be better years, I imagine. I hope. I couldn't hold out any longer. I was just hurting the ball club and myself."

UP CLOSE TO FRANK SINATRA

Fresh from Baltimore's World Series win, Orioles players and wives of the married ones headed to Miami Beach in late winter 1967. The south Florida city was where the Orioles would stage spring training before they began defense of the first Series title in franchise history. It wasn't all seriousness, though. They got to not only hear Frank Sinatra in person but to be so close to "Ol Blue Eyes" that they could touch him, courtesy of an Orioles teammate with show business connections.

Here's how Jim Palmer described a memorable night in Miami Beach, almost six decades after it happened.[4]

"Frankie Bertaina didn't really pitch that much for us ... (but) he knew Jilly (Rizzo), who was Frank Sinatra's friend and Dean Martin. Dean Martin and Frank had bet the Orioles forty-to-one odds, one thousand dollars, that the Orioles would win four straight (in the 1966 Series). Frank was coming to the Fontainebleau during spring training. Because we trained in Miami, Jilly called Frank (Bertaina)."

Bertaina relayed an invitation from Sinatra via Rizzo. Sinatra would see that three couples, Palmer and his wife, Susan; Wally Bunker and his wife, Kathy; Dave and Jean McNally; and Bertaina got front-row seats for Sinatra's performance at the famed hotel. "We met Frank, and he's either married to or dating Mia Farrow. We were that close to the stage." (Frank Sinatra had married the actress in 1966. They divorced in 1968.)

Reminded of this event in early 2023, Jean McNally said it changed her opinion of the singer. "I wasn't a big fan before, but after seeing him, I definitely was. Also, I saw Mia Farrow in the ladies' room! It was a great evening."

Two young people from Billings, Montana, who probably couldn't have imagined having a front-row seat to hear Frank Sinatra a few years earlier, got a night to remember, thanks to journeyman pitcher Bertaina, whose show business associations surpassed his pitching ability.

NO PAY FOR TV, RADIO INTERVIEWS

A few weeks into spring training in 1967, Dave undoubtedly was aware of—and may have taken part in—an early attempt to get a meager amount of workplace fairness for the Orioles. They wanted to get paid for talking to television and radio personalities. On March 5, Oriole players gathered for a late-morning clubhouse meeting before their daily workout. They named Steve Barber their new player representative and chose Dave Johnson as alternate.

Then they walked out of the hour-long meeting. Barber walked over to a Baltimore TV station's sports director, who had set up with camera equipment and cameramen in front of the first-base dugout.

Barber told the sports director that players had decided stations would have to pay them $50 for each first-person television interview and $25 for each first-person radio interview.[5] As a Baltimore sportswriter on the scene put it, "the fur flew thick and fast for about four and a half hours." Orioles management, unaware of the players' vote and ardently opposed to their demands, finally called Marvin Miller to get a ruling on the matter.

Miller, the Major League Baseball Players Association head, told the players they were "in the wrong" on the issue. "Revert to normal policy" was the course they should follow, he said. Explaining further, Miller said, "when in uniform and on the field, a player is under obligation to do anything the club requests in the area of club promotion."

Phil Jackman, a *Baltimore Sun* sportswriter, immediately mocked what he called the players "foolhardy and futile bid" for extra pay.[6] He said Barber's announcement to the electronic media was a holdup. If Miller hadn't told the players that their demand violated their contracts, it wouldn't have been just radio and TV stations who would have had to fork over money to get interviews. Newspapers would have had to join the new money game, too, Jackman claimed.

"You'd say, 'How's it going, Waldo?' And Waldo would answer, 'Not too bad. That'll be seventy-five cents please (twenty-five cents a word)." Or, Jackman said, a photographer would come up to "Old Spitball" and ask him for a couple of shots. The pitcher would hand the photographer a card with his rates: a head shot, $12, or smiling, $14; an action shot, $21.50, smiling $27.75; and sneaking in after curfew, $156, smiling, $156.50.

When Barber announced the team's decision, he said, "We feel there's a greater demand on us this year as World Champions, and if we're going to get it (extra money), this is the year." Fine. Except that if the Orioles dropped into the second division in 1967 or future years, they'd have to realize that they couldn't demand a "tariff" as high because the demand for their comments would have fallen.

Jackman faulted the Orioles for their lack of public relations skills, but he might have been harsh on a group who were mostly in their twenties and who largely lacked college education. The *Sun* sportswriter said the players goofed by not informing Orioles management first of their intentions before informing the press of their demands.

Barber said he had to handle the matter as he did because interviews were imminent. The Orioles office, however, was about 150 feet from the locker room where the team meeting took place, and it was the same distance to the outfield where the TV people were setting up their equipment. So, Barber's logic failed in Jackman's view. Barber tried to deflect blame for the botched plan, saying he had to carry water for the players as their representative. In fact, he acknowledged he was the player who came up with the idea in the meeting, according to Jackman.

Fully on the side of management, Jackman said a player's contract required him to do everything he could to promote baseball when in uniform. On his own time, though, a player could do as he wished. Bauer, the O's manager, sat in on the meeting, then did three TV interviews, all for free. He refused to comment on the kerfuffle. Barber said "only one or two" players voted against the proposal.

Although the initiative failed, was it a tiny cloud in the sky, a harbinger of the storm that the battle for player rights in the 1970 would bring? Dave would lead that effort, helping players earn workplace rights that were far more consequential than getting paid for TV and radio interviews.

TANGLING WITH AN UMPIRE

Dave wasn't known for dramatics or for being a troublemaker. Yet once, in May 1967, he got called on the carpet for losing his temper. The Orioles were at a low point then. Memories of the 1966 World Series triumph fading, the 1967 season reached a trough on May 8. By then, the Birds had lost three straight games to the Tigers in Detroit and were in eighth place in the American League, four and one-half games off the pace.

Slugger Frank Robinson hadn't gotten a homer in his last 44 at-bats. As he said, trying to lighten the clubhouse mood, "Only the home run hitters drive Cadillacs. That's my wife sitting out there in the Ford."[7]

That sense of malaise apparently rubbed off on Dave, who was on the losing end of a three-hit, 4–0 shutout thrown by Tigers' starter Joe Sparma. Detroit put the game out of reach with a three-run outburst in the fifth inning off "snake-bitten" Dave, as Jackman described his outing.

The frame started with Dave walking a Tigers batter and then throwing Sparma's bunt far above Luis Aparicio's head at second base. Dave next ran right by Don Wert's bunt, and the bases were loaded with no outs. It got worse. Dave threw three straight balls to Dick McAuliffe, and he became so angry with umpire Jerry Neudecker's calls that the ump threw Dave out of the game. Game watchers saw Dave appear to intend to walk over Neudecker as the enraged pitcher left the diamond.

Although baseball rules stipulated that a pitcher who came to the plate to dispute a call was subject to automatic ejection, few fans knew this. Even fewer could remember seeing a starting pitcher tossed out for this infraction.

Nine days later, AL president Joe Cronin summoned Dave to Boston for a session in Cronin's office. He wanted "a little talk" about the matter, Dave stated afterward.[8] Cronin levied a fine and a reprimand to Dave for his action; however, he was not suspended. Dave declined to say how much he was fined. He sounded chastened, though, saying, "Mr. Cronin treated me very fairly" after the first tantrum and banishment of his then four-and-one-half-year major-league career.

Dave made three starts, all no-decision outings, in April before he picked up his first win. It's hard to pinpoint the root cause of his troubles. On opening day against the Minnesota Twins, for example, he had a 4-0 lead and then the Twins scored three runs and had a man on second in the fifth inning.[9]

Bauer left McNally in to finish the inning so he could get credit for the win. Only problem was that the next batter up for Minnesota was slugger Harmon Killebrew, who blasted a McNally pitch upstairs at Memorial Stadium, but the ball fortunately went foul. McNally walked Killebrew and in came Drabowsky, who eventually got the win.

Then there was another game again against the Twins on April 11. The Orioles grabbed an early lead, helped by a Brooks Robinson homer plus some more of his defensive gems at third base … and McNally was wild. Drabowsky pitched three innings to pick up the win.

In the clubhouse afterwards, someone asked Etchebarren what was wrong with McNally.

"He couldn't get the ball to go where he wanted. Actually, I don't think he made that many bad pitches," said McNally's longtime battery mate. But, as a Baltimore writer pointed out, "The catcher was being kind. Mac's percentage of strikes was something like Wilt Chamberlain's percentage on free throws," a reference to the NBA star's troubles at the foul line. And when McNally did find the plate, the Twins teed off on him for seven hits in 4-2/3 innings.[10]

McNally's malaise seemed to come to a head on April 25, 1967, when he appeared at the Advocate Club's annual "Welcome Home Orioles" luncheon in Baltimore. McNally, a member of a five-man panel at the Emerson Hotel, fielded an audience question relayed to the panel: "What has been McNally's trouble this spring—why hasn't he been able to find the plate?"

"I don't think it's any of his business," McNally said, deadpanning into a microphone handed to him, and the crowded ballroom roared with laughter.

Veteran Orioles broadcaster Chuck Thompson, who moderated the panel, started the good-natured ribbing of McNally when he named him to the panel and then, as he worked his way forward to the head table, said, "Don't worry, Dave, it's not home plate. You can find it."

McNally laughed along with the crowd and later got in a comeback when he asked which team was giving him the most trouble.

"Lately, it's been my own team," he quipped. More seriously, "Basically, I think Minnesota and Detroit are the best clubs, while California also is tough."[11]

Relief came three days later, on April 28, when he went six innings, holding Detroit to eight hits in the Orioles' 5–3 win. Dave gave up all three Tiger runs and was the victim of two home runs, but he struck out six while walking three. Blefary keyed the Birds' win with a grand slam home run in the first inning. His blast wiped out the 2–0 lead the Tigers had built against McNally's pitching. The win gave Baltimore an early lead over Detroit for first place in the league standings, and just like Game One of the 1966 World Series, Drabowsky rescued Dave. The bullpen ace allowed one single over the last three innings.[12]

Dave's best stretch of pitching came in late June and for two weeks in July, when he put together a three-game winning streak. First, he beat the Cleveland, 8–1, on June 30, in the second game of a marathon doubleheader. Umpires stopped the game after five innings because a Cleveland curfew forbid starting any inning after 11:59 p.m. The game finished on July 1.[13] Dave limited the Indians to five hits and no runs in his five innings on the mound.

Next, on July 6, Dave beat the league-leading White Sox, 3–1, at Comiskey Park, holding Chicago to five hits and got the offense he needed from Paul Blair and Sam Bowens. Blair homered and added a single for two RBIs, and Bowen homered for the other Baltimore run.[14] Finally, on July 13, McNally shut out Boston on six hits as the Orioles cruised to a 10–0 win at Fenway Park. Gary Bell, Jose Santiago, Dan Osinski, and Galen Cisco paced Baltimore's battering of the Red Sox. The Orioles got sixteen hits for thirty-two total bases. Dave's first 1967 shutout also benefited from leaping catches by outfielders Curt Motton and Blair that prevented extra-base hits by Carl Yastrzemski and Joe Foy.[15]

On September 23, Bauer scratched Dave from his starting assignment that night against Boston because his sore left elbow, which had bothered him before, was aching again. Dave was out for the season and thoughts that his major-league career could be over might have swirled through his mind.[16]

Dave had been on the disabled list for three weeks late that summer because of his elbow. The Orioles restored him to active duty on September 11, and he threw one perfect inning of relief two nights later against Detroit. Then, on September 25, he showed his season wasn't over as he made his first start in almost five weeks. He pitched five scoreless innings at home against New York and got credit for the Orioles' 2–0 win, which gave him a 7–7 record for 1967.

Sitting in the locker room, Dave said, "I threw the ball well and felt fine, but (on) Tuesday, the elbow was giving me pain again. Not nearly as bad as it was earlier this summer, but it hasn't gone away. I can't see much reason for going out there with a sore arm."

Asked if he was worried that his days as a big-league pitcher might be over, Dave said in a flat voice, "Yes. There is something in there that is irritating the elbow. I don't know how to describe it." Dave said the arm hurt only when he held it in certain positions. He originally injured his elbow on March 30 while pitching an exhibition game in Florida against Boston. By mid-season, soreness spread to his shoulder. "I think that was from lack of throwing, though. It hasn't given me any more trouble, but the elbow definitely hasn't cleared up."

By July, the Orioles seemed to have lost the swagger they had had in the fall of 1966 and early in 1967 as baseball's reigning champions, and that drop in pride showed up in the team's front office. *Baltimore Sun* sports editor Bob Maisel wrote how, starting the day after the 1966 World Series finished, when he would call the Orioles office, the operator would answer with a cheery, "World Champion Baltimore Orioles." That continued for a while, Maisel said, but when he rang the Orioles office on July 6, 1967, the greeting was a plain, "Baltimore Orioles."

Maisel said he needled the operator soon after this happened. "I took so much guff from people who called that I finally decided to cut it out," she said. "I'd say, 'World Champion Baltimore Orioles,' and they'd say, 'What ya mean World Champions. Have you looked at the standings lately?' It got so I was wasting so much time explaining that I decided it wasn't worth it."[17]

Meanwhile, Dave's woes got worse. He had never had a sore arm in his life until 1967, but now, late in the season, he had an aching pitching wing. First, his elbow bothered him, then his shoulder, and he had pitched only eleven innings before being put on the disabled list in August.[18] Trying to find the cause, the Orioles sent him home to Baltimore for a doctor's examination on August 17.[19]

The Orioles season of discontent finally over with his Orioles mired in the second division, Orioles manager Hank Bauer considered a new approach in 1968. "I'm gonna be tougher," said the ex-Marine. "Maybe a few of these guys have been taking too much for granted. Maybe we're gonna have to tell a few guys what to do rather than expect them to do it."

Doug Brown, a veteran Baltimore writer whose bylined postseason account also appeared in *The Sporting News,* offered five question marks about the Orioles. Some of them, he wrote, "can only be removed via a shift in personnel."[20] Although Brown mentioned McNally only in passing, the Billings lefthander certainly was aware of the issues and how they affected his performance.

The trouble spots Brown mentioned were:

- Frank Robinson's eyes. His vision had turned fuzzy after he collided with Chicago's Al Weis in late June. Robinson seemed on track for a second straight Triple Crown; his average was .337, he had twenty-one homers, and he had batted in 59 runs. When he came back a month later, he batted .282 with nine more homers and 35 RBIs, giving him final season statistics of .311, thirty homers and 94 RBIs. Robinson's eyes had gotten better late in the year, but while they still weren't "100 percent at the end," that question mark would likely go away over the winter.
- The sore arms of McNally, Palmer, Wally Bunker and Marcelino Lopez. Although the Orioles knew they couldn't rely on four sore pitchers, they would not trade for new starters.
- Left-handed relief pitching. Here, a trade might be in the offing.
- Catching. Etchebarren had slumped to .215 and his backup, Larry Haney, was better at .268. The Orioles might be dealing for a first-string catcher.
- Bench. The Orioles had traded three solid bench players, Charlie Lau, Woodie Held, and Bob Johnson, and now needed to rebuild the bench via the trade route.

Also, Brown said, maybe the Orioles should consider trading Powell, only twenty-six. He suffered through a mediocre year—.232 batting average, fifteen homers, fifty-five RBI—but still was good trade bait.

After his troubled 1967 season, one would think 1968 would have to turn out better for Dave. And it did.

1958 Billings Legion team that went to the Little World Series. (Yellowstone County Museum - donated by the Billings Baseball Preservation Society.)

1959 Billings American Legion team. (Yellowstone County Museum - donated by the Billings Baseball Preservation Society.)

1960 Billings Legion team ready to leave on big trip though the Midwest. (Yellowstone County Museum - donated by the Billings Baseball Preservation Society.)

1960 Little World Series banquet in Hastings, Nebraska. (Yellowstone County Museum - donated by the Billings Baseball Preservation Society.)

1960 World Series team. (Yellowstone County Museum - donated by the Billings Baseball Preservation Society.)

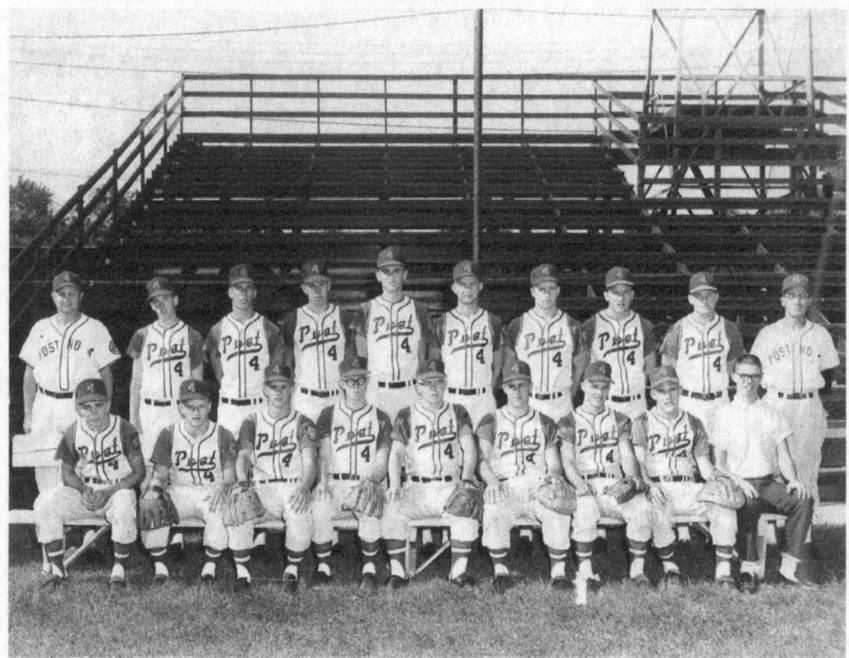

Billings American Legion team in Hastings, Nebraska, for 1960 Little World Series. (Yellowstone County Museum - donated by the Billings Baseball Preservation Society.)

Brooks Robinson, Andy Etchebarren, and Dave McNally home plate jubilation at the end of the 1966 World Series. (AP Photo)

McNally pitching during the 1969 World Series versus New York Mets. (AP Photo)

McNally clowning around with Jim Palmer and Mike Cuellar in 1970. (AP Photo)

McNally (second from left) is first to get 20 wins in 1971 as part of the greatest pitching rotation. (AP Photo)

CHAPTER FOURTEEN

RETURN TO GLORY

GOOD STEAK HELPED

Maybe a top cut of beef contributed to Dave's success in 1968 and 1969. A Baltimore guy ran a corner grocery store about six blocks away from the McNallys' house in Lutherville. This man, Larry Caldwell, supplied Dave with the filet mignon steaks he ate before games, starting in 1968 and continuing in 1969. The Caldwell steaks seemed to be the key to Dave's increased success those years.[1]

Every fourth day, coinciding with days when he pitched, Dave put a filet mignon on the barbecue on his patio. When he took it off the grill at about 3:30 in the afternoon, it was cooked the way he liked, medium with a hint of pink. He ate, and then Jean drove him to Memorial Stadium, where he arrived at 5:15, in time to get in his pregame warm-ups. Jean would return later, in time for the game to start.

The ritual started about halfway through the 1968 season when Caldwell gave Jean a free steak. "This is to get your husband going," he said. And it worked. Dave had an 8–8 record midway through the 1968 season. After that, he won fourteen of his last sixteen games to finish with a 22–10 record. He became the biggest winner in modern Orioles history and only the second Birds pitcher to win twenty games—Steve Barber was the other—since Baltimore rejoined the American League in 1954.

Dave wasn't fanatical about filet mignon. He enjoyed New York and porterhouse steaks, and Delmonico steak was top tier. His pregame ritual, however, required filet mignon grilled on his barbecue because his winning ways started when he began eating that cut of beef regularly. Caldwell didn't ship steaks to Dave on the road, but the grocer and the pitcher stuck to the habit at home in 1969–with one exception. "I didn't have a steak (on) Opening Day. And you know what happened," Dave said. Orioles manager Earl Weaver, who had taken over after Hank Bauer was fired, yanked Dave in the third inning that day. "Larry called me the next day and said, 'I forgot the steak.'"

Dave's next start after opening day was a day game, so he sliced up his steak at 9:45 that morning. Then he shut out the Washington Senators. On this game day in May 1969, Dave was at the ballpark with a full stomach. For the first forty-five minutes he was there, all he had to do was get dressed, and talk about steaks, salt tablets, and his nemesis on the Senators, Frank Howard. Dave escaped defeat in that game, a 5–4 Baltimore loss to Boston in extra innings. He yielded five hits and two runs in his short mound stint, and he walked three and struck out one.

Reliever Mike Adamson took the loss after the Red Sox brought in the winning run on a pinch-hit sacrifice fly in the twelfth inning.[2]

Dave also checked his mail; just one letter awaited him.[3] Like many athletes of that era, Dave often took salt tablets. "Yes, I take salt tablets every day–three when it's cold like this, up to six when it gets hotter." He said all the Orioles took salt tablets because trainer Ralph Salvon insisted on it. "He says muscles lose their elasticity when you sweat."

Howard? Yes, he still had Dave's number. He homered off Dave for the Senators' only run in their recent 2–1 loss to the Orioles. "Four last year," Dave said. "Last Sunday he hit the home run his third time up, but I really pitched him good the last time (Howard came up)."

What do you mean? "I threw him four straight balls. The last was intentional."

Kidding aside, Dave admitted he didn't know why Howard feasted on his pitching. "I think it's that I try so hard to make good pitches, I wind up making bad ones."

That night, facing the defending world champion Detroit Tigers, Dave knew he had to be wary of someone else: Willie Horton. "Three home runs off me last year, four or five in sixty-seven," he said. "I'll have to be careful with him tonight."

The clock in the clubhouse showed 6:05 p.m. It was time for Dave to have a half-hour of fun, doing something he rarely got to do in a game: hitting a baseball. Batting practice was starting. In 1968, Dave went 0-for-41 before he smacked a two-run homer off Denny McLain to help beat the Tigers, 5–3, on July 21. After that he hit respectably, by pitcher standards: 10-for-45, including a grand slam.

Now, as he prepared to face Detroit's Wilson, he was 0-for-7 at the plate for the season. "Let's see," he said. "At last year's pace, I've only got thirty-four at-bats to go before I get a hit."

Dave was back in the clubhouse by 6:45. He wasted time until 7:30 when he went into Salvon's cubicle to have a spot on his left foot taped up. "He drags his foot at the end of his delivery," Salvon said. "If we didn't put something over it, he'd scrape it raw." The trainer pointed to a jar containing salt tablets, and Dave dutifully took and swallowed three. As Dave sat on a table, Salvon bent his left arm; it seemed he was trying to remove it. First, Salvon lifted the arm up and back, and Dave winced when it would go no further. Salvon gave a satisfied grunt. Then he pushed the arm behind the back, across Dave's chest and out to the side. The player and trainer repeated their wince-and-grunt routine each time. Next, Salvon tugged at Dave's left scapula blade and carefully yanked his wrist until it cracked.

"Helps a pitcher get loose," he said. "You can save a pitcher ten or fifteen pitches in one night. If you loosen the tendons and muscles, stretch them before the guy goes out there, then tendons and muscles don't have a tendency to snap when he breaks a curve, say."

Salvon administered a rubdown of Dave's pitching arm, using a brown liquid. "Vital oil," he said. "It's for horses."

"And lefthanded pitchers?" an observer asked.

"For this lefthanded pitcher anyway," Dave said. "Keeps the heat in."

Salvon signaled he was done by slapping Dave on the back, and then he turned his attention to coach Charlie Lau, lying face down on a nearby table. Lau was waiting for a B-12 shot in his rump. "Let me give it to him, Ralph," Dave said. "Do I just jab it straight down?"

"Right," Salvon said. "Nothing to it."

Dave pretended to give Lau a shot, but it was Salvon who poked him. Although Lau knew what had happened, he played along with Dave's game. "You could have given the shot to me," he said to Dave. "You've got good hands." Dave grinned and added a make-believe tremble in his left hand for effect.

Brooks Robinson rushed in. He told Salvon to work on somebody who would make a difference that night. "Get out of here, McNally," Robinson said. "Who's pitching tonight, Ralph?"

Dave took the ribbing in stride. He finished putting on his uniform and went to the dugout for a briefing from Weaver. One Tiger was a good low-ball hitter, and when another Detroit batter was at the plate, Dave was told that they were going to signal Dave Johnson to shift over from second base to the right as a defensive move.

McNally left to warm up with catcher Clay Dalrymple and then pitched a methodical game. When it was over, the Orioles took home a 5–2 win. Dave threw a five-hitter to stay undefeated with his third win. He held Horton to two singles. Al Kaline and Dick McAuliffe homered against him, although Kaline's dinger resulted from Oriole left fielder Merv Rettenmund allowing Kaline's shot to pop out of his glove and sail over the fence.

Dave basked in the attention he was getting in the clubhouse. Someone asked him about his drive to right field in the third inning; Horton caught the ball on the warning track. "That's as far as I can hit a ball," Dave said. "It was the wind. Must have been blowing one hundred miles an hour."

Analyzing his performance, Dave said he had ducked out of two losses. "I got better as I went along, but I'm still not in a set groove. Last year, I could wind up and throw any pitch I wanted and just concentrate on the area I wanted the ball to go. Now, I find myself thinking about how to grip the ball." He said his arm felt fine, and the velocity of his pitches was all right. Yet, "I'm hanging curveballs and I'm just not comfortable," he said.

Detroit manager Mayo Smith saw little that was off in the Baltimore southpaw's pitching. "McNally looks just like he did last season. Maybe not quite as sharp as he was at mid-season, but he will be," Smith said after the game.[4]

Someone told Dave that Jean was waiting outside. He showered and joined her. They hadn't decided whether they'd pick up steamed crabs and take them home or go to a Mexican restaurant. Finally, fed and done for the day, Dave was home at around 1 in the morning, trying to sleep. He tossed and turned for a while, then dropped off. Four days later, he would repeat the routine.

Dave was no stranger to no-hitters. He threw several as a Billings Legion Post 4 pitcher. But on May 15, 1969, for the second time in his major-league career, he closed in on a no-no game only to be denied in the late innings. That night, playing Minnesota at Met Stadium, he held the Twins hitless into the ninth inning. Cesar Tolivar spoiled his bid for a gem with a single. He punched a line drive to left center field on a one-ball, one-strike pitch Dave said was a fastball down low.[5] Afterward, Dave took the near-miss in stride. "I have no regrets," he said. "I was throwing the ball as good or better in the last inning than I did all night. There's nothing you can do about it."

Jim McNally, one of Dave's two older brothers, was then a car dealer in Williston, North Dakota. He attended the game and got to see the second one-hitter of Dave's professional career and the fifteenth in team history. He also came close on October 1, 1964, against the Washington Senators. Don Lock spoiled the potential McNally no-hitter with a two-out double in the eighth inning.

As of Dave's one-hitter against the Twins, there had been three no-hitters in the Orioles' brief history, the most recent thrown by Tom Phoebus against Boston on April 27, 1968.

Dave recalled pitching five or six no-hitters in American Legion competition. That tally included two no-hitters in Montana's 1960 state tournament. When Ed Bayne's team advanced to the Legion Little World Series, Dave was the only pitcher there who had thrown a no-hitter in a state tournament.

Reflecting on his mastery of the Twins, Dave said, "This was probably as good or better than any game I ever pitched. I never threw all three pitches—fast ball, curve, and slider—through a whole game when they were working this good." Etchebarren praised Dave's showing: "Dave pitched exceptionally well. He had an exceptional curve, a good slider, and he threw his fastball in good spots."

The Orioles catcher said he thought Dave would get the no-hitter when the Orioles took the field in the bottom of the ninth. "I thought

Dave was going to get it, but I was afraid of Tolivar." Why? "You can't pitch to him any set way. He sprays the ball all over."

Maintaining baseball tradition, no one in the Orioles dugout said anything about a possible Dave no-hitter. "But fans all around me were hollering at me all night," Dave said.

Asked if he needed to be reminded that he was pitching a no-hitter, Dave said, "I had an inkling," and he laughed.

More glory was ahead of him.

CHAPTER FIFTEEN

THE STREAK

Unlike other pitchers who had to cope with disappointment and refocus themselves after narrowly missing a no-hitter, Dave had a goal even more lofty to set his sights on after the Twins spoiled his bid. He had won his last two games of 1968 and now, in late July 1969, he was closing in on the American League record of seventeen straight wins.

On July 25, 1969, he pitched the Orioles to a 4–2 victory over Chicago. That gave him a 14–0 season record, and it was his sixteenth straight win. Afterward, Dave didn't dispute the old saying that you have to be lucky to be good and good to be lucky.[1] Dave praised "numerous superb plays" by Mark Belanger, Merv Rettenmund, Frank Robinson, Don Buford, and Boog Powell for helping him win. In particular, Robinson and Powell made the difference; the former with a three-run homer in the first inning and the latter with a solo home run in the sixth.

As someone who liked to keep a conversation with the press on a light note, if possible, Dave said of his teammates, "I had to test them to see if they're still loose after the All-Star break."

Dave was all right with the kidding he took, that he had been living in a tree. He realized Weaver had pulled him out of eight games when the Orioles were behind, only to have them rally for a win and getting him off the hook with each no-decision outing. "You can kid me all you want when I'm fourteen-and-oh," he said. "When I'm seven-and-eight, though, watch out."

Now a winner in twenty-eight of his last thirty decisions, Dave said his pitching was as good as his record. "I think I have pitched well enough to win fourteen this year," he said, even though people in the clubhouse razzed him about the relief help he got in the eighth inning that night. "I probably should have some losses in there," he said, "but that's where the luck comes in." He pointed out that he had struck out twice as many batters as he walked, and that he had allowed "quite a few less hit than innings pitched." He added, "Those are always pretty fair measures of effective pitching." Also, his earned-run average then was something "you can never be ashamed of," less than 3.00.

Many people had asked Dave to compare his win streak to those that belonged to legendary AL pitchers. He knew that two more wins would tie, and three more would break the AL record of sixteen straight wins in one season. That mark belonged to Washington's Walter Johnson and Boston's "Smokey Joe" Wood, who accomplished the feat in 1912, and to Lefty Grove of the 1931 Philadelphia Athletics and "Schoolboy" Rowe of the 1934 Detroit Tigers.

In the National League, Tim Keefe and Rube Marquard, both New York Giants pitchers, won nineteen in a row in 1888 and 1912, respectively, Another Giants pitcher, Carl Hubbell, held the big-league record of twenty-four straight wins over two seasons, 1936 and 1937.

If Dave won his next game, he would tie the AL record of seventeen straight wins over two seasons, held by Cleveland's Johnny Allen, who set the mark in 1936–1937. But he said he wasn't focusing on those records. "If I had pitched a lot of real good consecutive games, I'd be worried about a bad one showing up sooner or later. But I've had my share of bad ones, so the pressure of bad games doesn't show up, if you know what I mean."

Beating the White Sox wasn't a lucky win, he said. "Two runs in eight innings I regard as pretty fair pitching." He attributed Chicago's two runs in the eighth inning to his "throwing some pretty fat pitches." Dave said he wasn't trying to take anything away from the White Sox, "but when I get a lead, I don't want to walk anyone. A base on balls is the same thing as a hit. I just try to concentrate on throwing the ball over the plate." He said he didn't want the White Sox to hit hard, but they did.

As the *Baltimore Sun's* Lou Hatter put it, "Shave it any way you want. A bushel of talent wrapped around that marginal little bit of luck which has projected Baltimore's All-Star lefthander into the forefront of baseball's modern-era pitchers."

Dave picked up his AL-record-tying seventeenth straight win on July 30, 1969, but not without an anxious moment. "You definitely need little favors along the way," he said after beating the Kansas City Royals, 4–2, at their park. He pitched eight innings and gave up nine hits while striking out seven and walking one.[2] The favor that Dave received came in the ninth inning when Kansas City's Bob Oliver, trying to reach third, was tagged out. He had tried to advance on Ed Kirkpatrick's pinch-single, but the game-ending out negated the Royals' rally. And in another fortunate play for Dave, what could have been a run, scored by Buck Martinez, didn't count either. Martinez raced from second base toward home plate after the hit, but Don Buford made a bullet throw to third base, where Brooks Robinson tagged out a sliding Oliver.

Thus, Dave was spared a third earned run, which earned him ribbing in the Birds clubhouse after the game. "How about that," said shortstop Belanger. "Mac not only won the game, but the run didn't count."

"Whattaya mean? That's the first break I've had all year," Dave hollered back. He had been nicknamed "Dave McLucky" and was used to getting good-natured guff from his teammates. "They can needle me all they want. I'm very happy. Very happy indeed."

Dave now was tied with Johnny Allen.

It might have been a good omen for Dave that the 13,648 fans on hand in the Royals' park included fifteen nuns. Sister Maureen Hall, a grade-school and high school classmate of Dave in Billings, organized the nuns' night of baseball. Sister Maureen was then a schoolteacher in Kansas City. "I hadn't seen her in eight or nine years, but I talked with her and the other fourteen nuns before tonight's game and this afternoon at our hotel," Dave said.

And if God helps those who help themselves, Dave did his part with his bat in the win. He singled off KC's Roger Nelson in the seventh inning and kept alive Baltimore's two-run winning rally, which Buford capped with a double. "I helped myself for a change," Dave said.

A day later, Dave's record rated mention on the floor of the U.S. Senate. Montana Senator Mike Mansfield boasted about the Treasure State product to his colleagues. "Dave McNally is feeling no pressure, he is feeling no pain, but in his own words, he is feeling very lucky," Mansfield said.[3] "We're following every game with trepidation."

THE STREAK ENDS

A delegation of Montanans traveled to Minneapolis to see Dave's try for the record on August 3. One well-wisher at a pre-game luncheon was ten-year-old Mark Lucas of Miles City. Holding a baseball signed by Dave, the youngster said, "I hope you end up twenty-five and zero." Grinning, Dave said, "So do I."[4]

An old friend surprised Dave by his presence at the event. When he spotted the man, Dave said, "What are you doing here? Why didn't you tell me you were coming?" He was speaking to Joe Pirtz, the man Dave often credited for his major-league success. Pirtz, a Billings barber, was Dave's pitching coach while he played for Legion Post 4. Although he spent eighteen years helping Ed Bayne build a youth baseball dynasty and made stops throughout the country for regular season and postseason Legion games, Pirtz was seeing his first major-league game.

The trip to Metropolitan Stadium came courtesy of Billings beer distributor Ralph Nelles, who flew Pirtz there in his own plane. "It's a pleasure and a privilege to be here. This is the happiest day of my life," Pirtz said. The lunch crowd included Dave's older brother, Jim, who showed up with fifteen fans from North Dakota, where he lived. At the lunch, an older Butte man shook Dave's hand and, lowering his voice, said, "I grew up on the same block in Butte as your dad."

Most of the fifty-plus fans were from Billings, but individuals from smaller Montana towns, such as Plentywood, Wibaux, and Melstone, also attended. One fan from Butte, Dick Leary, mentioned a personal tie to baseball history during a question-and-answer period: "I saw Schoolboy Rowe of Detroit set the record of sixteen straight victories against Washington … and I plan to see you break it Sunday."

Dave's answers during the Q&A time included:

- "Frank Howard has beaten me so bad I decided this winter I wasn't going to let him beat me anymore. I'll walk him on four straight pitches if I have to."
- "There's no place around that has a better Legion baseball program than Billings."

- "We (Billings) should have won the national Legion title in 1960, but I blew it first as a pitcher, then in the outfield."

Dave said the biggest thrill of his career was winning the last game of the 1966 World Series against the Dodgers. His first twenty-win season in 1968 "was fun, but it was an individual thing."

Alas, the well-wishers went home disappointed. McNally lost to the Twins, 5–2, on a grand slam by Rich Reese. The Orioles led, 1–0, in the Minnesota seventh, and Dave retired the first two Twins batters on flies to center field. The next two Twins singled, and a walk loaded the bases.

Pitcher Jim Kaat was due up next, and Twins manager Billy Martin sent in Reese to bat for him, going with the odds favoring a left-handed hitter in that matchup. McNally had a 3-2 count on Reese when he sent a waist-high fastball at him. "I did not think it was going out when it left the bat."

Said catcher Etchebarren: "I probably wouldn't have called for a fastball in that situation if his slider had been working, but we lost control of the slider in that inning." It was Reese's first at-bat against Dave during his two seasons in the majors.

When it was all over, Pirtz was left wondering if he was bad luck for Dave. "The last time I saw Dave pitch in person was in the American Legion final in 1960. He started the game for us against New Orleans, and we were ahead, three-zero, when he got wild. I took him out, put him in right field, and the ball went through him out there. We ended up getting beat."

Dave, although disappointed, also sounded relieved afterward. He told another Orioles pitcher that he had tired of apologizing for winning. The "McLucky" nickname had stuck, and when the Orioles "defrocked" Saint Christopher, the team drafted Dave to stand in for the saint who had long monitored plane flights.

The game still put McNally in the AL record books for most consecutive wins over two seasons, seventeen, and most consecutive wins at the start of a season, fifteen. During his 1969 streak, Dave finished ten of the fifteen games. During the 120-1/3 innings he pitched in that span, he gave up 22 earned runs, struck out 76, and walked 27.

Beth McNally continued to follow the feats of her youngest child closely. When Dave pitched, she went to a Billings restaurant and followed the game on a Western Union ticker. That day in August 1969, when Dave was trying for an American League record-breaking eighteenth straight win, was a Sunday, and the restaurant was closed. A friend could tune in a radio broadcast of the game from Minnesota and invited Beth over to listen. Weeks later, she attended the AL playoffs and the World Series.

The get-together of Montanans (and a few North Dakotans) before Dave's attempt to set the record was one example of his desire to stay connected with his hometown and native state and to preserve friendships built over the decades. One example involved Bohlinger, who owned a women's clothing store in downtown Billings for many years. That sent him once on a business trip to Los Angeles, where he stayed in the Biltmore Hotel, also where the Orioles stayed when they were in town to play the Angels.

"After work, I'd stop off at the bar. And here was Dave; we talked." Soon, teammates Andy Etchebarren, Brooks Robinson, and Boog Powell joined McNally, and Dave introduced them to John.

Holiday get-togethers in Billings involved Dave and his brothers, Jim and Dave, as well as Bohlinger. "He'd (Dave) come home at Christmas. We'd have a drink and sing Christmas carols."

Another time, Bohlinger was in New York on business and attended a Yankees-Orioles game. "I had a seat right by the clubhouse. Infield batting practice was going on. He saw me and came over. He said, 'I start tomorrow. I'll get you a ticket.'" Unfortunately, the Yankees (Bohlinger's favorite team) got to Dave that game, and he was pulled in the third inning.

Bohlinger remembered Dave as someone who, despite his fame—"he was a real celebrity"—was "real modest, open, friendly. He did not have an inflated ego."

CHAPTER SIXTEEN

ANOTHER SERIES

The win streak over, Dave and the Orioles could concentrate on winning the AL East pennant, capturing the league crown in the playoffs, and reaching the World Series for the second time in team history. In the first-ever AL playoffs, Baltimore, best in the Eastern Division, faced Western Division champion Minnesota. And this playoff series, which resulted in a three-game sweep for the Orioles, let Dave avenge two earlier setbacks to the Twins: his almost no-hitter on May 15, which became a one-hitter that he won, and the July 30 loss in Minnesota that snapped his consecutive win streak at seventeen games.

But on October 5, Dave completely mastered Minnesota. He blanked the Twins on three hits for an eleven-inning, 1–0 victory. "This is the best ever," he said afterward. "I had the same kind of stuff this time as I did back in May. My fast ball moved around well, and I got the breaking pitches over the plate. That one-hitter was a big thrill. It would have been a greater thrill if it had been a no-hitter. This time, though, so much more was at stake."[1]

Baseball writers learned after the game that Dave pitched the tenth and eleventh innings with cramps in his left forearm. That explained why he jabbed his throwing hand against his side several times. Between innings, trainer Salvon had relieved the discomfort with heat. Dave had encountered the same annoyance earlier in the season. That time, while he was pitching against Oakland, the cramping caused his fingers to draw up.

Dave said his cramps didn't cause his control problems in the eleventh inning, when Harmon Killebrew and Tony Oliva walked. Dave ended the threat by getting Bob Allison for the third out. "I was just rushing my body out front too far. It was just a matter of telling myself to slow down the body and let the arm catch up. I had to remind myself about six times before my mind got the message."

Dave struck out eleven and walked five. He got a scare in the tenth inning when Twins catcher George Mitterwald lifted the ball into the left-field upper deck. The ball sailed barely foul, and Mitterwald then struck out.

Dave also played a key role in Baltimore's only run on Motton's pinch-single that scored Powell from second base. Dave, who was the next batter up, signaled for Powell to slide at home. Powell, however, appeared to miss the bag after he got tangled up with of Mitterwald on Oliva's throw from the outfield. Dave escorted Powell back to the plate just to make sure he scored. "I almost tackled him," Dave said of how he got his burly teammate back for what seemed like a needed actual touch.

"He didn't just call me back," Powell said. "Dave hysterically screamed me back. I guarantee you, I touched it the second time." Powell's second touch turned out to be unnecessary, however. Umpire Ed Runge said Powell's heel nicked the edge of the bag on his first crossing.

The Orioles entered the 1969 World Series confident they could top the New York Mets, thanks to one of baseball's best pitching staffs. The Birds, however, were not cocky about their matchup with the underdog National League representatives. "The one thing the New York Mets have going for them is pitching. In young Tom Seaver and Jerry Koosman, they may have the best one–two punch in baseball," wrote *Baltimore Sun* sports editor Bill Tanton on the eve of the Birds' second appearance in the fall classic.[2]

But as George Bamberger, the Birds' pitching coach, analyzed the strength of the Orioles and the Mets mound personnel, he wasn't willing to concede the edge to Gil Hodges' crew. Bamberger offered his assessment as he sat in the team bus in Bloomington, Minnesota, waiting for the Orioles to finish celebrating their three-game sweep of the Twins in the AL playoffs and come out of the visitors' clubhouse. "I wouldn't trade our staff for theirs. Our pitchers have better records. More wins, better earned-run averages," he said.

Someone noted that the Birds pitchers also had a better defense backing them. "That's all part of pitching," said Bamberger with a New York accent, the result of living in Mets territory on Staten Island.

Bamberger had coached the Orioles pitchers for two years and had turned them into a premier contingent in 1969. Baltimore had two twenty-game winners: Mike Cuellar at 23–11, and Dave, who at 20–7 was coming into the Series with the second of what would become a string of four straight twenty-win seasons. Behind them were defensive stars, with Brooks Robinson and Mark Belanger regarded as the best. "Like the chicken and the egg," Bamberger said of the pitchers-defenders tandem.

On paper, the Orioles had the better of the pitching matchups. In Game One, the Mets planned to start Seaver, who Tanton wrote, "is an inspired performer who is so good that he was able to win even before the Mets got good." That was a reference to the Mets' sudden rise from being the butt of jokes as the worst team in baseball to pennant winners. If needed, Seaver could pitch Games One, Four, and Seven of the series.

But the Orioles gave up nothing in sending out Cuellar. His accomplishments included winning fourteen of sixteen games that year games since July. Hodges had pegged Koosman for his second starter. He went 17-9, and during the second half of the season, according to Tanton, he may have been the best pitcher in the National League if Seaver wasn't.

But neither Seaver nor Koosman stood out in the Mets' playoff sweep of the Atlanta Braves. In contrast, McNally displayed the best pitching of the playoffs in both leagues in his three-hit win over the Twins.

Game Three in New York was expected to feature Baltimore's Palmer, 16–4 in the regular season, against Mets rookie Gary Gentry, 13–12. "Call this matchup a plus for the Birds. Nobody in the game has a No. 3 man like Palmer," Tanton wrote.

Yes, Palmer gave up ten hits in the Orioles 11–2 playoff win over the Twins, but Jim was only being as good as he had to be.

Tanton rated the pitching matchups this way: Seaver-Cuellar, a tossup; Koosman-McNally, give Mac the edge; and Gentry-Palmer, "Palmer all the way."

Atlanta manager (and former Orioles manager) Paul Richards remained shocked that his Braves hammered the Mets pitching and still lost.

"I can't understand it. How can we shell their three starting pitchers the way we did and hardly be in any of the three games?" he said.

Continuing his comparison of the Mets and the Orioles, Tanton wondered where the New Yorkers could win if not by better pitching. "With the bat? Never. The Mets batted. 241 with 109 homers. The Orioles hit. 265 with 175 homers. With the glove? Of course not. The Orioles are far superior, particularly in infield defense."

What the Mets had, that the Orioles needed to be beware of, were intangibles that defied logic. On paper, they weren't as good as the Chicago Cubs but beat them. Nor were they as good as the Braves, but they dispatched of them, too.

"In this Age of Aquarius, some strange things happen. Logic does not always prevail," Tanton concluded.

Baltimore got off to a good start in the series. The Orioles' Cuellar bested Seaver and the Mets, 4–1, in Game One. Cuellar held the New Yorkers to six hits, and he logged eight strikeouts and four walks. He helped his cause by singling in the fourth inning with two out to drive in a run.

Dave, however, suffered defeat in the next game at the hands of a team that had been 100-to-1 preseason long shots to win the National League pennant. It took until the ninth inning for the game to be decided as a 2–1 win for the Mets. New York's darlings rapped out three singles by Ed Charles, Jerry Grote, and Al Weis, all with two out, to beat Dave, who earlier gave up a home run to Donn Clendenon.[3]

The Mets gave Koosman the lead in the fourth inning when Donn Clendenon socked a leadoff homer. Solid defense by third baseman Charles and shortstop Bud Harrelson helped Koosman hold the slim advantage until the ninth inning. That's when Koosman walked Frank Robinson and Powell with two out.

Next up for the Birds was Brooks Robinson, who had singled in Baltimore's only run in the seventh. That threat prompted Hodges to change pitchers. Koosman, who had no-hit the Orioles until Paul Blair's single in the seventh, came out to a standing ovation from the Memorial Stadium crowd.

In came Ron Taylor, who picked up his fourteenth save of the year.

"I made one real bad pitch when it counted, and it killed me," Dave said, calmly reflecting on the game afterward. "A batter goes to the plate looking for a pitch he can hit, and I gave him one," he said, regretting that pitch in an otherwise solid six-hit, nine-inning outing.[4] "It was a slider up in and I wanted it down. I felt I pitched a good game, and a similar pitch would have hurt me just as much against Minnesota (in the playoffs).".

Some second-guessers thought that Dave should have walked Weis. The Mets had runners on first and third, with Koosman up next, but it was likely that Hodges would have sent in a pinch-hitter, someone who was a more dangerous hitter than Weis. Dave, however, said he didn't consider intentionally walking Weis. "My intention was to make good pitches and get him out and at the same time not care if I walked him."

Dave said he didn't throw a bad pitch to Clendenon in the fourth inning, when the Mets first baseman connected for a homer that scored the visitors' only other run. "He hit a low fast ball—not a real bad pitch, although it didn't turn out well."

Dave was pitching with an uncustomary week's rest, but he said that wasn't a problem. "I felt good the whole day—very confident," he said after striking out seven and walking three. Usually, a long layoff leaves me feeling too strong, and I get wild, but that wasn't the case today."

He complimented Koosman for "pitching real good ball," but said he thought the Orioles quality hitters would connect on his pitches. "However, even the good hitters have a set way you can pitch to get them out, and Koosman did."

Dave looked ahead to Game Five and said he had no different plans for pitching to the Mets. "I felt I was doing what I wanted to do today, and I was getting them out. It was just the one real bad mistake."

After winning the Series opener, the Orioles lost the next three games. Thus, Dave, as the starter in the fifth game of the best-of-seven Series, took on a lead role in a "do-it-or-see-you-next-spring" game at Shea Stadium.[5]

Based on his experience pitching in his share of big games before, most notably the opener of the 1966 World Series, Dave said he was ready for the Mets. "In sixty-six, I was so nervous the day and night before the game, I was sure I wouldn't be able to walk, let alone pitch, but really, I was surprised when it was over. Actually, I was disappointed. There was no reason to be shook up. Well, some, but . . ."

Between the scouting reports and what he had learned in his close loss to the Mets, he said, "I think I can get them out." His six-hit performance, in addition to giving up two runs, would normally make him a winner for the Birds. Two runs by the Mets, however, had been enough to beat Baltimore three straight games.

Referring to the Mets' success against him, he said, "I can't do anything about that." Dave normally could count on hitting from the Robinsons, Brooks and Franks, plus Blair, Powell, Buford and others to boost him to victory, but the Mets had muffled the Orioles bats.

"I think we've hit the ball harder than the Mets right along. In the game I pitched, for instance, we hit eight hard shots off Koosman, and all of 'em ended up as outs. What can you do?"

Las Vegas bookies still believed in the Orioles, making them 23–20 favorites to win Game Five. But they favored the Mets to win the Series by seven-to-five odds.

The Orioles brought disappointment and frustration to the pre-game workouts. "We're going to break out of it today," said Brooks Robinson. "We're disgusted with ourselves. I've never seen our team this mad." And Powell patted Dave on the back and vowed, "We're going to get you two runs today. I promise, two whole runs."

To which Dave answered: "I hope I'm around in the fifteenth inning when it happens."[6] When he played in the next Fall Classic, at the end of the 1970 season, he wouldn't need extra innings to get the runs to produce a win. And he would help his own cause, surprisingly, with his batting.

The Cinderella Mets won the World Series with a 5-3 win in Game 5. Despite starting, McNally didn't suffer a second Series loss; reliever Eddie Watt was tagged with the defeat. Through the first five innings, McNally yielded three hits and two walks but had to escape Mets' threats twice, when the NL representatives got a runner to third base in one inning and second base in another. McNally came out for a pinch hitter in the eighth inning, with the score tied at three, and the Mets got the two runs they needed to win off Watt.[7]

CHAPTER SEVENTEEN

THE GRAND SLAM

After the tough loss to the Mets in the 1969 World Series, Dave relaxed during the winter as he looked forward to the next season.

For the second straight winter, he wasn't working—at least not in a traditional job. He made occasional banquet appearances and in January 1970, he planned to spend a week in Montana where he served as the state Easter Seals chair. The role involved recording TV spots in a half-dozen cities.[1]

Dave explained why he wasn't showing up at an office or punching a clock somewhere. "When I did work during the winter, I went to spring training tired. You can't have an eight-hour-a-day job and work out for two or three hours, too." To stay in shape, he played paddleball at a YMCA in the Baltimore area, often with teammate Eddie Watt and former Oriole Larry Haney.

Dave had won forty-two games in 1968 and 1969–the best two-year performance of his career—and he traced the sparkling record to not spending his winters working in a men's clothing store or calling on bars and liquor stores to sell beer from owner Jerry Hoffberger's brewery.

Dave took time in January that year to attend a screening of the Baltimore premiere of a film about the 1969 World Series. There, in color, he and other Orioles watched the McNally pitch that swung Game Two in the Mets favor and started what became four straight wins and a Series sweep.

Clendenon was at bat. Dave delivered a fastball down the middle and low, almost where he wanted it. He hoped the ball would nick the inside corner of the plate, but he missed by six inches. The Mets batter didn't.

He swung, connected and homered, and that solo shot ended McNally's string of twenty-three scoreless innings in post-season play, dating back to the 1966 World Series.

"I didn't expect to pitch shutout ball forever," Dave said.

Baltimore fans might have gotten on his case for the pitch that keyed New York's win that day, but they didn't. "I was surprised. I thought we'd hear a lot of guff. We didn't. All the people I talked to felt there was nothing we could have done about it."

Dave also started the fifth and final game of the Series. He again faced Koosman in a tight contest; Weaver pulled Dave in the ninth inning, and Watt took the loss in relief. Dave wanted to put that game behind him, too, except for one detail. He homered off Koosman for the Birds' first extra-base hit in 35 innings, since Don Buford doubled in the fourth inning of the opener. Was this a harbinger of Dave's upcoming historic grand-slam home run in the 1970 World Series?

Dave and Powell were the last two Orioles to sign 1970 contracts. They agreed to deals on March 5, the day before play in the spring-training Grapefruit League began. Both got $65,000 salaries for the season.[2]

By 1970, spring training for the Orioles in Miami had become a familiar routine for the McNallys. After spending part of the winter in Billings with their parents and other relatives and friends, Dave and Jean would head to South Florida with their three children in tow.

In March that year, Jean drove her leased Plymouth convertible into the players' parking at Miami Stadium. Manny DeCastro, a former welterweight boxer and Navy cook who kept unauthorized vehicles out of the lot, stopped her for a minute. "I'm Dave McNally's wife," Jean said. DeCastro waved her through, and that gave Jean and Dave's seven-year-old son, Jeff, a thought. Our family name means something, he said to himself. "She's the wife of Dave McNally. . . . Move over, President Nixon, I'm Dave McNally's son."[3]

By then, Dave and Jean could look back at a career in the majors that already ranked with the best for anyone who hadn't yet celebrated his twenty-eighth birthday. Dave had already topped the American League with twenty-two wins in 1969. He had won an AL record-tying seventeen straight games, starting in 1968 and continuing into 1969. He had played in two World Series, 1966 and 1969, and had won the Series clincher in 1966.

It's great to be young and an Oriole, is how McNally could have viewed his world. And baseball writers certainly noticed him in that era; he was a contender for the Cy Young Award as the best pitcher in the American League for three years running. He finished fourth in the balloting in 1969, second in 1970, and fourth in 1971.[4]

Along with Detroit's Denny McLain and New York's Mel Stottlemyre, he comprised the trio of AL pitchers who had won twenty or more games in back-to-back seasons. So, Dave was understandably optimistic about the Orioles' prospects in 1970. "We have good pitching and hitting, a solid defense and a strong bench," he said during spring training. "Maybe some trades still will be made, but we're in fine shape now without having made any offseason deals."

The Orioles headquartered at Miami's McAllister Hotel. Players, however, spent spring training with their families at housing they rented in the city, often close enough that players could carpool to the stadium.

Dave and Powell had been the last of the Orioles to come to terms that spring. Dave signed for about $5,000 less than he thought he deserved. Still, he sounded content as he chatted on a Saturday morning in the $800-a-month home he rented on Key Biscayne.[5]

Among the pleasant things in his life:

- Jean, his wife of eight years, going on nine
- Jeff, now seven and already his golfing pal
- Daughter Pam, almost six, who loved circuses, Saturday morning TV cartoons and looking after her new sister
- Susan, six months old, who woke the household up at five every morning with her need for attention.

Dave was a low-key athlete, not prone to temper tantrums. "I might throw a glove or a bat once in a while, but that's about all," he said.

Jean knew what to expect from her ballplayer husband. "If things don't go right, he's more quiet and reflective than usual," she said, "and maybe he'll make me wait for him longer than ordinary after a game if it's been particularly tough. But he never brings the game home with him." The McNallys chatted with a reporter over cups of coffee, the conversation ranging from crossword puzzles—Dave was hooked—to giving speeches, which he accepted in his role as a baseball celebrity.

He was hours away from pitching for the first time in 1970. Still fresh in his mind was the 1969 World Series loss. A vivid moment for him came in the fifth game when the Cleon Jones "shoe polish" incident deprived him of a win. Later in the game, Al Weis homered off Dave to pull the Mets into a tie. Watt, who relieved Dave after seven innings, took the 5–3 loss.

"I know that the pitch hit Jones, but the Orioles protested when umpire Lou DiMuro accepted the black-smudged baseball as the one that rolled into the Met dugout. We didn't feel DiMuro kept his eye on the ball, as he maintained."

Dave disputed the notion that the Orioles weren't prepared for the challenge of the Mets, perennial cellar dwellers in the National League before their miraculous rise to the top in 1969. "Some persons thought we were not mad enough," Dave said, "but we did everything possible to get ready. We were prepared mentally and physically."

Forget about claims that the Orioles had no "book" on the normally light-hitting Weis, allowing him to hit the key homer in the Mets' World Series-clinching win. "We had been successful pitching (to him) low and tight when he was with the White Sox. I made the mistake of getting the pitch up a little and there went the game."

After Dave won fifteen straight games to start 1969 and then lost four straight, some observers claimed he was pitching differently during his swoon. "Nope," McNally said. "We looked at movies of me when I was going good in both 1968 and '69, and we couldn't detect anything. Pitchers fall into slumps the same as hitters, and they pitch themselves back into the groove."

McNally possessed a passable fastball, but he was never considered to be in the same league as, for example, Nolan Ryan or Palmer in terms of pitching velocity. McNally's pitching speeds appears to have been unrecorded. The first radar gun used to measure the speed of a pitched baseball was invented in 1954, and the device was used in the 1955 Major League All-Star game.[6] The Orioles, though, didn't get a radar gun until the spring of 1975 when they used the $1,200 device in an exhibition game. By then, McNally was no longer an Oriole.[7]

Dave won five of his last eight games in 1969, and he said he changed nothing in his pitching style. For 1970, he was working on a new variation of his change-up. "I've used a palm ball change-up, but it tends to be erratic, and I'm looking for a pitch that acts like a fastball and one that I can throw with confidence and consistency. If I can develop it, fine. Otherwise, I'll drop it."

Dave, slick as a pitcher with 883 strikeouts to 424 walks, better than a two-to-one ratio, wasn't so neat in the kitchen where he enjoyed being an amateur chef. "Oh, his stuffed flounder, eggplant casserole, his breakfasts—they're all very good, but he always leaving the cleaning up to me," Jean said, showing no irritation.

Dave had reported to training camp weighing what the Orioles ordered in a letter to him. His weight reached 230 pounds a few years earlier when thought some more pounds would make him a better pitcher. This winter, he went on a crash diet and came to Florida weighing 189 pounds: one pound less than the team required.

That winter, he enjoyed being on an Orioles basketball team whose other members were Blair, Palmer, Brooks Robinson, Dick Hall, Ed Watt, Pete Richert, and coach Billy Hunter. They played eight games and lost once, to a team of amateur all-stars. When the weather allowed, Dave played golf. Swinging a club right-handed, the same way he batted, he posted scores in the low eighties.

He did such a good job as chair of the Montana Easter Seals campaign he was invited to serve again in 1971. "I've told 'em I will," he said.

During the early spring 1970 interview in Miami, Jean remembered watching her husband's attempt to set the league record for consecutive wins on TV in their home in Lutherville. "The news media had played up the occasion so that nobody could overlook the significance. I wanted to watch it alone so I could concentrate more." She said she shed a few tears when Rich Reese's grand slam spoiled her husband's chance for immortality.

Dave tapped his memories of that game, too. "I fell behind on Reese, 3–2 and threw a fastball out over the plate. He hit it well, but hardly anybody thought the ball would go out." The Orioles left fielder started tracking the ball, but then the wind carried it out of the park.

Dave said he tried to relax and keep his emotions in check because, in his words, "you pitch better than if you try too hard. There's a very thin line between the two, but it does exist and can mean the difference between winning and losing."

The conversation drew to a close. Norma Hall, Dick Hall's teenage daughter, was expected to arrive soon to handle babysitting duties for the evening. Jean would drive to Miami Stadium to see Dave make his 1970 debut against the Atlanta Braves.

That night, he pitched two shutout innings. He looked like the southpaw who had won ninety games as a big leaguer, the all-time best then by a Baltimore pitcher. Was it a sign of things to come since spring training was when players worked on their weaknesses, experimented, and didn't always give their maximum effort?

But, as writer Lowell Reidenbaugh put it, "Dave McNally does not deal in excuses, just superb pitching."

Dave put together another winning streak in 1970. He won nine straight games in late summer. Along the way, he beat Oakland, 5–1, on August 25 for his twentieth win of the season. He was the first AL pitcher to win twenty games three years in a row since Bob Lemon did that from 1952 through 1954.

Others may have thought Dave found winning twenty games a comfortable routine by now, but it wasn't. "I was more nervous today than when I went for number twenty-two years ago, last year, and in all the World Series games I've pitched," he said afterward. "Don't ask me why. I nearly drove my wife nuts today."8

Dave gave the Memorial Stadium crowd some anxious moments during the first two innings before he settled down and glided to victory. "I had a good curveball when I beat the A's in Oakland last week, so I wanted to get that started. But it never did really come. By the time the third inning came around, I was throwing strictly fastballs."

Oakland took advantage. With one out, Campy Campaneris singled, stole second, and scored on Felipe Alou's single. Tommy Davis then doubled, and Dave faced troublesome cleanup batter Sal Bando. "He always hits me pretty good, and I saw Earl Weaver giving the sign to put him on. In the middle of my stretch, though, Earl whistled. I assumed that meant everything was off, and Bando lined to second base." The A's loaded the bases with a walk, but Dave struck out Gene Tenace to end the threat.

Dave owned a 12–6 record at the All-Star break in July, and his earned-run average hadn't fallen below 4.00 since his second start. Then he took off and won eight of his next nine decisions.

Dave, who became the major league's first twenty-game winner that year with the win over Oakland, had never reached that plateau that early in the previous two seasons. He achieved the feat on September 25 in 1969 and on September 9 in 1968. The last win of his streak was a 6–1 triumph over the Milwaukee Brewers, which made him the winningest pitcher in Baltimore's American League history.[9] The seven-hit performance pushed Dave's season record to 21–7 and gave him win No. 111 of his career. He passed the previous record-holder, Milt Pappas, who won 110 games between 1957 and 1965.

Dave's batting, as much as his pitching, paced the win over Milwaukee. He contributed three hits to the Birds' ten-hit attack, including a pair of doubles. The first cleared the bases in Baltimore's four-run second inning. Dave had a shot at his second shutout of the season but lost it when Belanger, who played excellent defense earlier in the game, muffed a sure double play in the eighth inning. That set up the Brewers' only run.

The win, Baltimore's twelfth in fourteen games, increased the Orioles' lead in the AL East to twelve games over second-place New York.

Dave posted the best regular-season record of his career in 1970, a 24–9 mark. His ERA was 3.22, and he struck out 185 while walking 78.

Weaver's outfit reached the World Series again by defeating Minnesota in the American League playoffs. The Orioles' three-game sweep of the Twins included an 11-2 win in the second game, in which Dave throttled

Minnesota on six hits while walking five and striking out five. He helped himself at the plate where he hit a run-scoring double.

Then it was on to the Series against the National League champion Cincinnati Reds. Jim Palmer and Tom Phoebus pitched and won the first two games for the Orioles, by 4-3 and 6-5, respectively, at the Reds' park. That sent the Series to Baltimore's Memorial Stadium, and Dave got the call to pitch Game 3.[10]

On October 13, 1970, a national TV audience watched the NBC broadcast of the game that would give Dave lasting fame. Wyoming native Curt Gowdy was calling the play-by-play.[11]

Gowdy said that "a building hand" greeted Dave as he came to the plate with two out and the bases loaded in the sixth for his third at-bat of the game. The TV camera showed his wife, Jean, wearing a hat and dress, in the stands, and the screen displayed Dave's season batting average, 133.

Reds' reliever Wayne Granger worked the count to 2-2 "Trying to get McNally to chase a bad pitch," Gowdy said. Dave waited for the next pitch, a slight grin on his face. He fouled a pitch to left field. Then he connected.

After he missed two sinking pitches from Granger, McNally connected on a waist-high fastball.

"That's hit pretty good. Grand slam home run!" Gowdy told his audience. After rounding the bases, McNally headed to the dugout, where he got a pat on the back from Frank Robinson. McNally's dinger landed far into the leftfield bleachers, an estimated 360 feet away.[12]

"World Series history has just been made," Gowdy said. "Dave McNally has become the first pitcher to hit a World Series grand-slam home run."[13]

His home run, a blast that landed about ten rows back in the leftfield stands, gave Baltimore an 8–1 lead. It was the twelfth grand slam in Series history, and it wasn't as if Dave was the only Orioles pitcher with long-ball hitting ability in postseason play. Cuellar had damaged the Twins with a grand slam in their earlier playoff series. McNally's dinger allowed the Orioles to cruise to a 9-3 triumph in which he got credit for the win.

"It has become quite evident that the Orioles can do no wrong," Gowdy said.

The *Gazette* capitalized on the feat of its hometown hero by trumpeting the game story the next day with a big headline, "Dave Does It All."

It was Dave's second big-league grand slam home run, the other coming in 1968 against Oakland's Chuck Dobson. He joined St. Louis Cardinals' great Bob Gibson as the only pitchers who had hit two World Series home runs.

The Reds narrowed the lead to 8–3 in the seventh, prompting Bamberger to come to the mound for a few words with Dave. He stayed in.

In the middle of the seventh, NBC color man Tony Kubek tracked down Jean and her son, Jeff, in the stands. He asked Jean what she thought of her husband's homer. "Great. So exciting"

"I don't know why you're so nervous. Dave doesn't look nervous at all," Kubek said.

"I think he is," Jean said. "I'm having a tough time settling down. I'm sure he is, trying to pitch."

Then Kubek turned to Jeff and put his microphone in front of the seven-year-old, wearing a suit and a tie. "Jeff, when your pop came up with the bases loaded, what were you thinking about?" Kubek asked.

"I thought he wasn't going to get a hit. I thought he was going to get out," Jeff replied with a perfect youngster deadpan.

He would be reminded of his innocent, youthful doubts about his father's hitting ability fifty years later, almost two decades after Dave's death.

Although Dave had been a good hitter when he played Little League baseball in Billings, he wasn't a serious threat at the plate in 1970. A southpaw who batted right-handed, Dave drove in just six runs in 105 at-bats that year.

"It just took me all year to set them (the RBIs) up," he quipped in an interview thirty years later.[14]

A career .133 hitter, Dave hit eleven home runs during his fourteen-year big league career. That output included a two-run homer against New York Mets pitcher Koosman in the third inning of Game Five of the 1969 World Series. He also hit a regular-season grand slam home run against the Oakland A's on August 26, 1968.

Dave said he could hit one pitch, "a belt-high, inside fastball. That's the only pitch I could hit, and that happened to be where (Granger) threw it," he said. "I had no visions of hitting a home run."

"I knew it was a strike, and I swung. I knew I hit it pretty well, but I hadn't hit enough home runs to know for sure that it was out of the park."

Jeff wasn't the only one who doubted Dave's hitting ability during the 1970 World Series. Two thousand miles away, his sister, Dee, oldest of Beth McNally's four children, sat in the boardroom of a prestigious Phoenix law firm on that afternoon in October 1970. Dee wondered how her "baby brother," as she had called him when he was a Little League player in Billings, would respond in what became the biggest moment of his baseball career.

Dee Nobles—her married name—was a legal secretary who started her career in Billings. The prospect of better pay prompted her to move to Phoenix. There, she joined a firm in which John J. O'Connor was a principal. His wife, Sandra Day O'Connor, would become the first woman named to the U.S. Supreme Court after her 1981 nomination as a justice by President Reagan.

"He was one of the nicest persons I've met in life," Dee recalled of John O'Connor.[15]

The firm where Dee worked included lawyers who were baseball fans, enough so that they planned to watch the TV broadcast of Game 3 of the 1970 World Series in the firm's boardroom. O'Connor and others knew Dee was Dave's sister. Thus, it might have seemed natural to include her in the group watching the game on TV. Then and now, however, an unwritten rule in many law firms was that lawyers and legal secretaries didn't socialize. Lawyers in this firm, though, invited Dee to join them.

"That was very atypical," she said more than a half-century later. The group settled in to watch the game. Then, in the sixth, came the big moment for Dave—and his big sister.

"Dave came up to bat. I said, 'Oh, no, he can't hit the broad side of a barn.' And then he cracked that grand slam. I never lived that down around the firm."

Dee said Johnny Carson later had Brooks Robinson and her brother on his late-night TV show. Brooks, a lifetime friend of McNally, couldn't resist a wisecrack at his teammate's expense. "Brooks said, 'I always thought Dave would get in the record books, but for his pitching, not his hitting,'" Dee said, still smiling about the memory many years later.

The rest of the game was routine. Dave gave up the Reds' final two runs in the top of the seventh. The scores came on Concepcion's sacrifice fly that brought in Lee May, who had walked, and Rose's single that drove in Tommy Helms, who had reached base on a force out.

Dave gave up two more singles, to May in the eighth, and to Helms in the ninth, on his way to a complete-game victory. Afterwards, baseball writers headed to the locker rooms to hear Dave describe his home run for the ages, and to hear Granger tell what had gone wrong when he served the fateful pitch.

"I was vacant as I ran around the bases," Dave said.[16] "My head was ringing from the crowd noise. I was so excited by the time I got to the dugout that I didn't hear anything that was said. I don't even remember what I said. All I know is that I was screaming."

Dave described the setup to his homer: "I was standing flat-footed. I was trying not to bail out (step toward third base) and was trying to keep from striking out by just hitting the ball."

Granger didn't have any excuses for his pitch that Dave clubbed over the wall. "McNally swings the bat good. We knew he was dangerous. The place I threw the ball (fast ball up, about belt high) was right where you're not supposed to throw it."

It was the first grand slam home run the Reds' relief star had given up. He couldn't resist a sardonic comment about having his name go in the record books alongside Dave's. "I save those kind (of pitches) until there are sixty million people watching," Granger said.

A rueful Sparky Anderson wondered if his powerful Reds would ever get a break. "Every mistake we've made, they've hit out of the ballpark. They told us McNally would hit the high fastball out of there. And that's exactly what we gave him to hit. It's in that book (the Reds' scouting report on Baltimore). You definitely are not going to beat this club by expecting them to beat themselves."

The Orioles captured their second World Series with a 4–1 edge over the Reds. Winning pitchers for the Birds, besides McNally, were Palmer, Phoebus, and Cuellar. Now, the Orioles could enjoy the winter off-season, and the McNally family could enjoy living in Lutherville.

CHAPTER EIGHTEEN

LUTHERVILLE DAYS

Lutherville, Maryland, where the McNally family lived for most of their time when Dave pitched for the Orioles, was a community of about 24,000 people in 1970. The Baltimore suburb proved an attractive place for the McNallys to raise their family when they lived away from Billings. Before moving to Lutherville, Dave and Jean McNally and their oldest son, Jeff, lived in a house in Baltimore where their neighbors included Orioles' first baseman Boog Powell, his wife, Janet, and their children. "Dave's kids and my kids, we lived like two doors apart on a street in Baltimore," Powell recalled.[1] "He (McNally) bought Brooks Robinson's old house, and I bought two doors down."

Powell said he first met Dave in 1961 when they both played in the Arizona Winter Instructional League. As young major-leaguers, they both played on the same winter ball team in Puerto Rico for two years, the limit under baseball rules. Back home in Baltimore, the McNallys and the Powells often got together to play cards, and their eldest children, Jeff McNally and John W. Powell, nicknamed "JW," were playmates as kids.

Mark Braff's 2023 book, *Sons of Baseball: Growing Up with a Major League Dad*, includes Jeff McNally's memories of his early life in the Baltimore area. Jeff was born in Billings in 1963, his father's first full year as a major-leaguer, but his mother soon came back with him to Baltimore. Jeff remembered living "right around the corner" from the Powells. "I have this very vivid memory of those little fire trucks with pedals. (JW and I) were two or three years old or whatever, and we used to meet out on the sidewalk. We each had one of those things and we kind of tooled around on them."

The McNallys lived in Baltimore for about three years, and then they moved to the Lutherville-Timonium area and lived there from 1966 until 1975, when Dave retired from baseball, sold the Maryland house, and moved his family back to Billings. Jeff said he grew up in "a great neighborhood. We lived in a development in the suburbs, just kind of classic suburban life." Next to their housing development was a cornfield, a vestige of when the neighborhood had been a farm. Jeff, JW, and other youngsters rummaged in the cornfield and made a fort there. "We'd get in trouble with the farmer 'cause we didn't know what we were doing, but we were like killing his corn by rolling around, forming forts and trails and things like that."

Besides building forts, Jeff and his friends found large open lots where they played baseball, "and that was really fun."

Jeff remembered his father being around the house a lot in the winter. Jerry Hoffberger, owner of the Orioles, also owned a brewery, and Dave and other players worked there in the offseason. "I can remember (Dad) heading off to work a few times. He did sales or something, but that was just for maybe one or two winters."

Jeff's memories include seeing his father, wearing "those old, gray sweats," leave for the local YMCA where the former high school basketball star joined a group of Orioles players who played hoops as part of their off-season workouts.

Jean McNally took Jeff to most Orioles home games, starting when he was very young. When he got older, he got to spend time in the locker room after games. He and his mother sat in a section in the Memorial Stadium stands where players' families had tickets. "And I just remember that feeling of being around all those wives and kids, and it was a really fun experience," Jeff said.

When the McNallys moved to Lutherville, it was "a little outskirts town," Jean said, tapping memories from events almost sixty years old.[2] "It was just a new development that we bought in and a new house." The town's allure included good schools, she said.

In an August 1971 newspaper article, Jean described her family's life in Lutherville and the routine they followed as Dave pursued his big-league career. The McNallys lived in a "comfortable" tri-level house, on a quarter-acre lot. Old trees shaded the four-bedroom house, furnished in contemporary style. Jean was redoing the family room using wet-look vinyl and glass-topped tables: She was choosing the furniture herself and getting help to put together "a well-decorated" look.

The house, in the 800 block of Jamieson Road, still stood in 2024 and was well-maintained then.[3]

Dave and Jean then had three children: Jeff, eight; Pamela, seven; and Susan, who turned two in September 1971. The McNallys would add two more children, Anne and Mike, both born in Billings after their father retired from baseball and returned home.

Jean said she and her children socialized with neighbors when the Orioles were on road trips. The McNallys entertained little, but they occasionally hosted small dinner parties and occasional neighborhood get-togethers. The McNallys socialized with other Orioles players and their families who lived nearby in Lutherville: Brooks Robinson, Jim Palmer and Dick Hall.

Jean, born and raised in cold and snowy Billings, said she especially enjoyed traveling to warm, sunny south Florida every year for spring training. "I really look forward to just packing up and leaving the cold weather behind come February," she said. Jeff, Pamela, and Susan accompanied their parents on the Florida jaunts. The older two children got some tutoring, and their teachers in Lutherville prepared schoolwork for them to take with them when they were away.

"Right now, their education is not a problem," Jean said, "but I know as they get older and their lessons are more demanding, it will become more difficult for us to make the annual trip. Still, she hoped her children could keep going to Florida when the Orioles were in spring training. "Right now, I feel it's more important for us all to be together than to split up the family for those six weeks. Dave is gone so much anyway, and we always miss him."

Jean said she was glad for the late-winter phase of her family's lives because Dave didn't have to travel during spring training. She said she was used to and accepted his traveling during the baseball season. "That's why in the wintertime, I think we should be together as much as possible."

Jean said she thought that a mother should raise her children as much as possible instead of relying on a nanny or babysitter to handle those duties. She said her children were "so much company" and as they grew older, they stayed tight knit. "We do lots of active things together, and then we have our quiet times for playing games or reading stories."

That August, she and the children had vacationed in Billings while the Orioles were on a road trip. They also had a brief seashore holiday.

Jean, the youngest of her family of five children, didn't like being away from her own children too long. Because of that, she was cutting short the month-long trip to Japan that Orioles management had arranged for players and their wives in October. She and several other players' wives planned to go for just the first two weeks.

Jean and her children had a membership at a nearby country club where she played golf, and Jeff swam on the club team. Jean played golf every Tuesday, and her nine-hole score was usually about 58, "but that fluctuates." She said she took up the sport a year earlier so she could be with her husband playing the game he loved best besides baseball. "Now I'm getting hooked on it and can understand why my husband can jump out of bed at five a.m. to go play golf! I find myself getting up at six a.m. on a golf day, and I get very anxious to get out on the course."

Jean enjoyed baking, and her most successful recipes included several of Dave's favorite goodies: banana cream pie, chocolate cake, and chocolate chip cookies. The liking for those sweets, by all the McNallys, meant that "it seems I'm always baking those."

She acknowledged that being married to someone who had achieved the fame that Dave had brought with it drawbacks. "Sometimes I feel everyone knows what's going on in our life, and I get moments when all I want is for people to forget Dave's a major-league pitcher and give us some privacy." Still, "I really do enjoy almost everything about our life: the excitement, the travel, the pleasant times, and that wonderful winter trip I mentioned earlier."

And, as 1971 started, the Orioles would get Pat Dobson in a trade and add him to a standout, history-making mound staff.

CHAPTER NINETEEN

GREATEST PITCHING ROTATION EVER

After the 1970 season, Dick Cavett invited Dave and Brooks Robinson to appear on his nighttime TV show, but things didn't go as planned during Dave's interaction with the cerebral TV host. "I almost walked off when he introduced himself and asked which one of us was Brooks Robinson. We had been told he knew something about baseball," McNally said.[1]

As 1971 began, Dave knew he and the Orioles couldn't rest on the laurels of the team's World Series triumph over the Reds three months earlier, or his first-ever Series grand-slam home run by a pitcher. In early January, the winter banquet season was still a month away, and Dave and his teammates had received and banked their winners-share checks from the Series. Now it was time to get in shape before life became hectic.[2] "Starting early makes for a short winter," he said while in Baltimore, "but I'll be on the go just about the entire month of January and won't have a chance to work out at all."

Dave, who owned three twenty-win seasons in a row, didn't think he'd have many conditioning days at spring training camp in February. For two years, he had been a holdout and a late arrival, seeking a better contract, and he expected 1971 to be the third year he would try to use the only leverage he had in getting a better deal. For the first time, Dave had hired an agent, this from the Mark McCormack firm in Cleveland, and his goal was a $300,000 salary in 1971.

Meanwhile, away from the money talk, Orioles coach Billy Hunter and the team's promotions director Bud Freeman talked some Birds into taking a break from golf to work out and play basketball at a local YMCA.

Unlike a couple years earlier, when several players got together, formed a basketball team and played without club permission, earning two players fines of $300 apiece, having a hoops team this year was completely OK with the Birds brass. "We're all for it now," said Personnel Director Harry Dalton, "because the advantages far outweigh the disadvantages and face it, it's an ideal way to get the players out and close to the public in the offseason."

Many celebrity teams played games that degenerated into fooling around on the court. Not so the Orioles, with a team that included several players who had starred as basketball players in their youth, Dave among them. In 1970, the Birds basketball team won about twelve straight games, all by comfortable margins, before it lost, and that game, which Dalton saw, was marked by more than his guys being on the losing end. "It was a real close game, and it got a little rough at the end. That was the night Eddie (Watt) busted a finger. It was an accident, though, so we have no objections to the guys playing again."

Besides Dave and Watt, others on the basketball team included Richert, Hall, Blair, Motton, and Brooks Robinson. Robinson, however, wasn't expected to be around much since he was a headliner on the banquet circuit after earning Most Valuable Player honors in the 1970 Series.

"I'm kinda glad they're letting them play basketball again," Hunter said. "Doing calisthenics and running around the gym can get pretty boring."

The Orioles got Dobson in a trade with the San Diego Padres to start the season. A big righthander, he was one of three newcomers on the Orioles roster, and Dobson didn't quibble with a theory advanced by Weaver that a trade could rejuvenate a pro baseball player.

"Quite a few guys need it. They get self-satisfied. This shakes them up a little bit, gets them back on the right track," he said.[3]

Four years later, Weaver's theory would get another test involving McNally.

"Let's see," Dobson said, "in the past 11 years, I've been traded twice, and I ended up having my best years ever with the new club."

"Say, maybe Earl's got something there."

The Detroit Tigers had shipped Dobson to San Diego before the 1970 season began. If he had stayed in the Motor City, he might have gotten 100 innings of relief pitching, but going to the Padres allowed him to start and pitch more–250 innings in fact. And that caught the eye of Orioles executives.

They envisioned him as part of a rotation that included fellow righty Palmer plus southpaws Dave and Cuellar. But why had the lowly Padres given up a pitcher who, with 14 wins in 1970, tallied about twenty percent of their sixty-three wins?

"I had no problems in San Diego," Dobson said, "but if there's one thing the Padres have, it's young pitching. They obviously figured at 28 and coming off a good year was a good time to trade me, so they could open up a spot in the rotation for one of their young pitchers."

Dave's hometown *Billings Gazette* gave him more ink on January 21, 1971. When he came home, it gave him a full-page spread with the headline, THANKS AGAIN, DAVE. The paper pictured McNally with his Legion coach, Ed Bayne, and another former Legion star, Hahn, who had once played in the St. Louis Cardinals' farm system. Another photo showed a drawing of Dave, "Billings' Own Man of the Hour," with twelve-year-old Danny Fuchs standing next to it, waiting for Dave's autograph.

A writeup with the photos described Dave as "a homespun boy come home to Montana to help Montanans less fortunate than himself." They included six-year-old Rodney Fisher of Billings, Montana's 1971 Easter Seals child of the year. Dave was the featured speaker on January 20, 1971, at the Easter Seals society banquet, attended by about 400 people who showered their love on one of their own.[4]

A question-and-answer period followed the showing of the World Series highlight film, and one unidentified person harkened back to Dave's youth with his question. "You wouldn't have any trouble with Willie Horton if you would throw him a slider on the inside corner. I saw you throw two fastballs to Horton one day, and he hit them both for home runs," the man said. "I told you when you were fifteen years old that you had a great slider. If you would keep them around his knees on the inside corner, he wouldn't give you any trouble."

Dave grinned. "All right. I'll try it and if it works, I'll give you a call." The crowd roared.

Someone else asked Dave what pitch from Reds' reliever Granger he hit for his 1970 Series grand slam homer. "It was a low and inside slider," Dave said, getting another roar from the crowd.

Billings also capitalized on Dave's fame through a sale of baseball gloves autographed by him. Bayne said a few McNally gloves would go on sale in Billings in January. "This is the first time a pitcher's name has appeared on a glove," said a representative from the national firm making the glove.

And if Dave had another twenty-win season, the firm planned to produce the glove for national distribution. The glove, based on what Brooks Robinson used, was built with special modifications that Dave had suggested. Bayne called it an all-around glove for infielders, outfielders, and pitchers.[5]

The winter banquet circuit took Dave to Spokane, where he was a guest speaker at the Washington city's annual sports award banquet. A local sportswriter wanted Dave to talk about his accomplishments, but he focused instead on Brooks Robinson's heroics in the 1970 series. "He's a fantastic guy," Dave said. "Not only is he a greater hitter, but he's one of those kind of people that you really like to see good things happen to. There are a lot of great ballplayers in the majors, but Robbie also is a great person."[6]

Robinson had just won the Hickok Award as the top Professional Athlete in 1970, and Dave said, "I couldn't have been happier if I won it myself."

Dave again was Weaver's pick for opening-day pitching duties. On April 7, 1971, he pitched a complete-game, 3–2 win over Washington. The Senators got nine hits, but Dave's all-time nemesis, slugger Frank Howard, who dinged McNally for thirteen home runs during his career, could not hit one out of the park that day.[7]

Oakland Athletics pitcher Vida Blue was the talk of baseball in 1971, and Jean McNally joined the bandwagon of his fans. Dave pitched the Orioles to a 3–1 win over the California Angels on May 6 after hearing his wife sing the praises of the twenty-one-year-old strikeout whiz. "My wife is really impressed by him—pitching four shutouts and striking out twelve or fourteen almost every time he starts," Dave said.[8] "When I left home to come to the ballpark, Jeannie said, 'Pretend you're Vida Blue.' She usually doesn't make wisecracks like that."

Even though he had posted three twenty-win seasons, Dave acknowledged he wasn't comparable to the A's wunderkind. "Under no circumstances was I Vida Blue," he said after beating the Angels.

"Attaboy, Dave. You really dazzled them with that garbage," said a needling Powell.

Was Dave mad at Powell as he and the Orioles approached "Vida Blue Night," when they would play the Athletics at Memorial Stadium? Nope. "I just know he's telling the truth. Besides, Boog's too big to argue with anyhow."

Reviewing his three-hit, three-walk performance against the Angels, which gave him a 5–1 record for the season, Dave said, "I didn't have any curveball. All I was trying to do was throw fastballs, anyway." He said his fastball was "nothing exciting," but he "kept it away from their hitters pretty good."

Dave fanned two Angels on his new change-of-pace pitch, an off-speed, semi-screwball but preferred to discuss his hitting, although the Angels' Andy Messersmith held him hitless. "The first time, I had to bunt. The second time, Messersmith threw me two sliders and a hook. That'll put me down a lot of times."

Then it was time to shower and join his wife at home. Surely, Jean wouldn't mention Vida Blue again.

Now, members of the Big Four, as McNally, Palmer, Cuellar, and new arrival Pat Dobson came to be known, headed for membership in the twenty-win club. Dave joined first, on September 21 when he shut out the Yankees, 5–0, on five hits. Remarkably, in notching his first shutout of the season, he faced just thirty-three batters and didn't allow more than one hit in any inning.[9]

Ironically, it appeared early in the summer that Dave might struggle to post another twenty-win season or approach that exalted territory at all. He had to sit out for thirty-eight days, from July 6 to August 13, because of a sore arm.

"Where's the champagne?" Blair shouted as he entered the Orioles clubhouse after the win over the Yankees.

"We only have champagne for unusual events," Dave Leonhard hollered back.

Well, it was as good an occasion as any to crack open the bubbly stuff, given the history-making nature of what Dave had just accomplished. He was just the eleventh pitcher in AL history to have won twenty games four years in a row, and Dave posted the best winning percentage during that streak of all the others except Lefty Grove.

Dave, from 1968 through that point in 1971, had a won-loss record of 86–31 for a .735 winning percentage. Grove, playing for Connie Mack's Philadelphia Athletics from 1928 through 1931, compiled a record of 103–23 with an .818 winning percentage.[10] "I always dreamed when I was a kid of someday pitching in the big leagues, but I never dreamed of anything approaching this," said Dave, calling the win his best game of the year.

Next in the twenty-win club came Cuellar and Dobson, who won both games of a doubleheader in Cleveland on September 24 to clinch the American League East title with the Orioles' sixth straight win.[11]

Cuellar reached the plateau next with a 9–2 win over the Indians fueled by home runs from Johnson, Frank Robinson and Powell. It was Cuellar's third twenty-win season in a row, and, just like in the fifth game of the 1970 World Series, he got in trouble in the first inning when he gave up a two-run homer to Ray Fosse.

Cuellar, however, settled down and allowed just three hits in the final six innings. His eight-hitter included one stretch where he retired 12 Indians in a row. Dobson was even better in the nightcap when he threw a six-hitter to blank Cleveland, 7–0.

Palmer joined the twenty-win club on September 26 when he shut out Cleveland, 5-0, on a three-hitter. The Orioles' sweep of a four-game series with the Indians was their eighth win in a row.[12]

1971 was a turbulent time, with the Vietnam War continuing and the country still reeling from the shooting of students at Kent State

University in May 1970. So, Orioles owner Hoffberger couldn't help but contrast the world outside with what he saw in his team's visitors' clubhouse in Cleveland.

"Wouldn't it be nice if all the world could be this happy?" he said.

After he, executive vice-president Harry Dalton, formerly the team's personnel director, and Frank Cashen, who had just stepped down as executive vice-president, together made a complete round of the room. Congratulating all the players and coaches, they paraded through Weaver's office. "Gee whiz!" Hoffberger exclaimed. "This is just like the first one (the 1966 pennant). Everyone is a new one. It's really something to look around here–really great. How about that! This is one of the great things about baseball. It's a good game, a peaceful game, a happy game and a non-violent game."

The Orioles entered the World Series respecting the Pittsburgh Pirates but confident they had an edge on the Roberto Clemente- and Willie Stargell-led Bucs. Under manager Danny Murtaugh, they had won the National League East with a 97–65 record, then dispatched the NL West champion San Francisco Giants, 3–1, in the league playoffs. Baltimore had reeled off a 101–57 record to nab the AL East crown for the third year in a row, and then the Orioles had swept the AL West title-winning Oakland A's, 3–1, to reach the Series a third straight time.

On paper, it looked very good for the Orioles, playing their third full year with Weaver as manager; he had become skipper with eighty-two games left in the 1968 season. They had not only the AL's best four starting pitchers, but the best in the majors, in McNally, Cuellar, Palmer, and Dobson, the twenty-game winners who together had won 89 percent of their games, 81 of 112. Baltimore's mound staff ranked first among the twelve AL teams in six pitching metrics, runs given up, earned runs, earned-run average, complete games, walks given up, and, of course, total wins.[13]

Hitting? The Birds weren't shabby in that department either. Their .261 batting average topped the AL, and they had scored more runs, 742, than any other team in the junior league. They also ranked first in on-base percentage and walks awarded.[14] And none of the Memorial

Stadium faithful could complain much about the Orioles' defense, which ranked second in the league in fielding percentage (.981) and errors charged (112).[15]

Weaver tapped Dave to pitch the Series opener in Baltimore. He faced the Pirates' Dock Ellis, a nineteen-game winner. However, he was more famous, perhaps, for pitching a no-hitter the season before while under the influence of the hallucinogenic drug LSD.[16]

Weaver said he would use a left-right-left pitching rotation, with the option for change as needed. Palmer would start in Game 2, Cuellar to Game 3, and Dobson to Game 4, although Dobson would work out of the bullpen when the Series started that weekend.

Dobson's eventual status as starter or reliever would depend on Dave's effectiveness in the first game. "If the lefthanders are successful, I can use them in five of seven games, if necessary. If not, I can use righthanders in four games," Weaver said.

He called Dobson his "ace of trumps," someone he could bring in if a starter got an early lead but got in trouble. For Weaver, having Dobson available in long relief would be just like he started the game.

Weaver said he decided on Dave as the starter in the opener after consulting with super scouts Russo and Walter Youse. "Their report indicated that Pittsburgh has a balanced attack from either side of the plate, but we came up with more reasons to pitch a lefthander against them," he said.

Weaver said he had watched the Bucs' playoff win over the Giants on TV and was impressed with their power hitting, starting with Stargell, the major-league home run champ with 48, and continuing to Richie Hebner and Al Oliver. The latter two players were lefthanders, which prompted Weaver to peg southpaws McNally and Cuellar as Baltimore's starters in the first and third games.

Dave went through several nicknames during his big-league career. First, he was "Dave McLucky," a reference to his knack for winning, thanks to breaks, despite his pitching not being up to the highest standards. Then, in the 1971 Series opener, wags started calling him "McUnlucky" after he gave the Pirates three easy runs early in the game, but then Dave shut out the Bucs on one hit the rest of the way, leading the Birds to a 5–3 victory. That got him the moniker of "Dave McPlucky" from some in the press box.[17]

"That's what makes him such a great pitcher. He's some kind of competitor," said Orioles catcher Elrod Hendricks, who committed the error that contributed to the three unearned runs that Dave gave up in the second inning. "Dave never lets anything get him down."

"I'll tell ya," said coach Billy Hunter. "He's gutty son-uva-gun. He finds a way to win."

Dave stayed focused despite a serious matter off the field. His son, Jeff, then eight, was seriously injured three days before the game in a bicycle collision with another youngster near the McNally's Lutherville home. Doctors needed twenty-three stitches to close a deep, four-inch gash above and below Jeff's right elbow, next to the bone. "I was very worried," Dave said. "It bothered me a lot until Friday afternoon, when we were told that there was no nerve damage. Jeff had been complaining of numbness. It took the doctors an hour to sew it up."

The Orioles went up, 2–0, behind Palmer, who controlled the Pirates on seven hits in an easy 11–3 win, but the Bucs came back at their park, Three Rivers Stadium, to win Game Three, 5–1. Steve Blass held the Birds to three hits to beat Cuellar, who Weaver removed after the sixth inning. By then, he had given up seven hits and all five Pittsburgh runs, four of them earned. Frank Robinson provided Baltimore's only excitement with a solo homer in the first, but Pittsburgh answered with Bob Robertson's three-run homer in the seventh.

Next, Pittsburgh edged visiting Baltimore, 4–3, using three pitchers to beat the Orioles, who sent four hurlers to the mound. Bruce Kison got the win for the Pirates, and Dobson took the loss. Kison gave up one hit in 6 1/3 innings and got his most batting help from Al Oliver, who plated two runs.

Then it was Game Five, and Dave got another turn. He suffered the Orioles' 4–0 loss, lasting four innings in which he yielded seven hits and four runs, three of them earned. Two wild pitches hurt his chances, and Robertson dinged him with a solo homer to lead off the second inning.[18]

Stating what may have seemed obvious, Dave said, "I depend a lot on my control, and for some reason, I didn't have it today."[19]

Dave's fortunes improved in Game Six of the series. Palmer, the Birds' starter, pitched magnificently into the ninth inning before leaving for a pinch hitter. First, Weaver brought in Dobson in relief, but he gave up a Dave Cash single and an intentional walk to Clemente as the Pirates threatened to win. So, with two left-handed batters next in the Bucs' order, Weaver called on McNally for his first relief appearance since July 19, 1969.

He didn't make it easy; he walked Stargell to load the bases, but Oliver's fly ball to center field ended the threat. Then, in the bottom of the tenth inning, the Orioles got the winning run from Frank Robinson, who walked, advanced on a Rettenmund single and came home on Brooks Robinson's sacrifice fly.

McNally thus got his seventh and final World Series win.[20]

Baltimoreans mourned the next day. A Memorial Stadium crowd of 47,291 saw the Pirates win the seventh and deciding game, 2–1. They became just the sixth team in World Series to lose the first two games and become champions.[21]

CHAPTER TWENTY

WINDING DOWN

Dave didn't set the American League on fire during his final three years with the Orioles, 1972, 1973, and 1974. Yet, he remained a solid major-league pitcher as he marched towards becoming the Birds all-time winningest pitcher at that time.

Although he slumped to a 13–17 win-loss record in 1972, he pitched five shutouts that season, all complete-game performances. In 1973, he went 17–17 and opened the year by shutting out Milwaukee and Detroit; he threw three more shutouts to run his season to five again. And in 1974, his last year wearing an Orioles uniform, he blanked the Yankees twice and shut out Cleveland and Kansas twice for four shutouts en route to a 16–10 win-loss record, giving him 181 wins as a Baltimore pitcher.

Here are some McNally highlights from those seasons.

1972

Baseball's first player strike, a thirteen-day pension dispute, delayed the start of the season, but the time spent not playing didn't seem to affect Dave, who opened with shutouts over New York and Cleveland, the double blanking a first for him.

And, pun intended, Powell was just trying to avoid striking out when he clinched the win over the Indians with a ninth-inning grand slam home run.[1]

"I was very happy after Boog's home run. I was very relieved when that ball left the park," Dave said after the blast ended his pitching duel with Indians pitchers.

"I've never thrown two shutouts in a row before, though," Dave said.

"I think it's because of the strike. I just know I'm throwing pitches that are hittable, but the batters aren't hitting the pitches they usually do. I've noticed the same thing on our club, even more so. When they get their pitch, they're not hitting it. Their timing is off because of that layoff."

Under regular circumstances, when there hadn't been a strike to cause batters to become rusty, Dave said he still might have had a shutout, but it would have been a seven- or eight-hit showing instead of the three hits that the Indians got. He noted that while he wasn't a big strikeout pitcher, he only whiffed one batter that night.

Dave acknowledged he had near-perfect control against Cleveland, which got just one walk. "I stayed ahead of them most of the way, with a couple exceptions, but they were hitting my first pitch a lot. Since the strike ended, I thought control might be a problem for the pitchers. It has surprised me quite a bit that the pitchers have been so effective. The strike has affected the hitters more."

Powell agreed.

"I'd be crazy to say it hasn't," he said. "When the strike ended spring training, I felt as sharp as I've ever been at that time."

The Orioles first baseman said he didn't feel he was swinging the bat badly, but he only had a single and a double in sixteen at-bats before smashing the fifth grand slam of his career.

"But right now, I'm just beginning to feel closer to the way I was when spring training ended," and the strike began.

Dave had started 1972 with his lingering arm problems seemingly behind him, but by the end of the season, rumblings of a repeat of those problems were common in the country's newspaper sports sections.

KUDOS FROM NIXON

Six years after he met President Johnson, Dave's record was outstanding enough to rate the attention of another White House occupant. In 1972, he got recognition from the most highly placed baseball fan in the country, President Richard Nixon, who named Dave to his 1945 to 1970 all-time baseball team. Here's the story behind that acclaim.

At the end of a June 22, 1972, press conference, Cliff Evans, a reporter for RKO General Broadcasting, asked the president to name his favorite baseball players. Nixon started naming players, but he stopped when he realized he would have to choose between legends.[2] "Mr. President, as the nation's number one baseball fan, would you be willing to name your all-time baseball team?" Evans asked.

"Yes," said Nixon, an honorary member of the Baseball Writers Association. Nixon went to work on the project on the following Sunday while at Camp David, the presidential retreat. He enlisted his son-in-law, David Eisenhower, to help him, tapping Eisenhower's baseball knowledge as a former staffer with the Washington Senators. (That team had just moved to Dallas to become the Texas Rangers.)

Writing about the effort, Nixon said, "We sat down together and began to study the record books for the purpose of compiling a list of stars which would stand up under the scrutiny such a selection would receive from the sportswriters and baseball fans throughout the country."

Nixon and Eisenhower did most of the work at Camp David. The president continued to revise his selections when he returned to the White House. Once Nixon had completed his teams, White House Press Secretary Ron Ziegler distributed the list, carrying Nixon's byline through the Associated Press. Newspapers could publish the list in their Sunday, July 2, 1972, editions. Shortly before the list was released, Nixon allowed Evans to conduct a short, exclusive interview with him.

Instead of creating a single, all-time list, Nixon selected a pre-war and a post-war team for each league. He said he found it impossible to limit the team to nine men. Nixon also selected only players active from 1925 on because that was when he started following baseball. He stopped in 1970 to give his evaluations perspective.

And how good was the company McNally was keeping in Nixon's estimation? He joined four other pitchers, two lefthanders and two righthanders, on the 1945–1970 team. All others were inducted into the Baseball Hall of Fame. They were: Bob Lemon, Cleveland southpaw, who won 207 games; Bob Feller, Cleveland's right hander, who won 266 games; Early Wynn, a righthander who played for Washington, Cleveland, and the Chicago White Sox and won 300 games; and Dave's childhood hero, fellow southpaw, Whitey Ford, who won 236 games for the New York Yankees. By the end of the 1970 season, Dave had won 114 of the 184 games he would win as a major leaguer.

At the end of the article he wrote, Nixon said, "The list, of course, could go on and on." He said he regretted having to "leave off some truly great star." Still, "if some smart reporter asks me to name an all-star football team, the answer will be a flat—NO!"

Dave thus gained the satisfaction of knowing that he had caught the eye of a second president.

1973

Dave started the season in a way that reminded observers of the Birds ace who had dominated the AL from 1968 through 1971. He shut out Milwaukee on three hits in Baltimore's opener, a 10–0 romp over the Brewers on April 6, and he followed up with another three-hit shutout as the Birds edged Detroit, 1–0, at the Tigers' ballpark on April 12.

Baltimore Sun sports editor Bob Maisel said that Dave "made it look almost too easy" in his win over Milwaukee.[3] Brooks Robinson cranked out two home runs, and Don Baylor had a highlight day at the plate with two doubles, a triple, and a home run. Afterward, as praise rained on Baylor in Baltimore's clubhouse, Dave joined the chorus. "I know one thing. I'm not even going to watch that guy hit from now on. It's downright demoralizing for a pitcher to watch anybody hit the ball like that."

Someone said that Dave might get his old "Dave McLucky" tag back. "That's okay with me," he said, grinning. "I just hope I didn't use up our runs for a while. Hope they saved some for the other fellows. I know one thing: it sure makes pitching easier when you jump out in front like that. I got dizzy watching our guys run around the bases. Downright enjoyable, wasn't it?"

Dave got personal satisfaction from the win over the Tigers because he didn't allow his longtime nemesis, Howard, now playing for Detroit, another home run. Howard, who played most of his career for the Washington Senators, socked more home runs off Dave during his career, thirteen, than anyone else, but he didn't damage the Orioles' ace on that early-season day in 1973.[4]

It was the bottom of the ninth in a scoreless game, and the Tigers had a runner on second base with Howard at the plate. Weaver came out to the mound to discuss the situation with Dave. "Well, Mac, what do ya wanta do?" asked the Orioles skipper.

"I wanta go home," Dave said in deadpan fashion.

If he was worried, his fear went away when he retired the six-foot-seven, 280-pound Howard on an infield popup. The Orioles then scratched out a run, and Orlando Peña got the final out with the bases loaded in the Tigers' half of the ninth to save Dave's win.

Dave pitched three more shutouts that year, giving him five for the season, and put together a trio of three-game winning streaks to end the regular season with a 17–17 record. Again, the Orioles reached the AL playoffs, but this time, when they faced the AL West champion Oakland A's, Baltimore's run of playoff success ran out. The A's won the series, 3–2, and Dave suffered a memorable 6–3 loss to Catfish Hunter in Game two on October 7.

Baltimore had won ten straight playoff games, going back to the 1969 start of the format, before that day. That's when the A's pounded Dave for four home runs en route to 6–3 victory. During his post-game comments, Dave said he had no complaints about any of his pitches—except where they landed.[5] And Weaver said the win didn't mean a thing because he didn't expect to stay unbeaten forever in playoff games.

Still, Baltimore's loss contained unusual elements. Dave had allowed only 16 home runs in 246 innings during the regular season and then was victimized by the A's. Hunter, meanwhile, had given up 39 home runs in 256 innings, four less than the AL record 43 homers yielded by Washington's Pete Ramos in 1957.

Against the Orioles in the playoff game, however, Hunter held the home team to six singles and a double before the Birds drove him out of the game in the eighth inning.

Dave acknowledged Oakland had found the long-ball mark against him during the season.

"Yes, five out of 16 in the regular season—more than their share, I'd say. Now it's nine, isn't it?"

The playoffs moved to Oakland, and the A's got the edge in Game 3. They edged the Orioles, 2–1, in 11 innings. Ken Holtzman was the winning pitcher, and Cuellar took the loss. The A's now led, 2–1, in the five-game series. Baltimore stayed alive with a 5–4 win in Game 4. Grant Jackson picked up the win, and Rollie Finger shouldered the loss.

Now it was the day for deciding Game 5. This was the day that sealed Dave's antagonism toward Earl Weaver. It's not clear when the player's animosity towards his manager began, but Palmer frequently quoted Dave as saying about Weaver, in reference to Weaver's days as a minor league player and his inability to make a major-league roster: "The only thing Weaver knows about pitching is that he can't hit it."

A headline in the *Baltimore Sun* on October 11, 1973, set the scene for what would happen: ALEXANDER SET; MCNALLY HURT? Writer Doug Brown said twenty-three-year-old Doyle Alexander would start for the Orioles, "but if you're wondering why it's not Dave McNally, you're not alone."

It was Dave's turn to take the mound. Yes, Oakland had rocked him for four home runs, but Dave had gotten three days' rest since that debacle. He was considered the Orioles' number two pitcher behind Palmer. "Then why a kid like Alexander in such a crucial game?" Brown asked.

He allowed Weaver to explain. The short, stocky skipper—he stood only five-foot-seven—pointed to Dave's four-home-run outing. He said A's manager Dick Williams, well aware of how his team had feasted on Dave's pitching his last time out, would load his lineup with at least seven right-hander hitters to try to take advantage of Dave.

Also, Weaver, a forerunner of Moneyball strategy with its emphasis on data-driven analytics, kept fastidious records. He remembered that in April 1973, Alexander relieved Dave and retired thirteen straight A's batters. Weaver also remembered that Alexander pitched a five-hitter against the As in May.

More was going on, though. No one was saying it out loud. Dave was denying it, but observers suspected he was battling elbow problems. "My arm is fine," he said, but his manager thought otherwise. "He tells me his arm is okay, but he has thrown a lot of innings this year," Weaver said.

Dr. Leonard Wallenstein, the team physician, shared Weaver's worry. "He tells me his arm is fine, too," Wallenstein said, doubt in his voice. "Dave had tendinitis in his elbow a few years ago. I think maybe after the season we should take some X-rays." The record is not clear, but possibly it was the same injury that sidelined Dave for more than a month in 1971.

Palmer was firmly on Dave's side then and decades later, although he emphasized that he had nothing against Alexander. "Doyle ended up having a pretty good career, but he didn't have the experience, the track record, at the time," Palmer said, apparently putting himself in the camp of those who thought Weaver shouldn't have plugged in Doyle for Weaver in a crucial, late-season game."6

Alexander, meanwhile, seemed oblivious to the simmering dispute between Weaver and Dave.

"I'm glad to get the opportunity. We can only do one of two things—win or lose," he said before the game that would determine the American League representative in the 1973 Series.

Whatever the rationale, Weaver's gambit didn't work. Alexander could not repeat his earlier success against Oakland. The A's collected five hits and three runs, one of them unearned, in 3 2/3 innings before Weaver replaced him with Palmer. The right-hander shut out the A's on two hits the rest of the way, but Hunter silenced the Orioles' bats. They lost, 3–0. Oakland was headed to the World Series. They repeated as World Champions in 1973 and picked up their third straight crown in 1974.

1974

Dave took part in major-league baseball's newly instituted salary arbitration process before the season began. The experience would prove valuable a year later. Players and management agreed to salary arbitration in 1973, and at first, the sports world yawned about the new way of doing things or ignored it.7 But that indifference changed as the 1974 season dawned when arbitration changed into a major part of the game, with potentially far-reaching effects. "Players who normally limit their cover items to money and women have been whittling away their time in the clubhouse discussing the various arbitration cases," a *Baltimore Sun* correspondent wrote.

Orioles general manager Cashen and his peers on other clubs preferred to not discuss arbitration, but not because it wasn't on their minds. It was because they had spent so much time that winter working on players' arbitration cases when they would rather get back to more routine duties like fining a player for long hair.

Observers, however, pointed out that arbitration, now baked into the basic agreement between players and owners, would be part of the game at least until the two-year labor agreement expired. And it was likely to endure beyond that, and the concept was likely to spread to other professional sports, especially football. "I think the important thing is to keep arbitration in context," said Marvin Miller, head of the players union. "The first thing to ask is, what does it replace? It replaces a system where a club could say to a player, 'You take what I offer you or you don't play.' In that context, arbitration can't help but be positive and constructive."

Future Hall of Famer Brooks Robinson, by then starting his twentieth season with the Birds, took a measured view of arbitration. "I think it makes both sides realistic, and it's a good way to settle things. You've got to look at baseball as a business. The club is the employer, and it's their job to get you as cheap as they can."

Cashen, while he might argue Robinson's last point, conceded that arbitration was going to be lasting. "It's here, and I imagine it's going to stay. Yet, I don't think it's the panacea for all the ills in the salary system."

TRYING SALARY ARBITRATION

Dave dipped his toes in the salary arbitration pool on February 11, 1974. He and teammates Blair and Bobby Grich were among four dozen players who went down that route. The first hearing to use the recently gained right involved Harry Platt, a Detroit lawyer and labor arbitrator, who met with pitcher Dick Woodson and the Minnesota Twins for more than four hours.[8] Platt called the meeting historic because until then a player never had an option for pressuring his team's owner to meet his salary demands other than sitting out at the start of the season. And, given the relatively brief careers for most players, an average of about six years, that situation stacked the deck in favor of owners.

Dave was first up among the Orioles who desired arbitration. He was scheduled to meet in New York on February 21 with Cashen, the team's executive vice-president and general manager. Dave said there was about a $10,000 difference between what he wanted and what the Orioles offered him. His salary in 1973 was about $105,000.

"You can go back (to previous years of negotiations) when you thought you were not treated right, and that also has to be considered by the arbitrator," he said. He expected to have his agent, Ed Keating, and possibly a lawyer from the International Management Company of Cleveland accompany him at the hearing.

"I think we have always been fair in our dealings with the players and feel our offers are equitable and defendable," Cashen said.

Dave won his case. He learned of the ruling on February 26, but he greeted the victory with some bitterness.[9] "It was a helluva experience to go through," he said. "I learned a lot from it."

Dave said he didn't mind Cashen commenting on his playing ability or giving his opinion of his star pitcher. "But there were some things said during the hearing that I don't think should have been said. That's all I want to say about it."

Dave refused to elaborate, but he implied Cashen had violated some confidences during the hearing. "I don't want to discuss any of the cases publicly," Cashen said, referring to all three Orioles players who wanted arbitration. "It's over with. We won two cases and lost one."

Blair and Grich lost, but Dave was awarded a 1974 salary that was $10,000 more than the club wanted to pay him. That put his salary for the new season at an estimated $115,000, and he was aware that without arbitration, he and the Orioles would have remained $10,000 apart when he finally had to sign.

After his four twenty-win seasons in a row, Dave fell to a thirteen-win campaign in 1972 and a seventeen-win showing in 1973. He apparently based his case for more pay on the fact that the Orioles were shut out six times while he was pitching. Summarizing the three-and-one-half-hour hearing, Dave said the arbitrator asked few questions and was mostly a listener. "He seemed to know about baseball, but it was hard to tell what he was listening to and what he wasn't."

Dave described the hearing as more formal than he expected. "I had talked to Dick Moss (lawyer for the players association), and he told me it would be a very informal hearing with a relaxed atmosphere. But it was more like a regular court trial. Was I nervous? I sure was."

CHAPTER TWENTY-ONE

LIFE WITH WEAVER

Dave and Earl Weaver had a long history together, starting in 1961 when Dave played on the Fox Cities Foxes team Weaver managed in the Three-I League. Dave played for Elmira in the Eastern League in 1962, and again Weaver was his manager. Then, after Dave made the roster of the Orioles of 1963, the two went their separate ways until partway through the 1968 season when the Birds hired Weaver to manage. Dave played on three of the Orioles teams Weaver guided into the World Series, 1969, 1970, and 1971.

The sometimes-prickly relationship between the star southpaw pitcher and the future Hall of Fame manager appears to have heightened, if not started, late in the 1969 season. That's when Dave was aiming for his second straight twenty-win season, and the Orioles were cruising toward the AL East flag. Going into their game against the New York Yankees on September 20, 1969, the Orioles held a nineteen and one-half game lead over second-place Detroit, and their lead would bulge to twenty-two games before the Birds ended up nineteen games ahead when the regular season ended.

Weaver's crew had a shot at setting the league record for most wins in a season. At the time, the 1954 Cleveland Indians owned the mark with 111 wins; the Orioles ended up just short in 1969 with 109 victories, which today puts them at fifth on the AL all-time list.

Palmer witnessed a blowup between Dave and Weaver in 1969 and recalled it in a 2023 interview. The tiff occurred on September 20, when the Orioles survived the New York Yankees' two-run, ninth-inning rally, and posted an 8-7 win at Memorial Stadium. Earlier in the game, the Yankees built a 4-1 lead at McNally's expense, prompting his exit and replacement by Lopez. Lopez got the win, aided by reliever Pete Richert who picked up a save by stopping a Yanks rally in the ninth.[1]

The move that caused fireworks between Weaver and Dave occurred in the bottom of the fifth, with New York leading, 4-1. Bobby Floyd drew a walk from Yanks pitcher Al Downing, and number nine batter Dave was next up. Weaver called on Rettenmund to pinch-hit for Dave, leaving him stuck at nineteen wins that day. Dave was in the dugout, his batting helmet on, and he was holding his bat when Weaver told him he was pulling him for a pinch-hitter.

"I've got a chance to win twenty," an enraged Dave shouted at Weaver.

"I've gotta think of the other twenty-four guys," Weaver replied.

With an angry Dave positioned by the water cooler next to the dugout stairs, Weaver stood at the other end of the dugout. Dave threw down his helmet, his bat and his warmup jacket on the dirt. Then he went to the other end of the dugout, took three steps down, and went into the locker room, with Weaver running after him.

Palmer remembered his teammate's remarks. "Dave gives him a lecture on how you should treat your players who are getting close to (pitching) three hundred innings and starting forty games. And you know that you needed to give me an opportunity to win my twentieth game. ... You know, all you care about is setting the all-time record for wins. And not being loyal to the guys that are going to help you get to the World Series. And he was right."

"And Earl started crying. He made Earl Weaver cry. I never could do that," Palmer said.

Dave's sometimes contentious relationship with Earl Weaver flared up again in August 1970. *Baltimore Sun* writer Phil Jackman reported on a conversation between pitcher and manager that month. "A couple more weeks, and we'll start working you guys every fifth day instead of every fourth day–have you good and strong for the playoffs," Weaver said.

Dave gave Weaver a look resembling, as Jackman put it, "a prune sucking a lemon."[2]

"What for? Who needs four days' rest?" Dave said.

Dave had a point, and Weaver knew it. His ace southpaw had just pitched six starts, all on three days' rest, and had been an inning short of pitching six complete games. He had won all six games with a splendid earned-run average of 1.87. Meanwhile, in the same span, Palmer had gone 3–0 with a 1.88 ERA, and Cuellar went 5–1 with a 2.77 ERA. The Orioles' Big Three owned a combined 14–1 record in 17 starts and had pitched twelve complete games. Their ERA was 2.07 for 143 innings.

On August 21, the Orioles had forty regular-season games left. If Weaver didn't change the pitching routine, Dave would get eleven starts, and Palmer and Cuellar would get ten apiece. Lefties Dave and Cuellar had won eighteen games. Palmer had won seventeen, so all three wanted as many shots at more wins as they could get. Thus, Weaver would have a challenge convincing the three stars that missing a pitching start, or two or three, was in their best interest or the team's.

"Fertilizer," Dave said. "Right after the All-Star break, somebody said the same thing. Look how we're going. All of us are pitching better the way things are."

Weaver took a jab at Dave. "You know it took you four or five years to get money-hungry," he said, and Dave retorted with a dig of his own. "It took you two and half (years), so what?"

Weaver's reference was to Dave averaging ten wins a year before his breakout twenty-two-win season in 1968: the first of what would become four straight twenty-win years. McNally was reminding Weaver of how he wrangled a multiyear contract out of the Orioles with some fairy tale about him ending up in Missouri, possibly living in a boarding house the next summer.

Dave and Weaver laughed, but that didn't dispel the tension.

"(Pitching coach) Bamberger says it will be best this way," Weaver said.

But Dave had backers, too, in Palmer, who was making a bid for the Cy Young award, and Cuellar, a workhorse who thought a pitcher had to make forty starts to earn his pay.

In the early 1950s, Weaver had failed to make the major leagues as a player. Although Weaver became a Hall of Fame manager, Dave wasn't sold on his manager's knowledge of pitching. "The only thing Earl knows about pitching is that he couldn't hit," was a saying often heard from Dave.

Another Dave witticism about his longtime manager. "I once said: the only thing you have to realize about Earl is, he thinks out loud."[3]

In 2023, recalling October 1973, when Weaver started 23-year-old Alexander instead of the veteran Dave in the AL playoffs, fueling McNally's anger at his manager, Palmer remained firmly on Dave's side.[4] "Dave never forgave (Weaver) for that because he thought he should have gotten the opportunity. He had the experience. This wasn't the middle of the season." Instead, the Orioles' whole season was on the line.

Dave's annoyance carried over to the 1973 off-season when it was time to relax by playing golf. McNally, Palmer, and Weaver were avid golfers. They often played at two Baltimore-area courses, Pine Ridge, and Turf Valley. Sometimes, if the weather was good, the Orioles group would play twenty-seven holes or even thirty-six, Palmer recalled.

Thinking that the tradition would continue, Weaver called Dave at his home in Lutherville one day in the fall of 1973. Dave answered the phone. "Nine o'clock, Pine Ridge," Weaver said, although he may have suggested Turf Valley.

"Nope, I only play golf with my friends," Dave replied, as he slammed down the receiver.[5]

Dave never played golf with Weaver again. That set the tone for the 1974 season, Dave's last in an Orioles' uniform. Palmer contrasted his attempts at diplomacy with Weaver versus Dave's clipped, no-nonsense approach. "I would try to talk to Earl and reason with him. Dave would go, nope, yep. He'd give him one-word answers."

CHAPTER TWENTY-TWO

THE END... AND HISTORY

Dave McNally finished his career with the Orioles in late September 1974 on a high note—just as he had broken in with the Birds in spectacular fashion in September 1962. On September 19, 1974, Dave won his 181st game wearing an Oriole uniform, a three-hit shutout of the New York Yankees. Because Yankee Stadium was being renovated, that memorable win took place at Shea Stadium, home ballpark for the New York Mets and temporary home for the Yankees. This win thus partially exorcised Dave's memories of losing there to the Miracle Mets in the 1969 World Series.[1]

Palmer predicted Dave's gem before the game. As the team bus rolled along Seventh Avenue toward the stadium, Palmer looked back at Dave and said, joking, "What are you going to say to the writers after you throw your three-hitter?"

Afterward, Dave said that the Yankees, "were hitting me hard the first couple of innings, but after that, things started settling in. My control was so good; I couldn't believe it. It was the best control I've had all season." He needed just eighty-eight pitches to beat the Yankees. From the third inning on, only two Yankees got on base, and he retired fifteen straight batters during one stretch. "The reason I didn't throw many pitches was because I was throwing everything for strikes," Dave said, "I guess they all looked appetizing because the Yankees just kept swinging at them."

After beating the Yankees, Dave took the mound twice more for Baltimore, appearing in no-decision wins by the Birds against Detroit and Milwaukee, giving him a final season record in 1974 of 16-10. His win over New York represented Baltimore's eighteen victory in the past twenty-three games, a run that began on August 29 when Weaver's crew was eight games behind. When Dave beat the Yankees, the Orioles reclaimed their customary spot—first place in the AL East—and they went on to capture the divisional crown. Once again, however, they fell to the Oakland A's in the league playoffs, who won three of four games and advanced to the World Series.

Weaver praised Dave after he defeated the Yankees for his fourth straight win and his sixth win in seven outings, dating back to August 18. "Mac has always been tough in tight games. He's the kind of guy who likes to pitch in the big ones." But that feeling of camaraderie as a valued member of the Orioles was about to end.

Hoping for a new lease on his pitching life, McNally asked to be traded from the only baseball organization he'd ever known, and he got his wish in December 1974, when the Orioles dealt him to the National League's Montreal Expos.

"I'm excited about the trade," he said when it was announced on December 4. "I've never spent much time in Canada. I'm looking forward to playing there."[2] "It's a new life for me, and it should give me added incentive. I should be able to throw the ball like I'm capable of."

Baltimore immediately took notice of its loss of Dave and his classy demeanor on and off the field. For example, the *Sun's* Jackman mentioned a city organization that Dave had long been part of, the League for Crippled Children, which held a going-away party for him in February 1975. "The joint was packed and rightly so. Not a soul was there simply to be seen."[3]

And in March 1975, *Sun* sports editor Bob Maisel weighed in on Dave's ultimately unsuccessful contract negotiations with the Expos.

"(T)hose who doubt the ability, integrity and class of this Oriole organization should talk with Dave McNally about it," he wrote, noting that McNally was still sitting in his Lutherville home. His contract remained unsigned and and he was harboring doubts about whether he made a mistake in okaying the trade to Montreal.

"It's a bad situation. Right now, if these people (Expos management) said good morning to me, I'd look at my watch. When it comes time to put things in writing, it seems it just isn't there."

During his dealings with Cashen and the Orioles, McNally said, he and the Birds' brass would both present their cases, and though they "might disagree and get a little hot," he never felt he wasn't being dealt with honestly.

"If you agreed on something verbally, you could forget about it and go to the next point."

McNally said that, on the Wednesday night and Thursday of the week when he conversed with Maisel, he thought he and the Expos had come as close to agreement as possible without signing a contract, but the understanding fell apart when it was time to put it in writing.[4]

SURPRISE, SURPRISE

Dave pitched in Montreal for his new team, the Expos, on the afternoon of Sunday, June 8, 1975. So, his wife, Jean, more than five hundred miles away, wasn't expecting the knock on the door she heard at about 10:30 that night.

Who on earth could that be at this hour? she thought to herself as walked toward the door of her family's Lutherville house. When she opened the door, someone familiar stood there.

"Hi. Surprise, surprise," said her husband, suitcase in hand, whom she thought was lodged in a Montreal hotel, hundreds of miles away.

"Honey, I'm done with baseball."

Dave told his wife that he caught a plane from Montreal to Baltimore after he and the Expos lost to the San Diego Padres earlier that. Ironically, the winning pitcher in that game, the first of a doubleheader, was another major-leaguer born and groomed in Billings, Joe McIntosh.

McIntosh, a Padres rookie after being a standout at Washington State University, got the win by pitching a complete game for a 5–2 victory. Expos manager Gene Mauch lifted Dave in the sixth inning after he had given up all five San Diego runs—four of them earned—on six hits.

Dave wouldn't turn thirty-three until Halloween Day that year. Already, he had pitched in the major leagues for fourteen years and racked up a pile of accomplishments that made him a candidate for inclusion in baseball's Hall of Fame. Not one to rest on his laurels and seeking what he said was a "change in scenery," Dave asked for a trade from the Orioles after the 1974 season. They were the only big-league team the southpaw pitcher ever played for, and with little or no input from Dave, the Orioles shipped him to the Expos of the National League.

Dave got off to a promising start with the Expos. He won his first three games, pushing his major-league win total to 184 games. Then, he lost five straight games, his earned average ballooning to 5.26, a number that the hard-working Montanan found intolerable, and he came to believe that he could no longer pitch up to his high personal standards any longer. Dave had collected about $45,000 of his $115,000 Expos salary for 1975. Thus, he was leaving $80,000 on the table by walking away.

Jean McNally undoubtedly understood her husband's frustration. Still, Dave's sudden decision might have worried her. Adding onto this, Dave had left Expos manager Gene Mauch in the dark when he headed back home to Baltimore.

Trying to handle the matter as best she could, Jean undoubtedly asked her husband of fourteen years what the family was going to do instead of doing what he had loved since his youth—baseball, the source of his primary paycheck for the past fifteen years. The two Billings natives now had a family of three children, ranging in age from twelve to two-and-a-half, with a fourth child due on October 1.

Later, looking back to the day when he pitched his last big-league game for the Montreal Orioles and decided he was done with the game, Dave said, "I think I was really ready to get out of baseball…. The last couple years I played, I didn't enjoy it that much."

He traced that lack of enthusiasm for the game that had been his life since he was an eight-year-old Little Leaguer. His children were also growing up, and he wanted to be more present during that time. Also, "my arm was hurting, and I was getting no satisfaction from pitching."

Jean McNally needed to trust that the plan she and Dave had discussed for his future would prove a solid one for her family's future, and it turned out that the plan—joining his brother, Jim, in owning and operating the Archie Cochrane Ford dealership in Billings, the most prominent Ford dealership in Montana—became a solid foundation for the McNallys for the next quarter-century.

Someone else who welcomed McNally back to Billings was John Bohlinger. Referring to McNally, his longtime friend, Bohlinger said, "He was quite a guy. I loved his easygoing manner. When he left the

Expos, he said I don't have my stuff, and I can't take a paycheck when I can't deliver." He added: "What I think is remarkable about the McNally brothers—we had political differences—I ran as a Republican (and was labeled a RINO—a Republican in Name Only—by many Republicans in the area)" because that was the most practical way for Bohlinger, a Democrat at heart, to get into elected office in Republican-dominated Yellowstone County. "Jim and David were very conservative Republicans, but they always contributed to my campaign. With them, friendship was more important than political party."

THE SEITZ CASE

Later in 1975, finally off the field and back in Billings, Dave gained a spot in baseball history for his 1975 decision to join a case that led to a landmark labor decision. He and Dodgers pitcher Andy Messersmith signed on with MLB Players Union chief Marvin Miller to take on baseball's reserve clause. This provision dated back to the start of the twentieth century. It allowed a team to hold rights to a player's service until he was traded or released, in effect making him the property of a team that had signed him until he was traded or left baseball.

McNally and Messersmith's principled stand resulted in the landmark 1975 decision by arbitrator Peter Seitz, upheld in court, that toppled the reserve clause. The Seitz ruling gave players employment rights roughly equivalent to other American workers and opened the door to the modern era of free agency, in which players command multimillion-dollar salaries.

Miller, in his memoir *A Whole Different Ball Game*, said McNally and Messersmith's "willingness to challenge the reserve clause—what many called 'the backbone of the game'—led to the most important arbitration decision in the history of professional sports."

Here's the story of how Dave became involved in the Seitz case, as told by John Helyar in his book, *Lords of the Realm: The Real History of Baseball*.[5]

John McHale, president of the Expos, said it had become obvious to some club owners that "some relaxation on the reserve clause was needed." But baseball's leadership resisted the idea. The thinking of owners harkened back to the "pleasant and paternal" relations with players before Miller came along, and they still thought of baseball as a "privileged business." McHale could see "an accident waiting to happen. Somebody was going to do a number on us."

Miller, however, wasn't sure that Messersmith was the accident needed for a successful arbitration case. Messersmith was the Dodgers' ace, and LA had the "means and motivation to sign him." Would he go the distance on the case? Also, Dodgers owner Walter O'Malley seemed too smart to risk having the reserve system nullified over a no-trade clause, which was Messersmith's key demand. So, Miller sat down with Dick Moss, the lawyer for the players association, to discuss strategy. Then Miller remembered McNally. Dave hadn't signed voluntary retirement papers after his sudden departure from the Expos.

"They're (Expos) putting me on some other list," the former Orioles ace said in late June 1975, "a list that enables them to put another player on their twenty-five-man roster, and that doesn't thoroughly throw me out yet."[6]

Thus, McNally still was technically an unsigned player, not a retired one. Therefore, Miller likely reasoned, the player who had already shown a willingness to buck baseball's power structure might be willing to do so again, this time with nothing at stake beside his legacy and reputation.

Miller found Dave's home phone number in Billings and dialed it. The misery of his only season with the Expos, a 3–6 record with a 5.26 earned-run average, was still fresh on Dave's mind. Thus, when Miller asked him if he was coming back to play, Dave replied, "No, never."

"I'd like to add your name to the grievance as insurance if Andy decides to sign a new Dodger contract," Miller said.

Dave didn't hesitate. "If you need me, I'm willing to help," he said.

When O'Malley heard Dave had been added to the grievance, it changed his thinking about how to deal with Messersmith. "He had been willing to give him the moon to thwart a union test case. Now Miller had one anyway. There was no reason to capitulate to Messersmith," Helyar wrote.

John Gaherin, the top negotiator for the club owners, made a frantic call to McHale: "Go out to Montana. For Christ's sake, get the bastard drunk and sign him."

A stunned Dave picked up the phone one day that summer and heard McHale at the other end. "I happened to be passing through Billings," he said. "Can we sit down and talk about your situation?"

They met the next day at a hotel restaurant, where McHale presented Dave an almost unbelievable pitch. He offered Dave $125,000 to sign in 1976—more than he had ever made—and threw in $25,000 as a signing bonus. "Gee, I don't know," Dave said. "I'm not sure I can even pitch at the major-league level anymore."

McHale told him not to worry about it. He told Dave he'd get the $25,000 just for signing and coming to spring training in 1976. Dave talked to Miller on the phone the next day, and they laughed about how McHale supposedly just happened to be passing through Billings. Then Miller turned serious. "What are you going to do?" he said, knowing the money offered by the Expos would tempt any player thinking of making a comeback.

Dave said he wouldn't sign. "McHale wasn't honest with me last year, and I'm not going to trust him again," he said, referring to several oral promises the Expos executive made to McNally and then reneged on. Although it was tempting to go to spring training and collect a $25,000 check just for that, Dave said he had no intention of playing and "it wouldn't be right to take the money."

That set the case in motion. The union filed the Messersmith and McNally grievances in early October, and baseball was on edge. Its old order might end, and everyone knew it. The Lords of Baseball tried to stop the case by filing for an injunction to keep the Messersmith-McNally matter out of arbitration, but a federal judge said no to their request and ordered the hearing to proceed.

McNally and Messersmith won the arbitration case later that fall, and a federal judge upheld the decision in 1976. McNally had already started his new career as co-owner of the Archie Cochrane Ford dealership and did not take part in any of the hearings.

HICCUPS

Soon after Dave's surprise announcement he was retiring from professional baseball, life became busy at the McNally household in Lutherville.

In June 1975, Jean started packing for the family's move back to Billings, but there was a literal hiccup in her and her husband's efforts.

Starting on June 17, she tended to Dave, who had started hiccupping. His bout lasted thirteen straight days. Things reached the point at which Dave checked into Baltimore's Sinai Hospital. Dave and his physician, Dr. Leonard Wallenstein, had a conversation in which Walstein said he was concerned by signs of exhaustion he had seen in his patient. The doctor wondered whether Dave's hiccupping was caused by a small ulcer that might have started on the top of his stomach.

Wallenstein recommended Dave undergo tests that could pinpoint what was going on. Dave heeded the doctor's advice. He tried to put on a patient face, but his family's impending move back to Montana gave him a different outlook. He later told the *Baltimore Sun*: "Sometimes ulcers like that can take three or more weeks to heal and the doc didn't want this thing to drag on that long."[7]

The timing was not the best. Dave was preparing to join his brother Jim in running the Ford dealership. The McNallys had put their Maryland house on the market, and they planned to fly to Billings to begin househunting there in late June or early July 1975.[8] To further complicate matters, Jean was pregnant with their fourth child, their daughter Ann, who was born in Billings in October that year. "That's why we've got to get settled," she said. And then there was the matter of Jean's ten-speed bicycle, which had been stolen. She tried to take it in stride, saying, "That's the least of my worries right now."

Jean, while sympathetic to and supportive of her husband, found humor in the situation. "I know it's terrible to laugh about Dave's condition, but I think he just went to the hospital to get away from everything," she said.

When Dave checked into the hospital and got settled in his room, it seemed as if the whole country was trying to help him get rid of his hiccups. Phone calls flooded the hospital switchboard, leaving messages delivered to him. Letters poured in. After his ordeal ended, Dave estimated that he had received 200 "cure-alls" for his malady.[9] Tips Dave got included: standing on his head, breathing deep 652 times, looking at a full moon, holding a finger in an ear while drinking water, blowing in a paper bag, and holding a lump of sugar on his tongue.

Doctors, nurses, and patients on his hospital floor were aware of the famous baseball player in their midst. "I remember visiting him, and when I got off the elevator, I could hear his very loud hiccups from way down the hall," Jean said almost a half-century afterward.[10]

At least one person who tried to help apparently hadn't adjusted to the reality that Dave had given up major-league pitching. This individual suggested getting booed as a cure. "Craziest remedy I received was using a brown paper bag, cutting out a mustache, and putting it wet over my mouth," Dave said. "Yeah, I tried it."

He knew something about getting hiccups that lasted long enough to cease being a minor annoyance. In 1969, during spring training, his hiccups lasted three days. Dave remembered his mother's "real wacky remedy" for hiccups, advice she gave him when he was a kid. "She used to tell me to drink water out of a glass—backwards."

Hiccups were thought to be caused by nervous impulses that triggered spasms of the diaphragm. The only known cure then for serious cases that could last weeks, months, or years, was to interfere with the nerve leading to the diaphragm by an operation or local anesthetic. Walstein was preparing to take a last step when relief came to Dave after eight days of hospitalization. "He was one day away from a surgical procedure to stop them when, thankfully, they stopped," Jean said.

By July 2, 1975, Dave seemed to have conquered hiccups. He had been hiccup-free for three days and had been released from the hospital a day earlier. "Could be the best win of my career," he said as he prepared to play a round of golf.

Dave never was in danger of beating the Guinness World Book of Records listing for the longest hiccup attack. That belonged to Jack O'Leary of Los Angeles, whose suffering spanned seven years, from 1948 to 1956.

Dave later seemed to take his bout in stride. "No, I didn't worry about it, though I couldn't help but feel uncomfortable when I pulled a rib muscle."

Dave lost six pounds in the hospital, but he said he ate regularly when he didn't have tubes in his ears and throat. Jean, obviously pleased as June 1975 concluded, that her husband's hiccups had ended, said Dave "slept quietly and went the entire night without hiccupping, and I know he was quite relieved."¹¹ Jean said the family would delay its planned return to Billings until they were certain that Dave's health had returned.

As early as 1971, the McNallys were already thinking about coming home after Dave's baseball career was over. "We've talked about coming back to Montana after baseball," Jean said then. "That's where Dave would have the most business opportunities. We'd like to move back there." Jean said she *really* missed Montana's wide-open spaces.¹²

One morning in July 1976, Dave opened the *Billings Gazette* and read that major league players and owners had reached an agreement concerning contracts that incorporated the Seitz ruling, upheld earlier that year in federal court. "I'm very happy it's resolved. It's a very fair thing, and I'm just glad to see it resolved," he told the *Gazette's* Beth Bragg.¹³ "It was a tough, hard thing to go through," he said, adding that he received letters and calls from people who felt he was wrong in challenging baseball's reserve clause. Still, he felt it was worth it to take a stand in opposition to a bedrock provision in baseball's business model because the previous system was very unfair to players.

CHAPTER TWENTY-THREE

BACK HOME

HIGH HONOR IN BALTIMORE

With the Seitz case decided, and its finding affirmed by a federal court in 1976, Dave turned the page on baseball and became part of the Billings business community. Certainly, he paid attention to baseball, especially since his son, Jeff, was a budding junior baseball standout; however, Dave, now approaching his mid-thirties, showed no signs of wanting to return to the pitching mound. He also expressed no interest in managing or coaching professional baseball, but he was a supporter of and involved in junior baseball in his hometown.

In 1977, he joined other Magic City business leaders on the board of directors of the newly created Montana Bank of Billings. It was the fifteenth location of an affiliation of banking institutions located across Montana, from Missoula in the west to Baker, Fairview, and Richey in the east.[1]

Also in 1977, Dave became involved in a new Billings car dealership, D-J Volkswagen, the D referring to Dave and the J to his brother, Jim, his partner in owning and operating Archie Cochrane Ford. Dave had learned the car business as a salesman. Then, he worked as a sales manager before he switched to parts, service and administration.[2]

Asked what he liked about the automotive business, compared with baseball, Dave said, "That's easy. It's the competition. The hours are longer, but I get the same feeling of accomplishment."

Three years after he retired from baseball and returned to Billings, Dave remained adamant that his exit from the major leagues was final. "I probably get asked thirty times a week if I miss baseball. I don't," Dave, then a few months away from his thirty-sixth birthday, said in a June 1978 interview with the author, then a sportswriter for the *Billings Gazette*.[3] "Half the people don't believe it."

The interview took place after Dave and his doubles partner, Ernie Walters, had finished their match in the Muscular Dystrophy Association celebrity tennis tournament. Besides being involved in that benefit, Dave said he was being asked to help many other community groups and projects—more than he could accommodate. But he didn't consider the requests a burden. "I just have to explain. I can't do but half the things that I'm asked to do in town, but people are very understanding."

Dave said he was among the fortunate professional baseball players able to bow out with a promising future, in his case the car dealership he and his brother, Jim, owned and operated in the Magic City.

The changing landscape of baseball because of the Seitz ruling was becoming clearer, according to Dave. "They (players) aren't all in good shape. But there will be a heckuva lot more in good shape. As the salaries have gone sky high, even more should be better off. But some people can't stand to save a dime."

Dave's belief in personalized customer service went beyond words, into action, as an experience that one Billings man had can attest to. Larry Downer said that his interaction with Dave happened a few years after he bought a Ford station wagon in 1991 from Archie Cochrane when the dealership was still in downtown Billings; it later moved to King Avenue on the city's West End and remains there today. Downer said he brought the station wagon in for service one time, and the dealership arranged a courtesy car ride for him to the church where he was working.

"Shortly after being dropped off, the driver of the (courtesy) car returned and gave me a sorry story about how his grandmother had died in another state and he needed money to attend the funeral. I gave him fifty dollars," Downer said.[4]

That afternoon, Dave called Downer and asked if he had given the driver money. Downer said he had. "Then he informed me it was a phony story, and he had fired the driver. He also sent me the fifty dollars I was out."

Downer and Dave had a good chat over the phone, during which Downer told Dave that he and his family lived had lived in Maryland while Dave was pitching for the Orioles. The Downers never got to a game, but that was okay with Dave. Downer said he never learned how Dave detected the scam.

McNally's sense of humor never left him. In 1993, he wrote a check for $20 to Billings resident Deb Hofer, whose husband worked for Dave. The check memo said "Bribe," and Dave enclosed a note saying that the check was payable to "you (underlined for emphasis)" and "Please don't spend one penny on that TV-watching husband of yours." In a May 2024 Facebook post, Don Hofer, who shared a photo of the check and note, said, "Dave had a great sense of humor and was the best boss you could ask for."

After Dave and Jean McNally returned to Billings, their hometown, bringing their three children with them, they all quickly become fully engaged in life in the Magic City. That didn't mean, however, that their connections with Baltimore and the Orioles ended.

In late August 1978, Jean told her children about a trip they would soon make back to Baltimore. Baltimore writers and fans had selected Dave to the Orioles Hall of Fame, and all the family except their youngest child, Ann, would go back for the induction.

It was just before the school year started, and the McNally's oldest children, Jeff, then fifteen, and Pam, then fourteen, might have had some idea of what their mother was saying and what it meant, but she probably had to rephrase the news in terms her two youngest children, Susan, eight, and Ann, three, could understand.

Jean told her children that sportswriters in Baltimore had voted on who they thought were the best pitchers in Orioles history, and they had decided that their father was one of them and thus belonged in the new Orioles Hall of Fame.

The former star pitcher was ready for another trip to familiar haunts, Baltimore's Memorial Stadium, so he and Jean got ready to fly with their family to Baltimore.

They brought their three oldest children, Jeff, Pam, and Susan, along. But possibly believing that Ann was too young to appreciate the significance of the occasion, they left her in Billings, in the care of one of her grandmothers, Dave's widowed mother, Beth McNally.

When the McNally contingent got to Baltimore, a team representative drove them from the airport to the stadium's Hit and Run room for a luncheon. The room seated 150, and 150 people were there, "not because you had to be but because you couldn't pay them to be anyplace else," according to one of those present, *Baltimore Sun* sports editor Bob Maisel.

Discussing other Orioles greats that he had written on his ballot, Maisel said Palmer, Powell and Belanger belonged in the Hall and would eventually make it. Still, having stiff requirements for induction made sense because they left no doubt that someone was worthy of the honor. "Certainly, that applies to McNally, and everybody in that room yesterday knew it," Maisel said.

The function was "one of those entirely happy occasions," where people could temporarily forget labor problems and other issues then swirling through baseball and all professional sports. The McNallys were obviously delighted to be there, and everyone in the room was present because they wanted to be there. Attendees included everyone in the Birds' front office, from team owner Hoffberger on down. Weaver was there and so were many of McNally's teammates, including Jim Frey, Mark Belanger, Elrod Hendricks, Terry Crowley, Curt Motton (whose bat McNally used to hit his historic World Series grand-slam home run), Dick Hall, and team trainer Ralph Salvon. If McNally and Weaver chatted during the event, the sportswriters who were present did not capture their conversation in articles written afterward.

Hall, a former relief pitcher for the Orioles, got special mention from Dave when he chatted with Maisel. Dave thanked Hall for the many times he relieved him when he got into a jam. He might have cracked a joke about how, if he had trouble finishing his acceptance speech that day, perhaps Weaver would send in Hall to help him out, but Dave didn't need a reliever that day. He finished his speech fine, likely in his usual humble, self-effacing manner.

Brooks Robinson, one of Dave's best friends, was there. Frank Robinson, though, couldn't make it. He was a minor-league manager then, guiding the Orioles farm team in Rochester, New York, and he was trying to keep his team in its league playoff race.

Dave took time to point out to replicas of his locker along with those of the Robinsons to his children. He probably made special mention of a mop that Frank Robinson wore as a wig when he was the judge of the Orioles' kangaroo court. Jean and Jeff undoubtedly knew what the kangaroo court was—possibly Pam, too, but Susan McNally might have worn a puzzled look that caught her father's eye. He might have explained the kangaroo court's function to his middle daughter.

The kangaroo court, held in the spirit of fun, convened after some games the Orioles lost. Team members would talk about good plays—and bad ones, too, the ones that might have lost a game. The players were the jury, and if one of them was found guilty, Frank Robinson, as the judge, would fine him a modest amount. The money went into a fund to pay for fun activities the team did between games.

Getting this insight from their father undoubtedly reinforced what the McNally youngsters already knew. Their father's fourteen years as a major-league pitcher was more than a job. It was a passion. He had fun doing what he loved, and he became a beloved member of the Orioles family.

The gathering also heard from another longtime Baltimore sportswriter, Gordon Beard, who said, tongue in cheek: "Brooks and McNally belong in the hall together because they're the only players I know who left the game after long careers with more hair than they had when they started."

In Dave's case, Beard was referring to how the pitcher coped with premature balding. During one offseason, a Baltimore business that sold male hairpieces hired Dave to be photographed wearing one as a pitch for the wigs in newspaper advertisements. Dave eventually stopped wearing a wig and went back to what Maisel called "his old style with the hole on top." Said Maisel: "On him, it looks good. In fact, the whole McNally family could hardly look better. Must be that good Montana air."

Praise continued to roll in for Dave in the Hall of Fame event. More than one person in the crowd said if the Orioles had one big game to win, you'd want to have Dave on the mound going for it. When Brooks Robinson took the speaker's mic, he crystalized the sentiment. "If there was one guy to get out in the last of the ninth, and the season was hanging in the balance, Dave McNally would be the guy I'd like to have doing the pitching," said the man later named to the Baseball Hall of Fame, enshrined as perhaps the greatest third baseman of all time. "He was a super pitcher, is a great human being, and it was a pleasure to be on the same team with him. He had a certain something, intestinal fortitude, whatever you call it."

"How about guts?" Maisel wrote. The sportswriter related something he heard from Frank Robinson, another future member of the Cooperstown club: "There is something about McNally that makes you always feel like you're going to win when he's out there. You might be behind three or four runs, but something about the way he goes about the job makes you think everything will be all right."

Then the crowd heard from someone with a household name among Baltimore Orioles fans. That was master of ceremonies Jack Dunn, who had been around the Birds since his grandfather owned Baltimore Orioles teams that won seven straight International League pennants, from 1919 to 1925. "I've seen pitchers with great stuff, pitchers who were tremendous competitors, who had great character, were great gentlemen, and who had that certain something known as class," Dunn said, "but in my time in baseball, I've seen very few who combined all of these qualities as well as Dave McNally"

Then it was Dave's turn to speak. He said, "The ceremonies were a very emotional thing for me. My whole family and I loved our association (with) Baltimore. There is no way we could have gotten better treatment. I couldn't have asked for one more thing from the town and the Oriole organization."

And going into the Orioles Hall of Fame as the third player honored, joining original members Brooks Robinson and Frank Robinson, "Well, it means more to me than I can possibly explain."

As the festivities ended, Brooks looked at the blown-up picture on the wall from the end of Game 4 of the 1966 World Series. Gazing at the iconic photo that shows him leaping in the air and flying toward McNally and Etchebarren, waiting almost dazed at the mound, Brooks said people often asked him to pinpoint his greatest moment in baseball. "I've got to go back to that—the first world championship. It has to be my greatest moment in baseball. That picture shows it all."

Nobody apparently asked Dave to reflect on his triumphant time. They didn't have to. That series and that day became part of his being.

Now, the cheers that rocked Memorial Stadium were over, as was the adoration he experienced everywhere he went in Baltimore. Dave was happy to be back home in Billings; as he told the *Sun's* Jackman, he left baseball at the right time. "It was that simple," Dave said. "I watch guys on television today, guys like Jim Rice coming up to hit, and all I think is, hmmm, better put another pillow in the back of my head to get a better look."[5]

Besides his volunteer work for the Montana Easter Seals campaign, McNally also supported the Boys & Girls Club of Billings, the Ronald McDonald House, the city's American Legion baseball program, and his high school, Billings Central. He served on the Montana Highway Commission and the Billings Chamber of Commerce. His love of golf showed up in membership in three golf clubs: Hilands and the Yellowstone Country Club and the Springs Club in Rancho Mirage, California, where he and Jean often wintered in their later years.[6]

CHAPTER TWENTY-FOUR

MONTANA'S GREATEST ATHLETE

Sports Illustrated made it official in December 2000: Dave McNally was Montana's best athlete of the 20th century.[1] And his hometown pulled out all the stops to honor him after the accolade was announced. More than 600 people attended the tribute at a Billings West End hotel, including Governor-elect Judy Martz, herself an ex-Olympic athlete.

Master of ceremonies was another Billings major-leaguer, Jeff Ballard, another lefthander who pitched for the Baltimore Orioles from 1987 through 1991 after finishing his education at Stanford University, and that came after he earned a baseball scholarship based on his play as a star for the Billings Scarlets American Legion team.

Ballard and McNally got to know each other after the McNally's moved back to Billings in 1975, and Ballard got to know the McNally's oldest child, their son, Jeff, another Legion star in Billings who also earned a Stanford baseball scholarship. "Dave McNally was the dad of my best friend," Ballard said.

Those attending the dinner saw taped highlights of McNally's major-league career and a video "salute." They listened to speakers who talked about his American Legion baseball and golfing days.

Ballard, who paced the Orioles with eighteen wins in 1989, said, "McNally had been a big help in my career and he's been a good friend. It's an honor for me to do this. It's one of those things you get real excited about being a part of." The tribute was "long overdue," and it triggered "real excitement" among attendees, Ballard said. Proceeds from the event went to the March of Dimes, one charity helped by McNally's volunteer efforts.

"It is nice to be able to put an event together that can honor someone and at the same time can benefit a lot of others," Ballard said.

Although he had known Dave for more than two decades and knew that his thirteen seasons with the Orioles were extraordinary, Ballard said, "I never understood, to tell you the truth, the magnitude of his career until probably right now."

Preparing for his role as MC and as a former major-leaguer himself, Ballard said he came to realize that Dave was a special athlete. "Now that I'm really diving into his past and his numbers and the things that he did while he was playing for the Orioles, I was amazed. Now I have a full appreciation for how lucky I was to have somebody from Billings from time to time be there to give me his insights and his instruction on pitching."

Ballard recalled the help he got from Dave before he headed to Stanford to play Division One baseball. For a few weeks, following the American Legion season, they worked together on developing a sinking fastball and a slider that broke sharply to add to Ballard's repertoire. "He was very instrumental in my going to Stanford and being an impact player right away," Ballard said.

Along with Dave's competitiveness on the mound, his sharp wit and humility impressed Ballard. "For all the great things that he has done, he's probably the most humble person I've ever met. I think the way he looks back at (his career) is simply, 'They paid me to throw the ball, and I gave it my all. I tried to get outs and win games.'"

The ceremony included a review of Dave's big-league accomplishments.[2] "Those are big-time numbers and accomplishments that most major-league pitchers would take in a minute," Ballard said. "But most of you probably do not know how important he was to baseball for reasons that had nothing to do with statistics or box scores or achievements on the field."

He then read from a letter mailed to him by Hall of Fame pitcher Jim Bunning, winner of 224 games and by then a U.S. Senator from Kentucky. "In 1975, Dave played the entire season without a contract as part of a challenge to the century-old rule that gave baseball owners the complete right to keep players tied to their team forever," Bunning wrote. "In doing so, he stood up for the rights of ball players and for the American principles of freedom and economic independence."

"In these days of multi-million salaries and jaw-dropping contracts, it is easy to forget that just a few years ago, ballplayers were treated by owners as nothing more than servants. Under the rules of baseball back then, players had almost no rights whatsoever, no right to ply their trade except where the owners told them to go."

"The players today are indebted to you for the money they are making," said Brooks Robinson in a video salute to McNally played at the ceremony.

A last word from Bunning: "In making his stand, Dave McNally showed courage and conviction. He stood up not just for himself and for others, but more importantly, he stood up for his beliefs. That tells you what kind of person, what kind of man he is."

Billings, Montana, and the nation had just two more years to appreciate Dave's contribution to baseball and workplace fairness for professional athletes before he lost his final battle, the hardest of his life. By late summer in 2000, it had been more than two decades since he exchanged pitching mounds in Baltimore and Montreal for the comfort of his suburban home in Billings, complete with weekly golf games at nearby Yellowstone Country Club. Now as he approached his sixtieth birthday, Dave was trying to beat cancer.

CHAPTER TWENTY-FIVE

THE LAST BATTLE

By 2000, Dave no longer needed to outsmart the likes of this longtime nemesis, Washington Senators slugger Frank Howard. Nor did he have to strategize how to contain the murderers' row of hitters that the Pittsburgh Pirates presented to the Orioles in the 1971 World Series. Now he was engaged in the fight that topped all: he was trying to conquer, or at least hold off, the lung cancer he had been diagnosed with a few years earlier.

A lifetime smoker, Dave had given up cigarettes, hoping to better his odds of conquering the disease. Still, fighting cancer was a slog. Fortunately, Billings, on its way to becoming the top medical center in a 500-mile radius, provided treatment options almost equal to big cities. For example, the Rocky Mountain Cancer Center had started offering stem-cell transplants to cancer patients in 1997, and Dave had undergone the procedure.

Now, in September 2000, he could look back at his experience and offer wisdom to another former American League pitching standout preparing to have the same operation he had in 1999. That was Mel Stottlemyre, a right-hander who won 164 games for the Bronx Bombers from 1964 to 1974: the same period in which Dave had become a household name in Baltimore. He was expecting a phone call from Stottlemyre, who had been diagnosed with bone-marrow cancer. Like Dave, Stottlemyre was a product of the West, a native of Yakima, Washington. Dave hadn't yet heard from Stottlemyre when the Billings man recalled the misery that he had experienced.

"It was tough," he told a reporter for New York's *Newsday* in a telephone interview.[1] "They told me it was going to be darn tough. I prepared myself for it. I was laid up in the hospital for ten to twelve days. They took me down to the bare bones and I started coming back." He continued, "They just take you down as far as they can take you while keeping you alive. It was tough, but it was worth it. And I would do it again."

The *Newsday* account said that Stottlemyre that planned to call several people before his operation, including Dave, one of his top AL rivals for more than a decade. Dave said he would be glad to talk to Stottlemyre, another of the many people he had shared his cancer journey with recently. "We're a pretty small town, 100,000 people. The hospital will ask me to talk to someone who is maybe hesitating a little bit. I just tell them what I went through and what I did and how I would do it again. I say, 'Just prepare yourself for a hard time, but know that every day, you're getting closer to a better time.'"

Dave, however, detailed his treatment in a manner that left no doubt that it was an ordeal. He said that the operation made him sick to his stomach about ten times throughout ten days and left him without energy for a week. He added that the effects of the treatment were toughest on his family. When he was in the hospital, "I was out of it" for a couple of days, a fuzzy period when he couldn't remember half the people who visited him.

He returned to his job as a car dealer within two months, but it took three months before he regained the strength to play eighteen holes of golf. Dave had been a five-handicap golfer before the operation. His play ballooned to a sixteen-handicap, but he got his game down to an eleven-handicap before his tumor came back.

In June 2000, Dave went to his doctor, complaining that he was having trouble breathing. Tests showed two quarts of liquid in one of his lungs, along with a previously undiscovered tumor. A first round of chemotherapy failed to shrink the tumor, but Dave's fighter spirit prodded him to continue the battle. His doctors found the right chemical mix and were able to shrink the tumor by 78 percent.

"It's all on the plus side. I feel great," Dave said. "They said I was a stubborn mule the way I handled it. I just didn't let it get to me."

The stubborn mule held off death for two more years, but, on December 1, 2002, Dave McNally lost the last and toughest battle of his life and died in his Billings home, surrounded by his family.

Three days later, an overflow crowd of about 800 mourners packed St. Thomas the Apostle Church on Billings West End for Dave's funeral mass. Although it was almost winter, the temperature rose to 34 degrees that day, and no snowflakes dusted the windshields of cars at the Catholic church.[2]

Mourners viewed a casket decked with red roses and heard from the Rev. Steve Tokarski, a 1960 classmate of Dave's at Billings Central Catholic High School and co-celebrant with the Rev. William Hogan. "Dave's struggle with cancer was prolonged and increasingly difficult," Tokarski said. "But his death was peaceful, almost gentle. A peaceful death is something we all pray for, but it cannot take away the pain and the loss the family and friends experience."

Jeff, the oldest of the five McNally children, delivered a eulogy that was a mix of sadness and humor in recalling the man he knew as both his father and as a major-league pitcher, starting as a youngster in Baltimore through his retirement from the Orioles.

Jeff, an emergency-room physician in Salt Lake City, said that he remembered his father for more than being a star pitcher. "There has been a lot of press coverage talking about Dad's baseball career in the past few days. Although it's been fun reminiscing about a time in his life that was obviously very important to him, our family has spent most of our time since he died remembering what a great man he was. All of us who loved Dad are grateful to have had him as our guide, our companion, our ally and inspiration. Dad was funny and sharp, and he was sweet."

When it became obvious that Dave was losing his battle with cancer, his family worried about him and felt sad for him. "But at the same time, we were comforted because we knew he was at peace with himself and how he had lived his life," Jeff said.

Jeff reminded some and enlightened others about how his father could be "old school," with a mix of stubbornness and pride. He was strong-willed and, at times, bull-headed. "In fact, a lot of times, he was bull-headed," Jeff said to laughter in the church. "What he really was, he was true to himself and what he believed to be right."

Dave was an example of pure honesty and integrity in Jeff's eyes. "Dad didn't always have the best communications skills, and he occasionally lost his temper," Jeff said, singling out a 1974 event. "My favorite example of that is when he drop-kicked his glove from the mound to the outfield and was ejected over a controversial balk call."

Jeff mentioned his father's final attempt to lessen the seriousness surrounding his impending death. Dave purchased a big, fake bruise at a local novelty store and wore it on his abdomen where he had an injection the week before. Dave then went to what turned out to be his last doctor's appointment, and he feigned discomfort as he tried to cause a commotion. "He had a great sense of humor," Jeff said.

The crowd paying respect to Dave was so large that some mourners had to stand at the back of the church. Flowers, guest books, and memorial cards were everywhere. As *Gazette* sportswriter Bill Bighaus wrote, "There was nothing that indicated McNally wasn't one of baseball's greatest pitchers."

But some in the crowd were well aware of that fact. Jim Clevenger went to school with Dave's brother, Jim, and his daughters attended school with McNally's daughters and became friends with them. "Coming from a town of, what were we then, eighty thousand? It was really something to have a big-league ballplayer," Clevenger said. "It was really the greatest thing, even the fact that he was something we could all be proud of."

Tokarski, who knew Dave and Jean McNally when they all were teenagers, said, "Dave was a good, loving man who touched people's hearts and lives with his goodness. In the end, Dave suffered, but he suffered with dignity and grace. He never complained. He never surrendered his love of life. That may be his last and best gift to us."

Jeff said his father's accomplishments as a player were "quite astonishing." Yet, as Fraser McDonald, a longtime friend of the McNally family, said, "Dave was always considered a better person than he was a baseball player."

———

One of the casket-bearers was Andy Etchebarren. He and Dave began their professional baseball careers together when they were both eighteen-year-old bonus babies with the Orioles. They met in the Arizona Instructional League and played in their first major-league game together. For more than a decade, they also were roommates on Orioles road trips, and the Californian and the Montanan became best friends.

Etchebarren was in California visiting his mother and one of his daughters when he heard about Dave's death. He lived in Florida and planned to visit another daughter in Nashville, Tennessee, on his way home. He immediately changed his plans. "There was no question that I was going to get here one way or another," he said. "I had to find a suit and get the (plane) ticket changed."

Etchebarren said he talked to Brooks Robinson, who also lived in Florida, earlier in the week, before the funeral, and gave him the news. Robinson, who was driving from Baltimore to Boca Raton, Florida, said he would try to get a flight to Billings for the funeral, but he was unsuccessful.

Etchebarren said he came not just as a former teammate but to say goodbye to "my best friend." He continued: "You make a lot of acquaintances in life. If you can make one good friend, a friend that's there for you anytime, you're fortunate."

Reminiscing about the pitchers he caught for, Etchebarren said that McNally was the best. "I caught Jim Palmer and Nolan Ryan and a lot of good pitchers. When you ask me who's the best pitcher I ever caught, there's no doubt it was Dave McNally. Palmer and Ryan were overpowering. They should have been good. Dave made himself into a good pitcher."

McNally and Etchebarren are linked for all time in what's called the "Magic Moment" photograph in Baltimore. It shows Etchebarren running toward Dave, standing on the pitcher's mound. The photo also captures Brooks Robinson leaping toward him from third base after Dave finished beating Don Drysdale and the Los Angeles Dodgers to close out the 1966 World Series.

Although thirty-six years had passed since the photo was taken, McNally's funeral service allowed Etchebarren to reflect on how the two of them, plus Brooks Robinson, became forever part of Baltimore sports memories.

"It's the greatest picture ever taken in the history of Baltimore," Etchebarren said. "It was the first World Series that the Orioles were ever in and then to beat the Dodgers four straight when they had (Don) Drysdale, (Sandy) Koufax and those guys . . . For the guy to get that picture, I don't know. It was amazing."

By then, the Orioles no longer played in Memorial Stadium. They had moved to Camden Yards, and the 1966 Series photo was inscribed on two glass doors going into the Orioles office. "So that picture will be there forever with Dave in it," Etchebarren said.

Two days before the funeral, several of Dave's Oriole teammates remembered him as "an unyielding competitor who was stoic and focused on the field, but easygoing and friendly away from it."[3] Brooks Robinson and Don Buford were among those who shared memories. "He was one tough pitcher," Robinson said. "If there was one guy you wanted to get three outs in the bottom of the ninth, it was him." Added Buford: "He helped make our great clubs go. You knew every time he went out there, you'd get a complete game or close to it."

Marvin Miller, who enlisted Dave in the 1975 arbitration case that overturned baseball's reserve clause, called Dave, "a really bright guy. He said, 'You want insurance and I'll be glad to give it to you.' So, he joined the grievance. He didn't hesitate for a second. His contribution was a great one."[4]

Dave's manager for the longest period of his big-league career added praise for the southpaw. "Dave was an unbelievable competitor," said Earl Weaver, burying the hatchet between the two at last. "He did it with cunning and intelligence. He loved to set you up with a change, fool you with that tremendous curve and then throw the fastball by you.[5] Plus, he was one-hundred-percent gentleman. He was the kind of guy you wanted your son to be."

Weaver died a little less than eleven years after McNally, at eighty-two on January 19, 2013, of an apparent heart attack while on an Orioles fantasy cruise in the Caribbean Sea.

CHAPTER TWENTY-SIX

MCNALLY'S LEGACY

Further evidence of Dave's growing, post-career prominence in baseball began appearing in the late 1990s and continued after his death in the new millennium. His legacy was based on both his play on the baseball field: first in Billings as an American Legion standout, then in Baltimore as a star pitcher for the Orioles, and then his leadership in the battle to give players workplace fairness.

Nowadays, the average baseball salary stands at $4.5 million through the 2023 season.[1] Even before his death in 2002, McNally witnessed the stratospheric salaries that major leaguers were getting, yet McNally saw his fight as something more than helping players get big paychecks. His goal was to give baseball players fundamental fairness in the workplace. Just like other workers, baseball players deserved the right to choose their employers and negotiate their pay, he believed.

In 1999, when the Los Angeles Dodgers and the Boston Red Sox were getting set for the World Series, reporter Andy Price from Billings' KTVQ TV station interviewed Dave at Cobb Field, the place where he achieved glory as a Legion player. Price reminded viewers of Dave's crucial role in helping other players, but not himself since he had retired by the time of the Seitz ruling and didn't make a dime from free agency.

That prompted Dave to discuss what he felt was the most important aspect of the change he helped bring about. "When we had those really good teams in Baltimore, we had really great players in AAA that were stuck at that level. They'd played three years and were hitting .330 or .335, but they couldn't come up and they couldn't go anywhere else.

So, it helped everybody, by giving players the right, within limits, to shop their skills to other teams and to negotiate a spot on another team's roster."

The *Gazette's* Bighaus described the changed landscape of baseball in a December 15, 2000, column, twenty-five years after the Seitz ruling. "Any day now, thank-you notes from Alex Rodriguez, Manny Ramirez, and Mike Hampton should be arriving in Dave McNally's mailbox," he wrote. Those three players, all free agents, had signed contracts worth a total of $533 million earlier in the week. "And they've got McNally to thank for striking it rich."

Bighaus shared Dave's droll sense of humor as he commented on the richest deal of all at that time. Rodriguez, an all-star shortstop, had just signed a ten-year, $252 million deal with the Texas Rangers. "My first thought when I saw that was: Did Texas offer him $250 million, and he wanted two (million) more? How did they get to $252 million?" Dave quipped. "I just don't get them," he said of the headline grabbing contracts, specifically Rodriguez's. "Isn't ($250 million) about what (the Texas owner) paid for that club a couple of years ago? If they're going to bid that, I guess they have that and know what they want to do with it."

What a revolution Dave had triggered when he stood up to the entrenched baseball establishment. Dave retired from baseball in June 1975 and moved his family back to Billings where he began a new career as a car dealer. That employment plus his major-league player pension sustained him and his family for the rest of his life; his only compensation from the 1975 ruling was knowing that he helped baseball players, and all professional athletes, gain workplace fairness.

Six years after Dave's death, Billings gained a lasting symbol of his legacy and that of the man whose mentorship turned Dave into a major-league star. On June 29, 2008, several hundred people congregated at the new Dehler Park, which had replaced Cobb Field as Billings' primary baseball field. They were there to see the unveiling of larger-than-life bronze statutes of Dave and Ed Bayne.[2]

Two prominent Billings artists, Bill Rains and Lyle Johnson, created the statutes. Rains sculpted Dave's likeness and Johnson carved Bayne's.

Rains previously created monuments of ten Nashville legends for country music star Buck Owens. He said there was something special about working on a statue of Dave. "This is one of the greatest honors, to do a statue of one of our heroes here at home," he said.

Johnson said he never knew Bayne, who died in 2003 at age eighty-eight, but the more he learned about him, the more grateful he became to work on his statue. "The best sculptures are the ones you're most motivated to do," he said, describing his Bayne statue as one of his best works. It depicts the man who guided the Billings Legion Post 4 team to the Legion World Series four times in a five-year span, from 1958 to 1963, including the 1960 team with Dave as its top player that played for the national championship and finished second to a New Orleans team.

Bayne, himself a Billings Legion player in the 1930s, served as assistant coach of the Billings program before becoming head coach and was involved in twenty-two state championships that Billings won. Two of his former players, Greg Pekovich and Sam McDonald, commissioned his sculpture. Both spoke briefly before the unveiling. McDonald called Bayne, "a great friend and a terrific coach, one of the best coaches in Billings history." Johnson's sculpture shows Bayne giving advice to McDonald and Pekovich as teenagers.

Rains' son, Jim, describing the McNally project, said his father was "never more challenged by a project or more pleased with the outcome." Dave, he said, was a "genuine local hero, and his statute would grace "a truly wonderful baseball park." And Jeff McNally recalled how, when he was growing up in Baltimore, his father often talked about Billings, its Legion baseball program, and how both shaped him as a man.

Both statues still greet baseball fans as they enter Dehler Park to watch games featuring Billings' minor-league Mustangs and the city's two American Legion teams, the Royals and the Scarlets. Jeff McNally said his father would be honored to see his statue in front of Dehler Park. "It's really fitting, because this place never left him," he said.

Almost two decades after his death, Dave received additional recognition of his legacy. That came through two major articles in the *Billings Gazette*, an April 2020 piece about the day in June 1975 when Dave faced fellow

Billing product Joe McIntosh in Dave's final major-league game, and an October 2020 account of his record-setting grand-slam home run in the 1970 World Series.

The first article focused on the June 8, 1975, game between the visiting San Diego Padres and the Montreal Expos that pitted McIntosh, who had starred for Washington State University after playing Legion ball in Billings and was in his second year as a pitcher for the Padres, versus McNally.

What Gazette readers learned, if they didn't already know, were these details from the game forty-five years earlier:

It was a 57-degree day at the Expos field, and it was almost game time. McIntosh knew Dave well because one of his older brothers, Bill, was a teammate of Dave's on the powerhouse Billings Legion teams in 1959 and 1960. Dave lived on Elm Street in Billings through his eighteenth birthday, and he often went to the McIntosh family home on nearby Spruce Street to hang out with Bill.

In a break from convention then, which frowned upon fraternizing with opponents before a game, McIntosh went to the telephone in the Padres visitors' clubhouse. He called to the Expos clubhouse and asked for Dave. "Just a minute," someone answered. Dave came to the phone, and McIntosh said, "Hey, Dave, this is Joey McIntosh."

They chatted for a few minutes, and before he hung up, Dave spoke in the lingo of pitchers. "Nothing but fastballs down the middle," he said, describing the way he thought the two should pitch to each other at a time when the National League hadn't yet adopted the designated-hitter rule. That remark caught McIntosh off guard. He hesitated for a minute, then replied, "Right." The pitchers hung up and continued warming up for the first and still only all-Billings pitching duel in major-league history.

McIntosh, then twenty-three, didn't realize the significance of what was about to happen, but he did in 2020, when he was a still-practicing lawyer in Seattle. "A couple of Bayne boys who meet in the province of Quebec," he said. He probably was shaking his head as he pictured the long-ago scene in his mind. "How odd is it?" he said in wonder.

McIntosh never lost his admiration for Dave. "I followed him like crazy. I adored him. He was always so good to me and my family. I rooted for him the whole way."

That bond even survived Dave's trickery when McIntosh came to bat against him in the June 1975 game. McIntosh walked to the plate, ready to swing at fastballs. Instead, Dave served the youngster three curveballs and struck him out. As he walked back to the dugout, McIntosh glanced over his shoulder. He insists he saw Dave laughing. "He had a great curveball. There was no way I was going to hit that," McIntosh said. He realized that the deal was off. Dave had taken him for a ride in the long tradition of what baseball veterans did to rookies.

McIntosh knew he didn't have to stick to fastballs, either. He used his breaking pitches to get McNally to ground out in his first at-bat, and when Dave came up a second time, he tagged a long, foul fly out to left field that worried McIntosh a bit before Bobby Tolan gloved the ball.

The Padres gave McIntosh a three-run lead in the first and added two more runs in the sixth. That ended Dave's day—and his big-league career on a losing note. McIntosh said he talked to Dave only before the game that day, and the subject of retirement never came up.

In 2020, almost five decades later, McIntosh could joke about a possible scenario in June 1975: "Probably if he lost to me, he figured that's it."

No one ever asked Dave if that thought crossed his mind.

THE GRAND-SLAM AGES WELL

Readers of the *Billings Gazette* got an additional reminder of McNally's legacy during World Series time in 2020. Again, it was Bighaus who provided the memories in an article published on October 11, 2020.

Bighaus started with the story now familiar to many people in Billings, Baltimore and everywhere else where there were Orioles fans: Dave's sixth-inning grand slam home run in Game Three of the 1970 World Series against the Cincinnati Reds, and how Dave and Jean McNally's son, Jeff, the oldest of a family that grew to include five children, got his moment of fame, a brief appearance on national TV when NBC sportscaster Tony Kubek put a microphone in front of him.

Kubek found Jean and Jeff sitting in seats in Memorial Stadium a few minutes after the slam and asked both their thoughts. Jeff's were memorable.

"I thought he wasn't going to get a hit," said Jeff, then seven. "I thought he was going to get out."

Instead, his father entered the record books with the first and still only grand slam homer hit by a pitcher in Series play.

Recalling the event, Jean McNally said, "It was just pure excitement. I remember that day quite well."

Jeff, who earned a baseball scholarship to Stanford University and became a physician who practices in Utah, put the fifty-year-old moment in context during a phone interview with Bighaus. "It's kind of a defining sports event for our family," said Jeff, a high school basketball star in Billings and an American Legion baseball standout. (He was drafted by the Milwaukee Brewers before he was injured in college and decided to concentrate on his pre-medical studies.)

Dave's mother, Beth, also was at the game, a member of a crowd of 51,733 fans, most of whom looked on in disbelief when McNally sent Reds reliever Wayne Granger's pitch sailing over the left-field fence and several rows deep into the bleachers.

"Obviously, when Tony came up, I was almost too excited to even talk," Jean said. "And Jeff was so cute because he thought his dad was going to strike out. I think we were all just kind of speechless, you know. Did this really happen? It was so exciting."

The Major League Baseball Network had just broadcast a replay of the 1970 Series, which the Orioles won in five games. (Game Five, including Kubek's interview with Jean and Jeff McNally, can also be viewed on YouTube.) That allowed Jeff, Jean and others in the large McNally family to bask in Dave's glory. Thinking of her children, grandchildren and great-grandchildren, Jean said, "It was just a lot of fun for them to see." And "to see that I was young once, too," she said, laughing.

"It was very surreal. I had never seen it before," Jeff said of the interview, which occurred in the seventh inning. "I remember the interview and kind of what I said, but I had never seen it. It kind of threw me for a loop a little bit."

He watched the replay of Game Three with his wife, Cass, in their home in Utah while texting with three of their four children, who live in California. "I've used (the grand slam) many, many times in conversations. It's a super cool baseball trivia point," he said.

Jeff said he realized the importance of the moment as a youngster. "I totally remember as a seven-year-old being really into the game, recognizing that the bases were loaded and being excited. And then thinking, 'Oh, dang it, my dad is coming up and we're going to waste this opportunity.'"

Those watching the replay of the game heard commentary again from NBC announcer Curt Gowdy: "That looks pretty good," he said. "Grand slam home run!"

And the replay showed McNally beaming as he rounded the bases and then crossed home plate where a flock of jubilant Birds greeted him.

"It just gives you the shivers," Jean said. "There are a lot of baseball memories, but that's definitely the best."

"I remember thinking, 'That's going to be a home run,' and being shocked," Jeff said.

Jeff McNally gets another kind of kick from that day. "You should watch the interview. If for nothing else to see the plaid sport coat I was wearing and the super-wide tie. My kids just humbled me: 'Dad, you're the biggest nerd.'" Jeff shook off the good-natured grief he got, his memories sweetened by still having his ticket and program from the game.

Decades later, his mother remained amazed by her choice of gameday attire for Jeff.

"Before I first saw that interview, I would have bet I wouldn't have put a sport coat and tie on my seven-year-old. So, there was the proof, the evidence. I don't recall my thinking behind that. I just don't."

It's not as if their wardrobe that day—Jean wore a dress—was out of synch with the rest of the Memorial Stadium crowd. Most fans visible in the broadcast are wearing white shirts and ties or fancy dresses and necklaces.

Dave was a seasoned veteran by then, but he, too, got swept up in the historic moment. "His reaction was total excitement," Jean recalled. "I know he wasn't happy with his pitching, but that was completely overridden by the grand slam. I know he was pretty shocked and surprised. He was pretty happy with himself."

If Dave were alive in 2020, "He would remember it well, but he wouldn't want to fuss about it. It's also emotional that so many years have gone by, and Dave isn't here to enjoy his family and all this. That part is hard," Jean said.

Besides the broadcast replays, baseball fans across the country can enjoy another reminder of McNally's grand slam. His autographed thirty-two-ounce bat, a Louisville Slugger that he borrowed for that at-bat from teammate Curt Motton, as well as the ball that sailed out of the park, are both housed at the National Baseball Hall of Fame in Cooperstown, New York.

Jean summarized her late husband's legacy in three sentences: "A lot of people remember Dave for challenging the reserve clause. Winning twenty-games four years in a row was also a big deal ... But this grand slam stands out in most people's minds as what he is most famous for."

"A lot of people in Billings and Montana remember where they were and how excited they were. It's hard to imagine how many years have gone by."

The McNally family continues to celebrate Dave's 1970 World Series home run, and so do Orioles fans in Billings, Baltimore, and elsewhere. "I think it's just a pretty special feeling that he did that and no one else has broken the record," Jean said. "It's something, you know, that just sticks with our family forever. We do talk about it a lot."

She said she could only remember once that another pitcher came to bat in a Series game with the bases loaded. "Then you were kind of like, this will be great, they'll bring up Dave, and they'll say he was the only other pitcher to do that. Then you're kind of thinking, I don't want that to happen. Not at this point." Jean said her family considers the grand-slam record as something special. "We would rather keep it for ourselves."

It appears Dave's moment of immortality is safe. His record could have been matched after 1970 and then from the mid-1970s on even when the designated-hitter rule took effect in the American League. Until 2020, pitchers batted in National League ballparks during the World Series. But nowadays, with major-league baseball having adopted a universal DH-rule and other measures intended to liven up the game, pitchers don't bat even in postseason games.

That's OK with Jean, who with her five children, fourteen grandchildren, and eight grandchildren, as of 2020, hoped to keep Dave's grand slam record in the family. "I guess there are no more worries—that record is set in place," she said. "We're home free. But I think they're (major-league baseball) really missing out on an opportunity for another pitcher like Dave to get up there and cause a lot of excitement."

POSTSCRIPT

I owe the idea for this book to a Billings man, Tim O'Malley. When I was gathering material in 2014 for my first book, *Win 'Em All*, an account of the Laurel Locomotives' *Hoosiers*-like run to the 1969 Big 32 Montana state basketball championship, Tim shared a lot of useful material with me.

Tim, a product of the Billings Catholic and public school system (Fratt School and McKinley School), was a contemporary of mine, although I didn't know him when we were both in high school. He graduated from nearby Red Lodge High School in 1970, and I graduated the year before from Billings West High School.

Tim, well-known in Billings as someone who partnered with Chuck Schmidt to open the Suds Hut restaurant on Broadwater Avenue and then was an advertising salesman for three Magic City TV stations, was also an avid sports fan.

One of the main characters in *Win 'Em All*, Alan Campbell, a star guard for Billings Central High during his junior year, transferred to Laurel for his senior year and helped the Locomotives win their first state basketball championship. Tim knew Alan and shared his connections to Central. Tim told me that when he was a youngster, his family had a home near the Catholic high school and he got to know Dave, some nine years older and then a Central student.

I'll always remember Tim telling me several times, "Dennis, you gotta write a book about Dave McNally." Finally, I did, Tim. Sadly, you won't be able to read it, since I've learned that you passed away at age seventy-three on May 14, 2024. RIP, my friend. And, since heaven has a library, check out my book there. And thanks for inspiring me to chronicle the life of a man from our hometown, Billings, who championed workplace fairness for professional baseball players and whose principled stand helped bring that fundamental right to other pro athletes.

ENDNOTES

CHAPTER ONE: BILLINGS BEGINNINGS

1. *Daily Interlake*, Kalispell, Montana, January 6, 1971.
2. *Sidney Herald*, December 14, 1950.
3. *Billings Gazette*, August 20, 1950.
4. *Billings Memories II: the 1940s, 1950s and 1960s, Billings Gazette*, 2016.
5. *Billings Gazette*, October 5, 2010.
6. Ibid., September 27, 1952.
7. Ibid., September 28, 1952.
8. Ibid., June 15, 1952.
9. Ibid., June 7, 1952.
10. Ibid., June 10, 1952.
11. Ibid., June 18, 1952.
12. Ibid., June 21, 1952.

CHAPTER TWO: FOUNDATION FOR FAME

1. Ibid., March 14, 1959.

CHAPTER THREE: PRELUDE TO GLORY AND A LIFETIME MATCH

1. Baseball-reference.com.
2. Baseball-reference.com.
3. *Billings Gazette*, September 26, 1971.
4. Ibid., September 3, 1966.
5. Ibid., January 19, 1971.
6. Ibid., August 19, 2020.

CHAPTER FOUR: BEST IN THE LAND

1. Ibid., June 4, 1960.
2. Ibid., June 9, 1960.
3. Ibid., June 13, 1960.
4. Ibid., June 18, 1960.
5. Ibid., June 25, 1960.
6. Ibid., June 30, 1960.
7. Ibid., July 3, 1960.
8. Ibid., July 13, 1960.
9. *Helena Independent Record*, August 10, 1960.

10. Missoula *Missoulian*, August 14, 1960.
11. *Billings Gazette*, August 19, 1960.
12. Ibid., July 6, 1960.
13. *Coach: Baseball and Life-Eddie Bayne Style* compiled by his Billings American Legion baseball players, private printing, Billings, 2015.
14. Mays, ace of the New York Yankees pitching staff in 1920, had that season marred by his beaning of the Cleveland Indians' Ray Chapman on August 16, 1920. Chapman died soon after the accident. https://www.baseball-reference.com/bullpen/Carl_Mays.
15. *Billings Gazette*, August 25, 1960.
16. Ibid., August 25, 1960.
17. Ibid., August 28, 1960.
18. Baseball-reference.com.
19. *Billings Gazette*, January 11, 1964.
20. Ibid., May 2, 1964.
21. Ibid., February 8, 1998.
22. *The Hastings Daily Tribune* (Nebraska), August 19, 1960.
23. Evening World Herald (Omaha, Nebraska), August 30, 1960.
24. *Hastings Daily Tribune* (Nebraska), September 5, 1960.
25. *Hastings Daily Tribune*, August 30, 1960.
26. Billings Gazette, September 17, 1960.
27. *Baltimore Sun*, April 30, 1963.
28. Ibid., November 15, 1960.

CHAPTER FIVE: LEARNING IN THE BUSHES

1. Baseball-reference.com.
2. *Billings Gazette*, November 10, 1960.
3. *Arizona Republic*, November 5, 1960.
4. *Baltimore Sun*, October 28, 1960.
5. *Billings Gazette*, December 24, 1960.
6. Ibid., February 24, 1961
7. Ibid., December 29, 1960.
8. *Missoulian*, Missoula, Montana, February 28, 1961.
9. *The Post-Crescent*, Appleton, Wisconsin, April 6, 1961.
10. *Billings Gazette*, March 18, 1961.
11. *New York Daily News*, April 7, 1961.
12. *Billings Gazette* April 14, 1961.
13. *Post-Crescent*, Appleton, Wisconsin, April 14, 1961.
14. Ibid., May 9, 1961.
15. *Billings Gazette*, May 11, 1961.
16. *Lincoln Star Journal* (Nebraska), May 14, 1961.
17. *Post-Crescent*, Appleton, Wisconsin, May 26, 1961.
18. *Lincoln Star Journal*, June 4, 1961.
19. *Post-Crescent*, June 17, 1961.
20. *Billings Gazette*, September 13, 1961.
21. *The Sporting News*, November 8, 1961.
22. *Baltimore Sun*, November 29, 1961.
23. *Arizona Republic*, December 4, 1961.
24. *The Sporting News*, January 10, 1962.
25. *Billings Gazette*, January 7, 1962.

CHAPTER SIX: SERVING NOTICE

1. Ibid., March 31, 1961.
2. *The Sporting News*, January 31, 1962.
3. Ibid., March 31, 1962.
4. *Baseball Digest*, "Scouting Reports on 1962 Major League Rookies, March 1962.
5. *The Sporting News*, March 28, 1962.
6. *Star-Gazette* (Elmira, NY), July 17, 1962.
7. Kansas City was tops in the American League with a .276 batting average in 1962, Stathead.com
8. *Baltimore Sun*, September 27, 1962.
9. Ibid.
10. Ibid.
11. *Billings Gazette*, September 27, 1962.

CHAPTER SEVEN: BUILDING TOWARDS GREATNESS

1. *Baltimore Sun*, April 30, 1963.
2. *Billings Gazette*, April 23, 1963.
3. *Baltimore Sun*, April 24, 1963.
4. Ibid., April 28, 1963.
5. *Billings Gazette*, April 5, 1963.
6. Ibid., April 14, 1963.
7. *Baltimore Sun*, April 5, 1963.
8. *Billings Gazette*, February 13, 1963.
9. Ibid., April 16, 1963.
10. Ibid., April 28, 1963.
11. Ibid., June 12, 1963.
12. Ibid., September 15, 1963.
13. Baseball-reference.com.
14. *Billings Gazette*, August 28, 1963.
15. www.baseball-reference.com/bullpen/Winter_Leagues.
16. *The Sporting News*.
17. Ibid.
18. Missoula *Missoulian*, October 28, 1963.

CHAPTER EIGHT: NEARING THE PROMISED LAND

1. *The Sporting News*, January 2, 1965.
2. *Baltimore Sun*, February 28, 1964.
3. *Billings Gazette*, May 17, 1964.
4. *Baltimore Sun*, March 17, 1964.
5. Baseball-reference.com.
6. *Billings Gazette*, September 27, 1969.
7. *The Sporting News*, November 27, 1965.
8. *Baltimore Sun*, October 2, 1965.
9. *Baltimore Sun*, August 9, 1965.

CHAPTER NINE: BEST IN THE AMERICAN LEAGUE

1. Here's a snippet of Sarandon's monologue, now a classic part of American film: https://youtu.be/ECnlL4RY8PQ?si=bo1yvE-FNiVVQZZX.

ENDNOTES

2. *The Sporting News.*
3. *Intelligencer Journal* (Lancaster, PA), January 12, 1966.
4. *Havre Daily News* (Montana), January 12, 1966.
5. *Billings Gazette,* February 8, 1966.
6. *Baltimore Sun,* February 25, 1966.
7. *The Record American,* Mahoney City, Pennsylvania, February 26, 1966.
8. Plews, a Helena native, played second base, third base and was a pinch hitter during his four seasons in the majors with Washington and Boston, from 1956-1959. He had a 0.262 batting average. Barclay, born in Chicago, died in Missoula, Montana. He pitched for three seasons, 1957-1959, for the New York and San Francisco Giants and had a 10-9 win-loss record in the majors. baseball-reference.com.
9. *Billings Gazette,* November 12, 2020.
10. Baseball-reference.com.
11. *Baltimore Sun,* May 1, 1966.

CHAPTER TEN: SHAKY SERIES START

1. Baseball-reference.com.
2. Phone interview with Jim Palmer.
3. Ibid., January 24, 2023.
4. *The Baltimore Sun,* October 4, 1966.
5. *New York Daily News,* October 4, 1966.
6. *Baltimore Sun,* October 6, 1966.
7. *Billings Gazette,* October 6, 1966.
8. *Arizona Republic,* October 6, 1966.

CHAPTER ELEVEN: CHAMPS OF THE WORLD

1. *Baltimore Sun,* October 9, 1966
2. *Billings Gazette,* October 10, 1966.
3. *Baltimore Sun,* October 10, 1966.
4. Ibid., October 9, 1966.
5. *Billings Gazette,* October 17, 1966.
6. Interview with Pete Cochran, November 3, 2022.

CHAPTER THIRTEEN: POST-WORLD SERIES FUNK

1. *Billings Gazette,* February 7, 1967.
2. *Baltimore Sun,* February 26, 1967.
3. *Columbus News* (Montana), September 5, 1963.
4. Phone interview with Jim Palmer, November 3, 2022.
5. *Baltimore Sun,* March 6, 1967.
6. Ibid., March 6, 1977.
7. Ibid., May 8, 1967.
8. Ibid., May 17, 1967.
9. Ibid., April 18, 1967.
10. Ibid., April 12, 1967.
11. Ibid., April 26, 1967.
12. Ibid., April 29, 1967.
13. Ibid., July 2, 1967.
14. Ibid., July 7, 1967.
15. Ibid., July 14, 1967.
16. Ibid., September 23, 1967.

17. Ibid., July 7, 1967.
18. *The Sporting News*, September 9, 1967.
19. Ibid., September 2, 1967.
20. Ibid., October 21, 1967.

CHAPTER FOURTEEN: RETURN TO GLORY

1. Ibid., May 17, 1969.
2. *Baltimore Sun*, April 9, 1969.
3. *The Sporting News*.
4. *Baltimore Sun*, April 25, 1969.
5. Ibid., May 16, 1969.

CHAPTER FIFTEEN: THE STREAK

1. Ibid., July 26, 1969.
2. Ibid., July 31, 1969.
3. Ibid., August 2, 1969.
4. *Billings Gazette*, August 2, 1969.

CHAPTER SIXTEEN: ANOTHER SERIES

1. *Baltimore Sun*, October 6, 1969.
2. Ibid., October 8, 1969.
3. Ibid., October 13, 1969.
4. Ibid.
5. Ibid., October 16, 1966.
6. *The Sporting News*, November 11, 1969.
7. *Baltimore Sun*, October 17, 1969.

CHAPTER SEVENTEEN: THE GRAND SLAM

1. *The Sporting News*, January 10, 1966.
2. Ibid., March 21, 1970.
3. Ibid., March 28, 1970.
4. Baseball-reference.com.
5. *The Sporting News*, March 28, 1970.
6. https://baseballradarguns.com/evolution-of-baseball-radar-guns/.
7. *The Miami News*, April 19, 1974.
8. *The Sporting News*, September 12, 1970.
9. *Baltimore Sun*, August 30, 1969.
10. Baseball-reference.com.
11. NBC broadcast of Game 3 of the 1970 World Series, viewed on YouTube, last accessed on July 7, 2024.
12. *Billings Gazette*, October 24, 2000.
13. Video clip of McNally's grand slam home run: https://youtu.be/TVwXX-Mj5P8?si=DWrhWLWz2wGicZq-.
14. *Billings Gazette*, October 24, 2000.
15. Interview with Dee Nobles, October 26, 2022.
16. *Cincinnati Enquirer*, October 14, 1970.

CHAPTER EIGHTEEN: LUTHERVILLE DAYS

1. Phone interview with Boog Powell, 2023.
2. Interview with Jean McNally, January 20, 2023.
3. A sense of the house as it looks today provided by videos taken by retired *Baltimore Sun* sportswriter John Eisenberg and emailed to the author.

CHAPTER NINETEEN: GREATEST PITCHING ROTATION EVER

1. *Billings Gazette,* January 21, 1971.
2. *The Sporting News*, January 2, 1971.
3. Ibid., January 30, 1971.
4. *Billings Gazette,* January 21, 1971.
5. Ibid., January 14 1971.
6. *Spokane Chronicle,* February 3, 1971.
7. *Baltimore Sun,* April 8, 1971.
8. Ibid., May 7, 1971.
9. Ibid., September 22, 1971.
10. Other AL pitchers in the twenty-win for four years straight ranks were Cy Young, Red Ruffing, Walter Johnson, Addie Joss, Wes Ferrell, Rube Waddell, Urban Shocker, Stan Coveleski, and Eddie Plank.
11. *Baltimore Sun,* September 25, 1971.
12. Ibid., September 25, 1971.
13. www.baseball-reference.com.
14. Ibid.
15. Ibid.
16. *Baltimore Sun,* October 8, 1971.
17. Ibid., October 10, 1971.
18. www.baseball-reference.com.
19. *The Pittsburgh Press,* October 15, 1971.
20. *Baltimore Sun,* October 17, 1971.
21. *Baltimore Sun,* October 18, 1971.

CHAPTER TWENTY: WINDING DOWN

1. *Baltimore Sun,* April 22, 1972.
2. *Billings Gazette,* July 2, 1972.
3. *Baltimore Sun,* April 7, 1973.
4. Ibid., April 13, 1973.
5. Ibid., October 8, 1973.
6. Jim Palmer, phone interview, January 20, 2023.
7. *Baltimore Sun,* March 3, 1974.
8. Ibid., February 11, 1974.
9. Ibid., February 27, 1974.

CHAPTER TWENTY-ONE: LIFE WITH WEAVER

1. Ibid., September 21, 1969.
2. Ibid., August 21, 1969.
3. *Billings Gazette,* January 21, 1971.
4. Jim Palmer, phone interview, January 20, 2023.
5. Jim Palmer phone interview.

CHAPTER TWENTY-TWO: THE END... AND HISTORY

1. *Baltimore Sun*, September 20, 1974.
2. Ibid., December 4, 1974.
3. Ibid., February 8, 1975.
4. Ibid., March 3, 1975.
5. *Lords of the Realm: The Real History of Baseball.*
6. *The Sporting News,* June 28, 1975
7. *Baltimore Sun*, July 3, 1975.
8. Ibid., June 27, 1975.
9. Ibid., July 3, 1975.
10. Interview with Jean McNally, January 20, 2023.
11. *Billings Gazette*, June 30, 1975.
12. Ibid., January 19, 1971.
13. Ibid., July 14, 1976.

CHAPTER TWENTY-THREE: BACK HOME

1. Ibid., September 21, 1977.
2. Ibid., May 29, 1977.
3. Ibid., June 4, 1978.
4. Facebook message to author, February 24, 2024.
5. *Baltimore Sun*, September 1, 1978.
6. Funeral bulletin for Dave McNally, December 5, 2002.

CHAPTER TWENTY-FOUR: MONTANA'S GREATEST ATHLETE

1. *Billings Gazette,* December 12, 2000.
2. Ibid., December 15, 2000.

CHAPTER TWENTY-FIVE: THE LAST BATTLE

1. *Newsday*, September 14, 2000.
2. *Billings Gazette,* December 6, 2002.
3. *Baltimore Sun*, December 3, 2002.
4. *Great Falls Tribune*, December 3, 2002.
5. *Billings Gazette,* December 3, 2002.

CHAPTER TWENTY-SIX: MCNALLY'S LEGACY

1. https://apnews.com/article/mlb-average-salary-d7df2745aee8dd3dd59bf7a7c747841b.
2. *Billings Gazette,* June 30, 2008.

INDEX

A
Albie Pearson, 78
Al Downing, 181
Al Kaline, 72, 131
Al Oliver, 168, 169
Al Weis, 119, 143–44, 149
Anaheim, 96
Andy Etchebebarren
    longtime Orioles catcher and good friend of Dave McNally, 60, 68, 102–103, 139, 207
Andy Messersmith, 3–4, 8, 165, 188–90
Andy Price, 210
Anne McNally
    fourth-born of the McNally's five children, 159
Appleton, Wisconsin
    home of Tri-City Foxes, Dave's team for much of 1961, 62–64
Appliance Mart, 25, 29
Archie Cochrane Ford, 187, 190, 194
Ardmore, Oklahoma, 66
Arizona Instructional League, 60, 64–65, 93, 207

B
Babe Ruth, 25–26, 29–30, 55, 94, 103
Babe Ruth baseball, 25–26, 29–30, 55, 94, 103
Baltimore Orioles, 2, 4–5, 8–11, 21, 26, 32, 34, 53–65, 67–82, 84–89, 91–119, 128–29, 131–34, 138–53, 156–63, 165–69, 171–72, 174–80, 182–87, 189, 196–99, 201–202, 204, 206–10, 214–15, 217
Baseball Hall of Fame, 173, 199, 217
Baseball's first player strike in 1972, 171
Baseball Writers Association
    Richard Nixon an honorary member, 173
Bauer, Hank, 1–2
Beth Bragg, 193

Beth McNally, 2, 7, 10, 12, 14, 28, 34, 53, 62, 64, 70, 85, 103–5, 139, 155, 193, 197, 215
Big Boy Drive-In
    landmark Billings eatery, 41
Big Daddy Lipscomb, 72
Big Sky All-Stars
    Billings team that made first and only trip to the Little League World Series in 2011, 22
Bill Bighaus, 207, 211, 214–15
    longtime Billings Gazette sportswriter, 207
Bill Dixon, 12
Billings Central
    Billings Catholic high school, 17, 26, 28, 30–31, 40, 43–44, 53, 61, 110, 200, 206, 218
Billings Gazette, 1, 4, 7, 13, 17, 27, 34–35, 48, 73, 76, 89, 94, 107, 163, 193, 195, 212, 214
Billings Mustangs, 2, 17–19, 27–29, 47, 49–50, 95, 212
Bill McIntosh, 16, 18, 26, 42, 46
Bill Rains, 211–12
Bill Skowron, 93
Bill Tanton, 72, 141
Billy Hitchcock
    manager of Orioles when Dave McNally made the big team roster, 65, 78, 82
Billy Hunter, 89, 150, 161, 169
Billy Martin, 138
Blackie Johnson, 47
Bob Allison, 141
Bobby Floyd, 181
Bobby Grich, 178
Bobby Richardson, 76, 84
Bob Chilton
    home plate umpire in the 1960 Little World Series championship game, 52
Bob Daugherty, 102
Bob Feller, 83, 173

Bob Fry, 16–18, 27, 52
Bob Gibson, 97, 154
Bob Glasgow
    driver of Legion Post 4 team bus, 43
Bob Johnson, 87, 119
Bob Lemon, 151, 173
Bob Maisel, 118, 174, 185–86, 197–99
Bob Oliver, 136
Bob Robertson, 169
Boog Powell, 4, 60, 79, 134, 139, 157, 165, 171
Boston Red Sox, 109, 117, 129, 210
Brent Musburger
    Billings man, son of Cecil Musburger, who became famed TV sports broadcaste, 8, 21–22, 27
Brooklyn Dodgers, 2, 79, 95
Brooks Robinson, 32, 34, 89, 95, 101–2, 109–10, 115, 131, 136, 139, 142–43, 145, 150, 155, 157, 159, 161–62, 164, 174, 178, 198–99, 203, 208–9
Bruce Kison, 169
Buck Martinez, 136
Bud Freeman, 161
Bud Harrelson, 143
Burleigh Grimes, 54
Buster Narum, 75
Butte, Montana, 11–12, 27, 30, 33, 46–47, 53, 137
Byron Humphrey, 54

C

Cale Crowley
    Butte native and prominent Billings lawyer, 53
California Angels, 73, 86, 96, 165
California Winter League, 79
Camden Yards
    replaced Memorial Stadium as the Orioles home park in the 1990s, 209
Campy Campaneris, 152
Carl Hubbel, 135
Carl Mays
    scout for Cleveland Indians and former major-league pitcher, 39
Carl Yastrzemski, 117
Casey at the Bat, 94
Casey Stengel, 1
Catfish Hunter, 89, 162, 175, 177
Catherine McNally
    Dave's grandfather, 11

CBS
    owner of Yankees in 1960s before George Steinbrenner purchased the team, 55
Cecil Musburger
    "father" of Little League baseball in Billings, 8, 10, 21, 25, 29
Cedar Rapids, Iowa, 63
Central City, Nebraska, 43–44
Cesar Tolivar, 132
Charities and programs Dave supported, 14, 200
Charlie Lau, 119, 130
Chavez Ravine, 97
Cheney, Washington, 45
Chicago White Sox, 8, 34, 48, 76, 86, 117, 135, 149, 173
Chuck Dobson, 154
Chuck Estrada, 73–74, 77
Chuck Miller, 45
Chuck Stroup, 44
Chuck Thompson, 116
Cincinnati Reds, 2, 34, 77, 92, 153–54, 156, 161, 164, 214–15
Cleon Jones, 149
Cleveland Indians, 39, 48, 73, 77, 82–83, 86, 117, 135, 161, 166–67, 171–73, 179–80
Cliff Evans, 172–73
Cobb Field
    baseball park in Billings where Mustangs and Legion teams played for six decades, replaced in 2007 by Dehler Park, 14, 18–19, 29, 33, 37–38, 46–48, 210–11
Colorado Springs
    site of 1958 Little World Series, 37–39, 42, 53
Columbian League, 80
Comiskey Park, 34, 86, 117
Connie Mack, 166
Continental Plaza
    Gene Autrey-owned hotel in Los Angeles where Orioles stayed during 1996 Series games there, 96
Cuban Winter League, 79
Cuellar, Mike, 5
Curt Barclay, 92
Curt Blefary, 93
Curt Gowdy, 153, 216
Cy Young Award, 148

D

Dale Boudreaux
  catcher for Tulane Shirts, 51
Danny Fuchs, 163
Danny Murtaugh, 167
Dan Osinki, 117
Darrell Johnson, 71
Dave Johnson, 78, 93, 100, 113, 131
Dave Koslo, 1
Dave McNally, 1, 3–5, 7, 9, 13, 16–17, 21, 38, 43, 45, 47, 50–51, 68, 72, 75–76, 79, 83, 88, 91, 93, 108–9, 116, 136, 142, 147, 151, 153, 174, 176, 184–85, 199, 201, 203, 205, 208, 211, 218
Dave McNally Special
  house in Lutherville, Maryland, advertised in 1963 in Baltimore Sun, 75
Dave's favorite goodies, 160
David Eisenhower, 173
Dean Martin, 112
Dean Stone, 78
Deb Hofer, 196
Dee Nobles, 4, 7, 12–14, 28, 34, 53, 103, 107, 155
  Dave's sister, 13, 34, 53, 155
Dehler Park
  replaced Cobb Field as Billings' primary baseball park in 2008, 211–12
Denny McLain, 93, 130, 148
Dick Cavett, 161
Dick Hall, 4, 10, 32, 34–35, 50, 78, 83, 87–89, 150–51, 159, 162, 178, 180, 182, 186, 197–98, 202
Dick Harte, 26
Dick Leary, 137
Dick Letwak, 26, 46
Dick McAuliffe, 115, 131
Dick Moss, 179, 189
Dick Stuart, 102
Dick Woodson, 178
D J Volkswagen
  second car dealership in Billings that Dave and Jim McNally owned and operated, 194
Dock Ellis, 168
Dominican League, 80
Don Baylor, 174
Don Buford, 134, 136, 147, 209
Don Campbell
  owner of Big Boy Drive-In, 41
Don Drysdale, 92, 100–3, 108, 208
Don Harte, 26
Don Hofer, 196
Don Larsen, 87
Don Lick, 93
Don Lock, 132
Donn Clendenon, 143–44, 146
Don Wert, 115
Don Zupan
  sports editor of the Billings Gazette in the 1960s, 61, 69, 76–77
Doug Brown, 56, 68, 118–19, 176
Doyle Alexander, 176–77, 183
Dr. Leonard Wallenstein, 176, 191
Durocher, Leo, 1

E

Earl Knight
  Billings mayor in the 1950s, 28, 39
Earl Weaver, 10, 60–61, 63–64, 68, 129, 131, 134, 147, 152, 162, 164, 167–69, 174–77, 180–83, 185, 197, 209
Early Wynn, 173
Easter Seals, 146, 150, 163, 200
Ed Bayne, 30, 43–44, 47
  Billings American Legion coach who took the Legion Post 4 team to national prominence in the 1950s and 1960s, 10, 25, 33–35, 37, 43–44, 47, 51, 53–54, 103, 132, 137, 163, 211
Ed Bayne, Jr.
  one of Ed Bayne's sons and a player on his teams that reached the American Legion Little World Series, 34, 43–44, 47
Ed Charles, 143
Eddie Fisher, 98
Ed Gorilla
  coach of Fargo, North Dakota, Legion team, 47
Ed Hummel, 26, 30
Ed Kirkpatrick, 136
Ed Sadowski, 78
Elmira, New York
  city where McNally played in 1962, 64, 66–68, 72, 85, 180
Elm Street
  street in Billings where Dave grew up, 2, 8, 12, 54, 213

Elrod Hendricks, 169, 197
Emerson Hotel, 116
Ernie Walters, 195

F

Felipe Alou, 152
Felix Torres, 78
Fenway Park, 117
Flanagan, Mike, 5
Foxes
   Tri-Cities team based in Appleton, Wisconsin, 62–64, 180
Francis McCord, 25, 30
Frank Cashen, 167
Frank Howard, 19, 129, 137, 164, 174–75, 204
Frankie Bertaina, 112
Franklin Roosevelt, 107
Frank Pirtz, 33
Frank Quinn, 47
Frank Robinson, 34, 88–9, 101–103, 114, 119, 134, 143, 153, 166, 169, 198–99
Frank Sinatra, 112
Fraser McDonald, 207
Fratt School
   Billings Catholic school system, 2, 7, 218

G

Galen Cisco, 117
Gary Bell, 117
Gary Gentry, 142
Gary Rostkowski, 5
Gene Lissa
   longtime Billings grocer who donated the lot used for Little League baseball, 13
Gene Mauch, 186–87
Gene Tenace, 152
Gene Woodring, 88
George Bamberger, 141–42, 154, 182
George Mitterwald, 141
George Staller, 66
Gil Hodges, 141
Glendive, Montana, 30, 46–47
Gordon Beard, 74, 198
Grant Jackson, 175
Great Falls, Montana, 27, 31, 48–49, 94
Greg Pekovich, 212

H

Hank Aaron, 83

Hank Bauer, 1, 2, 74, 82, 86–89, 97–98, 102, 104, 110, 114–15, 117–18, 129
Hank Soar, 74
Harmon Killebrew, 115, 140
Harry Brecheen, 65, 80, 102
Harry Dalton, 70, 89, 91, 162, 167
Harry Platt, 178
Harvey Haddix, 87
Hastings, Nebraska
   site of 1960 American Legion Little World Series, 38, 50, 53–54
Herbie Plews, 92
Hiccups
   Dave's bout with hiccups in 1975, 190, 192
Hickok Award, 164
Hilands Golf Club, 14, 46
Hit and Run room
   site inside Memorial Stadium for Hall of Fame luncheon, 197
Hubert Humphrey, 100, 103, 108
Huntington Beach
   California team that defeated Big Sky All-Stars for the 2011 U.S. Little League championship, 22

J

Jack Dunn, 199
Jackie Brandt, 78
Jackie Robinson, 79
Jack Skinner, 2
James E. McNally
   Dave's grandfather, 11, 12
Jean McNally, 4, 17, 40–41, 53, 62, 64, 67, 69, 75, 85, 103, 107, 112, 128, 131, 147–51, 153–54, 157–60, 165, 186–87, 191–93, 196–98, 200, 207, 214–17
   Dave's wife, 4
   she married Dave in December 1961, 40, 53, 62, 64
Jean McNally and golf, 160
Jeff Ballard, 201–2
Jeff McNally, 4, 75, 85, 147–48, 154–55, 157–60, 169, 194, 196–98, 201, 206–7, 212, 214–16
Jerry Grote, 143
Jerry Hoffberger, 100, 103, 146, 158
Jerry Koosman, 141–45, 147, 154
Jerry Narum, 26

Jerry Neudecker, 115
Jerry Walters, 33, 38–40, 48
Jilly Rizzo, 112
Jim Bunning, 34, 202
Jim Clevenger, 207
Jim Frey, 197
Jim Gentile, 68, 79
Jim Kaat, 138
Jim Lefebvre, 101
Jim McLaughlin
    Orioles farm team director, 54
Jim McNally, 12, 132
Jim Michel, 26
Jimmy McNally
    Dave's father, who he never knew because he died in World War I, 7
    Dave's father, who he never knew because he died in World War II, 9, 11–12, 55
Jim Olsen, 45
Jim Palmer, 4–5, 10, 94, 96–97, 99, 103, 111–12, 119, 142, 149–50, 153, 156, 159, 163, 165, 167–69, 176–77, 180–84, 197, 208
Jim Russo
    Baltimore Orioles scout, 48, 68
Jim Scarborough
    Billings Central High classmate of Jean Hoffer and Dave McNally, 40
Jim Wilson
    Baltimore Orioles scout, 48, 68
Joe Cronin, 115
Joe Foy, 117
Joe Gaines, 78
Joe McIntosh
    youngest brother of Bill McIntosh, played Legion baseball in Billings, then for Washington State University and San Diego Padres, 106, 186, 213
Joe Paparella, 74
Joe Pepitone, 76
Joe Pirtz, 10, 98, 137
Joe Sparma, 115
John Bohlinger
    retired Billings businessman who was lieutenant governor and served several terms in the state legislature, 31–32, 139, 187
John Gaherin
    top negotiator for baseball team owners in 1975, 189

John Helyar, 188
John Houson, 38
John J. O'Connor, 155
John McHale
    president of the Montreal Expos in 1975, 188
John Miller
    young Orioles player, 61, 68, 75
Johnny Allen, 135–36
Johnny Carson, 155
Johnny Podres, 35
Johnny Unitas, 99
John Roseboro, 101
John W. Powell, 157–58
Joseph McMahon
    catcher for Tulane Shirts, 51
Jose Santiago, 117
Judy Martz
    former Montana governor, 201

K

Kangaroo court, 198
Ken Holtzman, 175
Ken Hunt, 77
Kent State University, 167
Kerry Feldman, 61
Koslo, Dave, 1
KTVQ
    Billings TV station, 34, 210

L

Larry Caldwell, 128
Larry Downer, 195–96
Larry Haney, 119, 146
Larry Shepard, 27
League for Crippled Children, 185
Lee MacPhail, 72
Lee May, 156
Lefty Grove, 135, 166
Legion Post 4
    Billings original American Legion team, now called the Billings Royals, 10, 14, 25, 29, 33, 35, 37–38, 41–43, 45, 47–50, 52–54, 61, 68, 77, 80, 98, 105–6, 132, 137, 212
Leo Durocher, 1
Leon Wagner, 76
Les Rohr, 92
Les Smith, 10, 98
Lincoln, Nebraska, 63
Lissa Field, 7–8, 14, 18, 25–28

Little League
  Little League baseball program, 2, 4, 7–8, 10, 13–14, 18, 20–29, 83, 95, 154–55, 187
Los Angeles Angels, 73, 76, 86, 96, 165, 189
Los Angeles Dodgers, 3, 9, 48, 60, 92, 94, 107, 110, 208, 210
Los Angeles Herald-Examiner
  use of "junior league" term puzzled young Orioles in 1966, 96
Lou Hatter, 135
Louisville Slugger
  the bat Dave borrowed from teammate Curt Motten to hit his World Series grand slam, now enshrined along with the home run ball in the Hall of Fame, 217
Lou Johnson, 100, 102–3
Lowell Reidenbaugh, 151
Luis Aparicio, 74, 101–3, 115
Lung cancer
  disease that took Dave's life in 2002, 4, 204
Lutherville, Maryland, 75, 128, 150, 156–59, 169, 183, 185–86, 190
Lyle Johnson, 211
Lyndon Johnson, 107

M

Magic City
  Billings longtime nickname based on its explosive population growth early in the 20th century, 13, 18, 22, 25, 27, 30, 33–34, 37, 39, 48, 50, 76, 83, 106, 108–9, 194–96, 218
Major League Baseball Players Union, 188
Manny DeCastro, 147
Manny Ramirez, 211
Marcelino Lopez, 119
Mark Belanger, 134, 142, 197
Mark Lucas, 137
Marvin Miller, 11, 113, 178, 188, 209
Maureen Hall
  Kansas City nun and high school classmate of Dave, 136
Maury Wills, 100
Mayaguez Indians, 80
Mayo Smith, 131
McAllister Hotel
  hotel in Miami that functioned as Orioles spring-training headquarters, 148

McNally, Beth
  Dave's mother, 2
McNally, Dave, 1, 3–5
McNally, Jeff
  oldest of Dave and Jean's five children, 4
Mel Stottlemyre, 148, 204
Memorial Stadium, 67, 73–74, 78, 96, 101, 115, 128, 143, 151, 153, 158, 165, 168, 181, 197, 200, 209, 214, 216
Merv Rettenmund, 131, 134, 181
Mexican Pacific League, 80
Mia Farrow, 112
Miami
  site of spring training for Orioles during Dave's career, 61–62, 65, 76, 85, 91, 110, 112, 147–48, 150–51
Mickey Mantle, 34, 84, 101
Midget Baseball
  early name for what became Little League baseball in Billings, 13
Midland Roundtable
  Billings organization that promotes local sports and athletes, 13, 25–27, 83, 109
Mike Adamson, 129
Mike Cuellar, 5, 142–43, 153, 156, 163, 165–69, 175, 182
Mike Flanagan, 5
Mike Hampton, 211
Mike Mansfield, 136
Mike McCormick, 71, 77, 89
Mike Mussina, 5
Miles City, Montana, 27, 45–46, 137
Milton Richman, 91
Milt Pappas, 82, 152
Milt Wester, 25
Minnie Green
  Catherine McNally's sister, 11
Minot, North Dakota, 40, 46
Moe Drabowsky, 98, 103–4, 115–16
Montana Bank of Billings, 194
Montana State University
  name for state university in Missoula until 1962, 12, 50
  state university located in Missoula, renamed University of Montana in 1962, 10–11, 50, 80
Montana State University (Bozeman)
  formerly Montana State College, 80

INDEX

Montreal Expos, 2, 11, 185–90, 213
Mudville, 94
Muscular Dystrophy Association, 195
Mussina, Mike, 5

N

National Baseball Golf Championship, 85
National Brewing Company, 109
New Orleans, 51–52, 77, 108, 138, 212
New York Giants, 1, 135
Nicaraguan League, 80
Nobles, Dee
  Dave's sister, 4
Nolan Ryan, 149, 208
Norm Clarke
  sports editor of the Billings Gazette in the 1960s, 111

O

Occidental League, 80
Okinawa
  island in Pacific where Jimmy McNally died in June 1945, 7, 12, 55
Orioles Hall of Fame
  Dave third player inducted, 4, 196, 199
Oshkosh, Wisconsin, 45

P

Palmer, Jim, 4–5
Pam McNally
  second-born of the McNally's five children, 85, 148, 196–97, 198
Panama League, 80
Pat Dobson, 160, 165
Paul Blair, 100, 102, 117, 143
Paul Richards
  manager of Orioles when they signed Dave McNally, 61, 66, 142
Pete Cochran, 14, 16–18, 27, 30, 48, 105
Pete Richert, 150, 181
Pete Rose, 77
Peter Seitz, 1, 3–4, 9, 11, 188, 193–95, 210–11
Philadelphia Athletics, 135, 166
Phil Jackman, 10, 113–15, 181, 185, 200
Pine Ridge
  Baltimore-area golf course, 183
Pioneer League, 2, 18, 27
Pittsburgh Pirates, 64, 80, 94, 167, 168–69, 204
Powell, Boog, 4

President Richard Nixon, 172
Puerto Rican Winter League, 80
Puerto Rico, 79–80, 157

R

Ralph Nelles, 79, 137
Ralph Salvon, 129, 197
Rev. Steve Tokarski
  co-celebrant at Dave's funeral service, 206
Rev. William Hogan
  co-celebrant at Dave's funeral service, 206
Richard Nixon, 147
Rich Reese, 138, 150–51
Robb Madgett, 50–51
Robert M. Ball
  Social Security commissioner in 1966, 108
Roberto Clemente, 80, 167
Rocky Mountain Cancer Center, 204
Rodney Fisher, 163
Roger Nelson, 136
Rollie Finger, 175
Ron Taylor, 143
Ron Ziegler, 173
Rostkowski, Gary, 5
Roy Anderson
  Billings Gazette sports editor in the 1950s and early 1960s, 28, 48, 95
Rube Marquard, 135
Russ Powers, 33
Russ Snyder, 81–82, 87, 101–2
Rusty Staub, 77

S

Salary arbitration, 177–78
Sal Bando, 152
Sam Bowens, 117
Sam McDonald, 212
San Diego Padres, 106, 162, 186, 213
Sandra Day O'Connor, 155
San Francisco Giants, 34, 60, 64, 94, 167
Saturday Evening Post, 21
Scottsbluff, Nebraska, 41–43
Scottsdale, Arizona, 64
Seitz decision
  result of salary arbitration case that overturned baseball reserve clause, 3
Seitz, Peter, 1, 3–4
Sheridan, Wyoming, 46
Sidney Eagles, 31

Sinai Hospital
    Baltimore hospital where Dave was treated during his bout of hiccups, 191
Skinner, Jack, 2
Social Security
    headquarters in Woodlawn, Maryland, 107–8
Socony Vacuum Oil Company
    Jimmy McNally's employer as a salesman in Mandan, North Dakota, and Billings, 12
Sparky Anderson, 156
Special-edition gloves autographed by Dave, 164
Spokane, Washington, 61, 164
Sports Illustrated, 8, 201
Springs Club, 200
Stanford University, 201, 215
Stem-cell transplants, 204
Stengel, Casey, 1
Steve Barber, 66, 88, 92, 113, 128
Steve Dalkowski, 75
St. Louis Browns, 55, 58–59, 94
St. Louis Cardinals, 48–49, 95, 154, 163
St. Patrick Catholic Church
    chuck in downtown Billings where Dave McNally and Jean Hoffer were married, 62, 64
St. Thomas the Apostle Church
    site in Billings of Dave's funeral in December 2002, 206
Stu Miller, 87, 93
Sunset Boulevard, 96–97
Susan McNally
    third-born of the McNally's five children, 88, 112, 148, 159, 196–98

T

Terry Crowley, 197
The Sporting News
    Bible Hyperlink, 35
    "Bible of Baseball", 66, 118
Thomasville, Georgia, 62
Three-I League
    Dave played on Fox Cities team managed by Weaver in this league, 180
Three Rivers Stadium, 169
Tim Keefe, 135
Tim O'Malley
    Billings man who passed away in 2024 and who encouraged the author to write about McNally, 218

Toby Kangas, 31
Todd Musburger
    Billings man, son of Cecil Musburger, who became professional athlete agent, 27
Tom Costello, 31
Tom McIntosh
    older brother of Bill McIntosh, played Legion baseball in Billings, then for University of Arizona and became a physician, 31, 93, 106, 132, 141, 153
Tommy Davis, 101, 152
Tommy Helms, 156
Tom Phoebus, 132, 153, 156
Tom Seaver, 141–43
Tony Kubek, 76, 154, 214–15
Tony Oliva, 140
Tony Robello
    scout for New York Yankees, 39
Topps Chewing Gum Company, 77
Tulane Shirts
    New Orleans-area team that defeated Billings in the 1960 Little World Series championship game, 51
Turf Valley
    Baltimore-area golf course, 183

V

Veracruz League, 80
Victoria, Texas, 62–64
Vida Blue, 165
Vietnam War, 166

W

Wally Bunker, 88, 99, 103, 112, 119
Walt Alston, 102
Walt Dropo, 89
Walter Johnson, 135
Walter O'Malley
    owner of the Los Angeles Dodgers in 1975, 189
Walter Shannon
    farm director of St. Louis Cardinals, 48
Walter Youse, 168
Washington Senators, 38, 45, 49, 52, 61, 82, 86, 88, 106, 108, 129, 132, 135, 137, 164, 173–75, 186, 204, 213
Washington State University
    alma mater of Ed Bayne, Woody Hahn, Bob Fry and Joe McIntosh, 49, 52, 106, 186, 213
Wayne Bell, 30, 33, 42–43, 51, 53, 80

Wayne Granger, 153, 155–56, 164, 215
Wes Stock, 89, 111
Western Union, 139
Whitey Ford, 35, 173
Wilbur J. Cohen, 108
Willard Fraser
    Billings mayor in the 1960s and early 1970s, 104, 109, 207
Will Foy, 70
Williamsport
    Pennsylvania city, birthplace of Little League baseball, 22–24, 67
Willie Davis, 100–2
Willie Horton, 129, 131, 163
Willie Mays, 34
Willie Stargell, 167
Wilt Chamberlain, 116
Wimpy
    term for hamburgers made popular in the Popeye comic strip, 111
Woodie Held, 119
Woody Hahn, 49–50, 163
Worland, Wyoming, 46

Y

Yankee Stadium, 1, 86, 184
Yellowstone Country Club, 106, 200, 203
Yellowstone County Welfare Department
    Beth McNally's employer for about three decades, 7, 13, 104

AFTERWORD

I'm now the author of five published books, all centered on topics of Montana history. The titles include: *Win 'Em All* (2016), *Mid-way Bravery* (2019), *Sky Dreamer* (2022), *Lindbergh in Montana* (2023), and the biography of Dave McNally that you're reading.

While you can find the print versions on Amazon, I encourage you to visit your local, independent bookstore and ask for the titles by name. Book store people can consult the Ingram catalog, find them and order them for you. And if I come to your city or town for a book event, bring along your copy/copies), and I'll be pleased to sign them.

Failing that, email me (dennis@treasurestatepress.com) and provide your physical address in the message. I'll then mail you a signed book plate that you can place inside your book.

You can order books directly from me, at this website: https://www.treasurestatepress.com/buy-the-books/. And while you visit my website, I encourage you to sign up for my free, no-spam email newsletter, allowing you to keep up to date on my books plus supplying you with other Montana history stories.

My books also are available in e-book format for Amazon Kindle readers, and as Apple Books, for Kobo readers, Barnes & Noble readers, etc. Look for those in your usual online outlets.

Finally, I maintain a YouTube channel devoted to stories about McNally. It can be found at:
https://www.youtube.com/watch?v=FsiiS8PD55o

ABOUT THE AUTHOR

A Montana native **Dennis Gaub** received his journalism degree from Northwestern University and worked twenty-five years as newspaper reporter and editor in the Treasure State and in Colorado, Wyoming and Michigan. He started as a parttime sportswriter for the *Billings Gazette* while in high school and was a reporter for the *Gazette* for twenty years. He later changed careers and worked in the tech field (software) before he retired from corporate life, returned to creative writing, with four books, all published, to his credit, and his McNally biography will become the fifth book. Gaub and his wife, Cathie, live in Billings, Montana, where they tend a community garden plot, enjoy restaurants and other cultural attractions in the state's largest city and leave on occasion to explore the country in their motor home

ABOUT THE AUTHOR

A Montana native, Dennis Gaub received his journalism degree from Northwestern University and worked twenty-five years as newspaper reporter and editor in the Tri-Cities area and in Columbia, Wyoming and Michigan. He started as a part-time sportswriter for the Billings Gazette while in high school and was a reporter for the Casper Star Tribune. He later changed careers and worked in the tech field so that he could retire from corporate life, returned to creative writing with out books, all published, to his credit, Idol Ilis McNally biography will become the fifth book. Gaub and his wife Cathie live in Billings, Montana, where they lead a community, except for easier restaurants and other attractions in the state's larger city and leave on occasion to explore the country in their motorhome.